Mathematics for Finance and Accounting

M L Ruscsak

Trient Press
3375 S Rainbow Blvd
#81710, SMB 13135
Las Vegas,NV 89180

Ordering Information:
Quantity sales. Special discounts are available on quantity purchases by corporations, associations, and others. For details, contact the publisher at the address above.
Orders by U.S. trade bookstores and wholesalers. Please contact Trient Press: Tel: (775) 996-3844; or visit www.trientpress.com.

Printed in the United States of America

Publisher's Cataloging-in-Publication data
Ruscsak, M.L
A title of a book :
    The New Era of Finance: Technology, Sustainability, and Globalization
ISBN
Paper Back   979-8-88990-089-4
Ebook   979-8-88990-090-0
Hard Cover   979-8-88990-088-7

M.L.Ruscsak

Useful mathematical tables and formulas for financial mathematics
Bibliography: A list of references cited in the book

Index: An alphabetical list of terms and concepts discussed in the book

PART 1: INTRODUCTION TO FINANCIAL MATHEMATICS

Financial mathematics is a field of study that applies mathematical and statistical techniques to the analysis and management of financial data. The field has grown significantly in recent years due to the increasing complexity of financial markets and the growing demand for quantitative analysis in the finance industry.

In this section, we will provide an overview of financial mathematics, its history, and its importance in the modern financial world. We will also discuss the various career opportunities available in the field and the skills and knowledge required to succeed in them.

Overview of Financial Mathematics

Financial mathematics is a multidisciplinary field that draws on mathematics, statistics, economics, and computer science. It involves the use of mathematical and statistical models to analyze financial data and make informed decisions about investments, risk management, and other financial matters.

The field encompasses a wide range of topics, including calculus, linear algebra, probability theory, stochastic processes, optimization, and differential equations. Financial mathematics is used in a variety of applications, such as portfolio management, option pricing, risk assessment, and financial engineering.

History of Financial Mathematics

The origins of financial mathematics can be traced back to the 17th century when French mathematician Blaise Pascal and Dutch mathematician Christiaan Huygens developed the concept of probability theory. In the following centuries, mathematicians continued to develop mathematical models for financial analysis, including the Black-Scholes option pricing model and the efficient market hypothesis.

M.L.Ruscsak

The field of financial mathematics gained significant attention in the 1980s and 1990s, with the emergence of financial derivatives and the increasing complexity of financial markets. Today, financial mathematics is a rapidly growing field with numerous applications in the finance industry.

Importance of Financial Mathematics

Financial mathematics plays a critical role in the modern financial world, where large amounts of data are analyzed and complex financial instruments are traded on a daily basis. The ability to accurately analyze financial data and make informed decisions is essential for success in the finance industry.

Financial mathematics also plays an important role in risk management, helping investors and financial institutions to mitigate risk and manage their exposure to market fluctuations. In addition, financial mathematics is used to develop innovative financial products and services, such as exchange-traded funds (ETFs) and index futures.

Career Opportunities in Financial Mathematics

The growing demand for quantitative analysis in the finance industry has created numerous career opportunities for individuals with a background in financial mathematics. Some of the most common career paths in financial mathematics include investment banking, actuarial science, portfolio management, quantitative analysis, securities trading, financial planning, and financial analysis.

These careers require a strong foundation in mathematical and statistical analysis, as well as an understanding of financial markets and instruments. Successful professionals in financial mathematics are able to use their analytical skills to make informed decisions and identify profitable opportunities in the market.

Skills and Knowledge Required for Success in Financial Mathematics

To succeed in a career in financial mathematics, individuals must possess a strong foundation in mathematics and statistics, as well as an understanding of financial markets and instruments. They must also be able to apply their knowledge and analytical skills to real-world financial problems.

In addition to technical skills, successful professionals in financial mathematics must possess strong communication and teamwork skills, as they often work in interdisciplinary teams to analyze financial data and develop solutions. They must also be able to adapt to changing market conditions and evolving financial instruments.

Conclusion

Financial mathematics is a rapidly growing field that plays a critical role in the modern finance industry. The ability to accurately analyze financial data and make informed decisions is essential for success in the finance industry. Financial mathematics offers numerous career opportunities for individuals with a strong foundation in mathematics and statistics, as well as an understanding of financial markets and instruments.

CHAPTER 1: OVERVIEW OF FINANCIAL MATHEMATICS AND ITS APPLICATIONS

In today's world, financial mathematics has become an indispensable tool for those working in the finance industry. Financial mathematics involves the application of mathematical models, techniques, and methods to financial problems and is an essential aspect of financial analysis, planning, and management. This chapter provides an overview of financial mathematics, its applications, and the various areas where it is used. We will also discuss the importance of financial mathematics in modern-day finance and its role in the global economy.

Overview of Financial Mathematics

Financial mathematics is the application of mathematical principles and techniques to finance, with the aim of solving complex financial problems. The field is also known as quantitative finance, mathematical finance, or financial engineering. The applications of financial mathematics are vast and varied, and include portfolio management, risk management, investment analysis, derivative pricing, and more.

In addition to finance, financial mathematics has numerous applications in other fields such as insurance, economics, and engineering. It involves using mathematical models and methods to analyze and solve real-world problems related to financial markets, investments, and financial products.

Applications of Financial Mathematics

Financial mathematics is used in various fields, including investment banking, actuarial science, risk management, and more. In investment banking, financial mathematics is used to create financial models and analyze the performance of financial instruments. Actuaries use financial mathematics to model and analyze insurance risks, while risk managers use it to evaluate and manage financial risks.

In addition, financial mathematics is used to analyze and price derivatives, such as options and futures contracts, and to manage the risks associated with these instruments. Portfolio managers use financial mathematics to analyze and manage portfolios of securities, while quantitative analysts use mathematical models to develop trading strategies and analyze financial data.

Importance of Financial Mathematics

Financial mathematics plays a critical role in modern-day finance and the global economy. Financial institutions, including banks, investment firms, and insurance companies, rely heavily on financial mathematics to analyze, manage, and mitigate risks associated with their investments and financial products. Financial mathematics is also used in financial regulation, accounting, and auditing.

Moreover, the increasing complexity of financial markets and products has made financial mathematics an essential tool for understanding and predicting market behavior. Financial mathematics helps investors and financial professionals make informed decisions, optimize their portfolios, and mitigate risks. It also helps to develop new financial products and services, such as exchange-traded funds (ETFs), hedge funds, and other alternative investments.

Conclusion

Financial mathematics is a critical component of modern finance, providing a framework for analyzing and solving complex financial problems. Its applications are vast and varied, and it is used extensively in finance, insurance, economics, and other fields. Understanding financial mathematics is essential for those seeking careers in the finance industry, as well as for anyone interested in investing, financial planning, or risk management. In this chapter, we have provided an overview of financial mathematics and its applications, setting the stage for a deeper exploration of the subject matter in subsequent chapters.

Definition of financial mathematics and its importance in finance

Financial mathematics is a branch of applied mathematics that focuses on the quantitative analysis of financial markets and investments. It is concerned with developing mathematical models, tools, and techniques to aid in the valuation, analysis, and management of financial assets and risks. In today's rapidly evolving financial landscape, the importance of financial mathematics cannot be overstated. This section will provide an overview of the definition of financial mathematics and its importance in finance.

Financial mathematics is a multidisciplinary field that draws upon a diverse range of mathematical concepts and techniques, including calculus, probability theory, linear algebra, statistics, and optimization. The application of these mathematical tools enables financial analysts, portfolio managers, traders, and risk managers to make informed decisions about financial investments and to manage the risks associated with them.

One of the primary areas of focus in financial mathematics is the valuation of financial assets, such as stocks, bonds, options, futures, and derivatives. This involves the development of

M.L.Ruscsak

mathematical models that can estimate the fair value of these assets based on various underlying factors, such as market conditions, interest rates, volatility, and other risk factors.

In addition to asset valuation, financial mathematics is also concerned with risk management. Financial institutions face a range of risks, including market risk, credit risk, liquidity risk, and operational risk. Financial mathematicians develop models and tools to help institutions manage these risks and to ensure that they have adequate capital and liquidity to withstand unexpected events.

The importance of financial mathematics in finance is underscored by the fact that many of the world's leading financial institutions rely heavily on quantitative analysis and mathematical models in their decision-making processes. For example, investment banks use financial mathematics to price and trade complex derivatives, hedge funds use it to identify and exploit market inefficiencies, and insurance companies use it to manage their portfolios and to price insurance products.

Moreover, financial mathematics has become increasingly important in the modern economy as financial markets have become more globalized and interconnected. The 2008 financial crisis highlighted the need for sophisticated risk management tools and mathematical models to help institutions identify and manage systemic risks.

In conclusion, financial mathematics is a critical discipline that plays a vital role in the world of finance. Its importance lies in its ability to help financial institutions make informed decisions about investments, manage risk, and navigate the complexities of today's financial markets. As the financial landscape continues to evolve, the role of financial mathematics is only set to become more important.

Applications of financial mathematics in business and finance

Financial mathematics has numerous applications in various fields of business and finance. It helps in analyzing, understanding, and managing various financial risks associated with investments, insurance, and other financial products. In this section, we will explore some of the most common applications of financial mathematics in business and finance.

✧   Investment Management:
One of the primary applications of financial mathematics is in investment management. It helps investors in making informed decisions by analyzing various factors like risk, return, volatility, and liquidity of different investment options. Financial mathematics plays a critical role in portfolio management, helping investors to maximize their returns while minimizing their risk exposure.

✧   Risk Management:
Financial mathematics also plays a vital role in risk management. By using statistical models and tools like value at risk (VaR), financial institutions can quantify and manage their financial risks.

This helps them to mitigate the impact of unfavorable market movements and make better-informed decisions.

✧   Insurance:
Financial mathematics is also used in the insurance industry to price various insurance products like life insurance, health insurance, and auto insurance. Insurance companies use sophisticated mathematical models to calculate the premiums and the expected payouts associated with different policies, thereby ensuring that they can remain financially stable even in the event of significant losses.

✧   Derivatives Trading:
Derivatives trading is another field where financial mathematics plays a critical role. By using mathematical models like Black-Scholes, traders can price various derivatives like options, futures, and swaps. These models help traders to make informed decisions based on the market movements, volatility, and other factors affecting the price of the derivative.

✧   Corporate Finance:
Financial mathematics is also widely used in corporate finance. It helps companies to analyze the financial risks associated with different projects and investments. This enables them to make informed decisions about investments, financing, and other financial activities.

✧   Financial Planning and Analysis:
Financial mathematics is also used in financial planning and analysis. By using mathematical models, financial planners can forecast various financial metrics like revenue, expenses, cash flow, and profit. This helps businesses to plan their financial activities and make informed decisions about investments, financing, and other activities.

✧   Algorithmic Trading:
Algorithmic trading is a rapidly growing field in finance, and financial mathematics plays a significant role in this field. By using sophisticated mathematical models and algorithms, traders can analyze market data in real-time and make automated trading decisions.

In conclusion, financial mathematics has numerous applications in various fields of business and finance. It helps businesses and individuals to make informed decisions based on data analysis and mathematical modeling. The use of financial mathematics has become increasingly important in today's complex financial markets, and its importance is expected to continue to grow in the future.

Historical background of financial mathematics

Financial mathematics has a long and storied history, with roots dating back to ancient civilizations such as the Babylonians and Greeks. The use of mathematical models and tools for financial analysis and decision-making has evolved over the centuries, with significant contributions

M.L.Ruscsak

from scholars and practitioners from various fields. This section will provide a historical background of financial mathematics, tracing its origins to ancient times and highlighting key developments up to the present day.

Ancient Times:

The earliest known use of mathematical concepts for financial purposes dates back to ancient civilizations such as the Babylonians and Greeks. The Babylonians developed a sophisticated system of arithmetic and geometry that allowed them to calculate interest rates, taxes, and other financial metrics. The Greeks, meanwhile, made important contributions to the field of geometry, which would later prove to be crucial for the development of financial models and tools.

Middle Ages:

During the Middle Ages, European merchants began to develop sophisticated systems for accounting and bookkeeping, which laid the foundation for modern financial accounting. However, it wasn't until the Renaissance that significant advances were made in financial mathematics. Italian mathematician Leonardo Fibonacci introduced the concept of the "Fibonacci sequence," which has since become a fundamental tool for modeling financial markets and analyzing trends.

Modern Era:

The 20th century saw significant advances in financial mathematics, driven by the increasing complexity of financial markets and the rise of modern finance theory. The development of calculus and other advanced mathematical tools allowed researchers and practitioners to create more sophisticated models for pricing and hedging financial instruments, such as options and futures contracts.

In the mid-20th century, mathematician Harry Markowitz introduced the concept of "modern portfolio theory," which provides a framework for optimizing investment portfolios based on risk and return. This theory revolutionized the field of portfolio management and has since become a cornerstone of modern finance.

In the latter part of the 20th century, the rise of computer technology and the internet revolutionized the way financial markets operate. The ability to process vast amounts of data and execute trades in real-time has led to the development of algorithmic trading, which relies heavily on mathematical models and tools for decision-making.

Recent Developments:

Today, financial mathematics continues to evolve, with ongoing developments in areas such as machine learning, artificial intelligence, and blockchain technology. These new tools and techniques are being applied to a wide range of financial applications, from risk management and investment analysis to fraud detection and cybersecurity.

Conclusion:

The historical background of financial mathematics reveals a long and rich tradition of using mathematical models and tools for financial analysis and decision-making. From ancient civilizations to the modern era, scholars and practitioners have made significant contributions to the field, advancing our understanding of financial markets and paving the way for new innovations and applications. As technology continues to evolve, it is likely that the field of financial mathematics will continue to play an increasingly important role in the world of business and finance.

Current and future trends in financial mathematics

Financial mathematics is an ever-evolving field, and as technology advances and new financial instruments are developed, the applications of financial mathematics continue to expand. In this section, we will discuss some of the current and future trends in financial mathematics.

One of the most significant trends in financial mathematics is the increasing use of machine learning and artificial intelligence. Financial institutions are generating vast amounts of data, and the use of machine learning algorithms to analyze this data can provide valuable insights into market trends and risk management. For example, investment banks use machine learning algorithms to analyze market data and identify patterns that can be used to inform investment decisions. Similarly, insurance companies are using machine learning to evaluate risk and price policies more accurately.

Another trend in financial mathematics is the use of blockchain technology. Blockchain is a distributed ledger technology that allows for secure, transparent transactions without the need for intermediaries such as banks. The use of blockchain technology in finance has the potential to reduce costs and increase efficiency, and it is being explored in areas such as payment systems, asset management, and securities trading.

In addition to machine learning and blockchain, financial mathematics is also being applied to new financial instruments, such as cryptocurrencies and digital assets. Cryptocurrencies are digital currencies that use cryptography to secure transactions and control the creation of new units. The development of cryptocurrencies has created new challenges for financial mathematics, including the need to develop new models for pricing and risk management.

Another area of growth in financial mathematics is the development of environmental, social, and governance (ESG) investing strategies. ESG investing considers the impact of a company's environmental, social, and governance practices in addition to financial performance when making investment decisions. ESG investing requires the use of new models and tools to evaluate non-financial data, and financial mathematics is playing an increasingly important role in this area.

Looking to the future, there is no doubt that financial mathematics will continue to play a critical role in finance. As technology continues to advance and new financial instruments are developed, financial mathematics will be required to provide the tools and models needed to manage risk and make informed investment decisions. In particular, the continued development of machine learning and blockchain technology is likely to drive significant innovation in financial mathematics, while ESG investing and the rise of new financial instruments will require new approaches and models.

In conclusion, financial mathematics is a constantly evolving field that is shaped by technological advancements and new financial instruments. The current trends in financial mathematics include the increasing use of machine learning and blockchain technology, the development of cryptocurrencies and digital assets, and the growth of ESG investing strategies. As these trends continue to develop, financial mathematics will continue to play a critical role in finance, providing the tools and models needed to manage risk and make informed investment decisions.

CHAPTER 2: THE ROLE OF MATHEMATICS IN FINANCIAL DECISION-MAKING

Mathematics plays a critical role in financial decision-making, helping professionals make informed decisions about investments, risk management, and financial planning. Whether you are an investment banker, portfolio manager, financial planner, or securities trader, you need a deep understanding of mathematical concepts and techniques to succeed in the field of finance.

In this chapter, we will explore the various ways in which mathematics is used in financial decision-making. We will begin by discussing the different types of financial decisions that professionals make, and how mathematics can help inform these decisions. We will then delve into specific mathematical concepts and techniques that are commonly used in finance, such as statistical analysis, calculus, and probability theory. Finally, we will discuss some of the challenges that arise when applying mathematical models to financial decision-making, and how professionals can overcome these challenges.

Types of Financial Decisions

Financial professionals make a wide range of decisions on a daily basis, ranging from investment decisions to risk management strategies. One of the key challenges of financial decision-making is balancing risk and reward. While taking on more risk can lead to higher returns, it can also result in significant losses. On the other hand, being too conservative can limit returns and hinder growth.

Mathematics plays a crucial role in helping financial professionals make informed decisions about risk and reward. By analyzing historical data and using mathematical models to predict future outcomes, professionals can make informed decisions about investments, hedging strategies, and other financial decisions.

Mathematical Concepts and Techniques in Financial Decision-Making

There are many mathematical concepts and techniques that are used in financial decision-making. Here are a few examples:

Statistical analysis: Statistical analysis is used to identify trends and patterns in financial data. By analyzing historical data and looking for correlations, financial professionals can make informed decisions about future trends and potential risks.

Calculus: Calculus is used to model complex systems and predict future outcomes. In finance, calculus is used to model the behavior of financial instruments and predict the impact of market changes on investments.

Probability theory: Probability theory is used to assess the likelihood of different outcomes. In finance, probability theory is used to calculate the probability of a given investment performing well or poorly, and to identify potential risks.

Linear algebra: Linear algebra is used to model complex systems and solve equations with multiple variables. In finance, linear algebra is used to model the behavior of financial instruments and optimize investment portfolios.

Challenges of Applying Mathematical Models to Financial Decision-Making

While mathematical models can be incredibly useful in financial decision-making, they also come with some challenges. One of the biggest challenges is the unpredictability of financial markets. Financial markets are influenced by a wide range of factors, including economic trends, geopolitical events, and investor sentiment. These factors can be difficult to predict, making it challenging to create accurate mathematical models.

Another challenge is the risk of overreliance on mathematical models. While mathematical models can provide valuable insights into financial markets, they should not be the sole basis for financial decision-making. It is important for financial professionals to use their own judgment and experience in addition to mathematical models when making important decisions.

Conclusion

Mathematics plays a critical role in financial decision-making, helping professionals make informed decisions about investments, risk management, and financial planning. From statistical analysis to calculus, there are many mathematical concepts and techniques that are used in finance. While mathematical models come with some challenges, they can be incredibly useful in helping professionals make informed decisions in a fast-paced and complex field.

Overview of financial decision-making and its importance in finance

Financial decision-making is a crucial aspect of the finance industry. It involves a process of identifying financial problems, analyzing the available options, and selecting the best course of action that maximizes financial returns and minimizes risks. Financial decision-making is essential for individuals, businesses, and governments to manage their finances efficiently and effectively. This section provides an overview of financial decision-making and its importance in finance.

Overview of Financial Decision-Making:

Financial decision-making involves a series of steps, including the identification of financial problems, gathering of relevant data, analysis of available options, and selection of the best course of action. The goal of financial decision-making is to maximize returns and minimize risks.

The first step in financial decision-making is to identify the financial problem. This involves recognizing a situation where financial resources are not being used efficiently or effectively. Examples of financial problems include cash flow problems, poor investment decisions, and excessive debt.

The next step is to gather relevant data. This includes information about the financial problem, such as the amount of debt, cash flow, and investments. This information can be obtained from financial statements, financial reports, and other sources.

After gathering relevant data, the next step is to analyze the available options. This involves evaluating the different courses of action that can be taken to solve the financial problem. Financial decision-makers need to consider the potential risks and returns associated with each option.

Finally, the last step in financial decision-making is to select the best course of action. This involves choosing the option that maximizes returns and minimizes risks. Financial decision-makers need to consider factors such as the expected returns, risks, and time frame of each option.

Importance of Financial Decision-Making:

Financial decision-making is essential for individuals, businesses, and governments to manage their finances efficiently and effectively. The following are some of the reasons why financial decision-making is important in finance:

✧ Maximizing Returns: Financial decision-making helps to maximize returns by choosing the best course of action that generates the highest returns.

✧ Minimizing Risks: Financial decision-making helps to minimize risks by identifying potential risks and choosing the course of action that minimizes them.

✧ Effective Use of Financial Resources: Financial decision-making ensures the effective use of financial resources by identifying situations where resources are not being used efficiently and taking corrective actions.

✧ Meeting Financial Obligations: Financial decision-making helps to meet financial obligations by ensuring that there is enough cash flow to meet the financial needs of individuals, businesses, and governments.

M.L.Ruscsak

✧   Achieving Financial Goals: Financial decision-making helps to achieve financial goals by choosing the best course of action that aligns with the financial objectives of individuals, businesses, and governments.

Conclusion:

Financial decision-making is a critical aspect of the finance industry. It involves a process of identifying financial problems, gathering relevant data, analyzing available options, and selecting the best course of action. Financial decision-making is essential for individuals, businesses, and governments to manage their finances efficiently and effectively. By maximizing returns, minimizing risks, effectively using financial resources, meeting financial obligations, and achieving financial goals, financial decision-making plays a crucial role in the success of the finance industry.

How mathematics can assist in financial decision-making

Financial decision-making involves a wide range of activities, such as identifying investment opportunities, assessing risks, evaluating costs and benefits, and making trade-offs between conflicting objectives. These activities require a deep understanding of financial markets, economic theory, statistical analysis, and mathematical modeling. Mathematics plays a crucial role in all these areas, providing a powerful toolkit for financial analysts, investors, and decision-makers.

In this section, we will explore some of the key ways in which mathematics can assist in financial decision-making. We will start by looking at the role of mathematics in financial modeling, including its use in valuation, risk assessment, and portfolio optimization. We will then examine the importance of mathematical tools in financial analysis and forecasting, as well as their applications in asset pricing, derivative pricing, and trading strategies. Finally, we will discuss the broader implications of mathematical modeling in finance, including its impact on financial regulation, corporate governance, and social welfare.

Financial Modeling
Mathematical models are used extensively in finance to describe the behavior of financial markets, instruments, and institutions. These models are based on a variety of assumptions and techniques, ranging from classical finance theory to modern stochastic calculus. The goal of financial modeling is to provide a systematic and rigorous framework for analyzing financial data, making predictions, and testing hypotheses.

One of the most important applications of mathematical modeling in finance is valuation. Valuation is the process of estimating the intrinsic value of an asset, such as a stock, bond, or real estate. There are many methods of valuation, but most of them involve some form of mathematical modeling. For example, the discounted cash flow (DCF) model uses mathematical formulas to estimate the present value of future cash flows from an asset. The Black-Scholes model, on the other hand, uses stochastic calculus to estimate the fair price of options and other derivatives.

Risk assessment is another area where mathematical modeling is widely used. Risk assessment involves identifying, measuring, and managing the risks associated with financial investments. This can include market risk, credit risk, liquidity risk, operational risk, and many other types of risk. Mathematical models are used to estimate the probability and severity of different types of risks, as well as to design risk management strategies and financial instruments, such as insurance policies and hedges.

Portfolio optimization is a third area where mathematics can assist in financial decision-making. Portfolio optimization involves selecting a portfolio of assets that maximizes the expected return for a given level of risk. This requires a sophisticated mathematical framework that can handle multiple assets, risk factors, and constraints. One of the most popular techniques for portfolio optimization is the mean-variance optimization model, which was developed by Harry Markowitz in the 1950s. This model uses statistical methods to estimate the expected return and variance of different assets, and then identifies the optimal portfolio that balances risk and return.

Financial Analysis and Forecasting
Mathematics also plays a critical role in financial analysis and forecasting. Financial analysts use mathematical tools to analyze financial data, such as balance sheets, income statements, and cash flow statements, and to make predictions about future trends and performance. These tools include statistical methods, regression analysis, time series analysis, and machine learning algorithms.

Asset pricing is one of the most important applications of mathematical tools in financial analysis. Asset pricing is the process of determining the fair value of financial assets, such as stocks, bonds, and commodities. This requires a deep understanding of the underlying economic and financial factors that affect asset prices, as well as sophisticated mathematical models that can capture these factors. One of the most influential models in this area is the Capital Asset Pricing Model (CAPM), which uses statistical methods to estimate the expected return of different assets based on their risk characteristics.

Derivative pricing is another area where mathematics is widely used. Derivatives are financial instruments that derive their value from underlying assets, such as stocks, bonds, commodities, currencies, or indices. They are commonly used for hedging, speculation, or arbitrage purposes. Examples of derivatives include options, futures, swaps, and forwards.

Derivatives pricing involves the use of advanced mathematical models and techniques to determine the fair value of these instruments. One of the most famous models used in this area is the Black-Scholes model, which was introduced by Fischer Black and Myron Scholes in 1973. This model allows for the calculation of the theoretical price of European-style options, which are options that can only be exercised at a specific point in time.

M.L.Ruscsak

The Black-Scholes model is based on the assumption that the underlying asset follows a geometric Brownian motion, which means that its price movements are random and follow a log-normal distribution. The model also assumes that there are no transaction costs, no dividends paid on the underlying asset, and that interest rates are constant over the life of the option.

Despite its assumptions, the Black-Scholes model has been widely used in the financial industry to price and hedge derivatives. It has also been extended and modified to handle more complex situations, such as American-style options, where the option can be exercised at any time before expiration.

In addition to pricing derivatives, mathematics is also used to manage the risk associated with these instruments. This is known as financial risk management, and it involves the use of mathematical models and techniques to identify, measure, and manage various types of financial risks.

One of the most common types of financial risk is market risk, which is the risk of loss due to changes in market prices, such as the price of a stock or a commodity. Market risk can be managed using various mathematical models, such as value-at-risk (VaR) and expected shortfall (ES), which provide estimates of the potential losses that could occur under different market scenarios.

Another type of financial risk is credit risk, which is the risk of loss due to the failure of a counterparty to fulfill its financial obligations. Credit risk can be managed using mathematical models such as credit scoring models, which use various financial and non-financial variables to assess the creditworthiness of borrowers.

Operational risk is yet another type of financial risk, which arises from inadequate or failed internal processes, systems, or human error. Operational risk can be managed using mathematical models such as scenario analysis and stress testing, which involve simulating different scenarios to identify potential weaknesses in the operational processes of a financial institution.

In conclusion, mathematics plays a crucial role in financial decision-making by providing tools and techniques to price and manage financial instruments, as well as to identify and manage financial risks. It is important for finance professionals to have a strong understanding of mathematics and its applications in finance to make informed decisions and succeed in the industry.

Understanding the relationship between financial models and decision-making

The use of mathematical models in finance has become increasingly important in recent years. Financial models are used to forecast future trends, simulate various scenarios, and predict the impact of different decisions. In order to fully understand the role of financial models in decision-making, it is important to first understand the basics of financial modeling.

At its core, financial modeling is the process of using mathematical formulas and statistical analysis to predict future outcomes based on historical data. These models are used to make important financial decisions, such as whether to invest in a particular stock, whether to acquire another company, or whether to issue debt.

There are many different types of financial models, but they all share the same goal: to provide insights into potential outcomes and inform decision-making. For example, a company might use a discounted cash flow model to determine the value of a particular investment. This model would take into account the expected future cash flows generated by the investment, the time value of money, and the risk associated with the investment.

Financial models are often used in conjunction with other forms of analysis, such as fundamental analysis and technical analysis. Fundamental analysis involves analyzing a company's financial statements, industry trends, and other qualitative factors to determine its intrinsic value. Technical analysis involves analyzing past market data to identify patterns and trends that can be used to predict future market movements.

While financial models can be incredibly useful tools for decision-making, it is important to remember that they are not infallible. Financial models are based on historical data, which means they are only as accurate as the data they are based on. They also rely on a number of assumptions, which can sometimes be inaccurate or misleading.

One of the challenges of using financial models in decision-making is understanding the limitations of the models. This requires a deep understanding of the underlying assumptions and the data used to create the model. It also requires a willingness to accept that the model may not always be right and that there is a degree of uncertainty involved in any financial decision.

Another challenge of using financial models is balancing the benefits of the model with the costs of developing and maintaining it. Financial models can be complex and time-consuming to develop, which means that they can be expensive to create and maintain. Additionally, the outputs of the model can be difficult to interpret, which means that it may require significant training to use effectively.

Despite these challenges, financial models remain an essential tool for decision-making in finance. The insights they provide can help companies make informed decisions and stay ahead of the competition. To be successful in using financial models, it is important to approach them with a critical eye, understand their limitations, and use them in conjunction with other forms of analysis.

Examples of successful financial decision-making using mathematical models

The use of mathematical models in financial decision-making has led to numerous successful outcomes in various fields. Here are some examples of successful financial decision-making using mathematical models:

✧ Option Pricing: In the 1970s, Fisher Black and Myron Scholes developed a mathematical model that revolutionized the way options were priced. The Black-Scholes model allowed traders and investors to calculate the theoretical value of options based on a range of inputs, including the underlying asset price, strike price, time to expiration, and volatility. This model provided a significant improvement in option pricing accuracy and efficiency, making it possible for traders to make more informed decisions on buying and selling options.

✧ Risk Management: The use of mathematical models in risk management has become increasingly popular in recent years. Risk management models help financial institutions to quantify, measure, and manage risks associated with their business activities. One example of successful risk management using mathematical models is the Value at Risk (VaR) model. VaR is a statistical measure used to estimate the maximum amount of loss that an institution can incur over a specified period of time, with a given level of confidence. VaR models are widely used by banks, insurance companies, and investment firms to manage their risks.

✧ Portfolio Optimization: Portfolio optimization is the process of constructing an investment portfolio that maximizes expected returns for a given level of risk. Mathematical models play a crucial role in portfolio optimization by helping investors to select an optimal mix of assets. One example of successful portfolio optimization using mathematical models is the Markowitz model. The Markowitz model uses a set of statistical methods to estimate the expected returns and risks of various assets, and then calculates the optimal portfolio allocation based on the investor's risk preferences.

✧ Credit Scoring: Credit scoring models use statistical techniques and mathematical models to predict the likelihood of borrowers defaulting on their loans. One example of successful credit scoring using mathematical models is the FICO score. The FICO score is a credit scoring system developed by the Fair Isaac Corporation that is widely used by lenders to evaluate the creditworthiness of borrowers. The FICO score takes into account various factors, such as payment history, amount of debt, length of credit history, and types of credit used, to assign a credit score to an individual.

✧ Algorithmic Trading: Algorithmic trading refers to the use of computer programs to execute trades based on mathematical models and algorithms. Algorithmic trading has become increasingly popular in recent years due to its ability to execute trades quickly and efficiently. One example of successful algorithmic trading using mathematical models is the High-

Frequency Trading (HFT) strategy. HFT strategies use mathematical models to analyze large volumes of market data and identify opportunities for high-speed trades.

Conclusion

In conclusion, mathematical models play a critical role in financial decision-making. They enable investors and financial institutions to make informed decisions by providing accurate and efficient estimates of various financial parameters, such as asset prices, risks, and returns. The examples listed above demonstrate how mathematical models have been successfully applied in different areas of finance, including option pricing, risk management, portfolio optimization, credit scoring, and algorithmic trading. As financial markets continue to become more complex and data-driven, the use of mathematical models is likely to become even more important in the future.

CHAPTER 3: REVIEW OF MATHEMATICAL CONCEPTS USED IN FINANCIAL MATHEMATICS

Financial mathematics is a branch of mathematics that applies mathematical models to financial markets and transactions. Financial decision-making often involves complex mathematical models, which require a solid understanding of mathematical concepts and techniques. This chapter provides a review of some of the most important mathematical concepts used in financial mathematics.

Linear Algebra

Linear algebra is a branch of mathematics that deals with linear equations, matrices, and vector spaces. It is an essential tool for understanding financial models and their applications. In financial mathematics, linear algebra is used to represent and manipulate large sets of data, such as stock prices, interest rates, and bond yields.

One of the most important concepts in linear algebra is the matrix. A matrix is a rectangular array of numbers or symbols that can represent a system of linear equations. Matrices are used extensively in financial mathematics to represent the returns on different assets, the weights of different portfolio holdings, and the relationships between different financial instruments.

Calculus

Calculus is a branch of mathematics that deals with rates of change and the accumulation of small changes over time. It is an essential tool for understanding financial models that involve continuous processes, such as interest rates and stock prices.

One of the most important concepts in calculus is the derivative. The derivative measures the rate of change of a function at a given point. In finance, derivatives are used to value financial instruments such as options, futures, and swaps. Derivatives pricing involves solving complex partial differential equations, which requires a solid understanding of calculus.

Probability Theory

Probability theory is a branch of mathematics that deals with the study of random events and the likelihood of their occurrence. It is an essential tool for understanding financial models that involve uncertainty, such as stock prices and interest rates.

One of the most important concepts in probability theory is the probability distribution. The probability distribution describes the likelihood of different outcomes of a random variable. In finance, probability theory is used to model the distribution of stock prices, interest rates, and other financial variables. It is also used to develop risk management strategies, such as hedging and diversification.

Statistics

Statistics is a branch of mathematics that deals with the collection, analysis, and interpretation of data. It is an essential tool for understanding financial models that involve empirical data, such as historical stock prices and interest rates.

One of the most important concepts in statistics is the regression analysis. Regression analysis is a statistical technique used to model the relationship between two or more variables. In finance, regression analysis is used to model the relationship between asset returns and other financial variables, such as interest rates and inflation. It is also used to develop trading strategies, such as mean reversion and momentum trading.

Conclusion

In conclusion, financial mathematics is a complex field that requires a solid understanding of mathematical concepts and techniques. Linear algebra, calculus, probability theory, and statistics are some of the most important mathematical concepts used in financial mathematics. This chapter has provided a brief overview of these concepts and their applications in finance. A deeper understanding of these concepts will be necessary for the reader to fully understand the financial models presented in later chapters.

Introduction to calculus and its applications in finance

Calculus is a branch of mathematics that deals with the study of rates of change and continuous processes. It is a powerful tool in financial mathematics that is used to model financial systems and make predictions about future outcomes. This section will provide an overview of calculus and its applications in finance.

Calculus has two main branches: differential calculus and integral calculus. Differential calculus is concerned with rates of change and the slopes of curves, while integral calculus is concerned with the accumulation of quantities and the areas under curves. Both branches of calculus have important applications in finance.

One of the key concepts in differential calculus is the derivative. The derivative of a function is a measure of its rate of change at a particular point. In finance, derivatives are financial instruments that derive their value from underlying assets. The pricing and valuation of derivatives requires a thorough understanding of the principles of differential calculus. For example, the Black-Scholes model, which is used to price options, is based on the principles of differential calculus.

Integral calculus is also widely used in finance. One important concept in integral calculus is the definite integral. The definite integral of a function is the area under the curve between two points. This concept is used in finance to calculate the value of assets that generate income over time. For example, the present value of a bond, which is the sum of the discounted future cash flows, is calculated using the principles of integral calculus.

Another important application of calculus in finance is optimization. Optimization involves finding the maximum or minimum of a function. In finance, optimization is used to find the best investment strategy or portfolio allocation. For example, an investment manager may use optimization techniques to find the optimal mix of assets that maximizes returns while minimizing risk.

Calculus also has applications in risk management. Value at Risk (VaR) is a widely used measure of risk in finance. VaR is calculated using the principles of calculus and provides an estimate of the potential loss that a portfolio may suffer over a given time period with a given level of probability.

In conclusion, calculus is a powerful tool in financial mathematics with a wide range of applications. It is used to model financial systems, price derivatives, value assets, optimize portfolios, and manage risk. A thorough understanding of calculus is essential for anyone seeking a career in finance.

Overview of linear algebra and its applications in finance

Linear algebra is a branch of mathematics that deals with linear equations, matrices, vectors, and vector spaces. It is a powerful tool for solving a wide range of problems in finance, including portfolio optimization, risk management, asset pricing, and regression analysis. Linear algebra can also be used to model complex financial systems, such as option pricing models, credit risk models, and interest rate models. In this section, we will provide an overview of linear algebra and its applications in finance.

Linear Equations:

Linear equations are mathematical expressions that describe a linear relationship between two or more variables. In finance, linear equations are often used to model the relationship between two or more financial variables, such as the relationship between stock prices and interest rates. Linear equations can be solved using matrix algebra, which is an important tool in finance.

Matrices:

A matrix is a rectangular array of numbers that can be used to represent a system of linear equations. In finance, matrices are used to represent the relationships between financial variables, such as the covariance matrix, which is used to model the relationship between the returns of different assets in a portfolio. Matrix algebra is also used to solve systems of linear equations, which is important in finance for solving problems related to risk management, asset pricing, and portfolio optimization.

Vectors:

A vector is a mathematical object that represents a quantity that has both magnitude and direction. In finance, vectors are often used to represent financial quantities, such as asset returns or portfolio weights. Vectors can be added, subtracted, and multiplied by scalars, which makes them a powerful tool for modeling financial systems and solving problems in finance.

Vector Spaces:

A vector space is a collection of vectors that can be added, subtracted, and multiplied by scalars. In finance, vector spaces are used to represent the space of all possible portfolio weights or the space of all possible returns of a portfolio. Vector spaces can be used to solve problems related to portfolio optimization, risk management, and asset pricing.

Applications of Linear Algebra in Finance:

Portfolio Optimization:
Portfolio optimization is the process of selecting a portfolio of assets that maximizes the expected return while minimizing the risk. Linear algebra is used to model the relationship between the returns of different assets in a portfolio and to calculate the optimal portfolio weights that maximize the expected return while minimizing the risk.

Risk Management:
Risk management is the process of identifying, assessing, and mitigating risks in a financial system. Linear algebra is used to model the relationship between different financial variables and to calculate the risk measures, such as value at risk (VaR) and expected shortfall, that are used to assess the risk of a financial system.

Asset Pricing:
Asset pricing is the process of valuing financial assets, such as stocks and bonds. Linear algebra is used to model the relationship between the returns of different assets and to calculate the expected return and risk premium of a financial asset.

Regression Analysis:
Regression analysis is a statistical technique used to model the relationship between two or more variables. Linear algebra is used to solve the system of linear equations that describes the relationship between the variables and to estimate the coefficients of the regression model.

Conclusion:

Linear algebra is an important tool in finance that is used to model complex financial systems, solve problems related to portfolio optimization, risk management, asset pricing, and regression analysis. Linear algebra provides a powerful framework for solving problems in finance and has applications in a wide range of fields, including investment banking, portfolio management, quantitative analysis, securities trading, and financial planning.

Introduction to differential equations and their applications in finance

Differential equations are a branch of mathematics that deals with equations involving derivatives. They are used in finance to model a variety of phenomena, such as stock prices, interest rates, and economic growth. Differential equations can be used to analyze financial data and make predictions about future trends.

One of the most common types of differential equations used in finance is the Black-Scholes equation, which is used to price options. Options are contracts that give the holder the right, but not the obligation, to buy or sell an underlying asset at a predetermined price within a certain time frame. The Black-Scholes equation takes into account the current price of the underlying asset, the exercise price of the option, the time until expiration, the volatility of the underlying asset, and the risk-free interest rate. By solving the Black-Scholes equation, one can determine the fair price of an option.

Another application of differential equations in finance is in the modeling of interest rates. The dynamics of interest rates are complex, and can be affected by a variety of factors, such as inflation, economic growth, and central bank policies. The Vasicek model and the Cox-Ingersoll-Ross model are two commonly used models for interest rate modeling. These models use differential equations to describe the dynamics of interest rates over time.

Differential equations can also be used to model the growth of a portfolio. The growth of a portfolio over time can be affected by a variety of factors, such as interest rates, stock prices, and economic growth. Differential equations can be used to describe the dynamics of these factors and their impact on the portfolio. This can help investors to make informed decisions about their investments.

One of the challenges in using differential equations in finance is the need for accurate data. The models used in finance are only as good as the data they are based on. Inaccurate or incomplete data can lead to incorrect predictions and unreliable models. Therefore, it is important for financial professionals to ensure that the data they are using is accurate and up-to-date.

Another challenge is the complexity of the models. Differential equations can be difficult to solve, and may require advanced mathematical techniques. Financial professionals who wish to use differential equations in their work must have a strong mathematical background and be able to apply their knowledge to real-world financial problems.

In conclusion, differential equations are a powerful tool in finance that can be used to model a wide range of phenomena. They are used to price options, model interest rates, and describe the dynamics of portfolios. While they can be challenging to work with, the insights they provide can be invaluable in making informed financial decisions. It is important for financial professionals to have a strong understanding of differential equations and their applications in finance in order to make the most of this powerful tool.

Basic statistical concepts used in finance

Statistics plays a crucial role in finance. Financial analysts and professionals use statistical tools and techniques to analyze data and draw meaningful insights to make informed decisions. In this section, we will discuss some of the basic statistical concepts that are commonly used in finance.

Mean, Median, and Mode:

The mean, median, and mode are the three measures of central tendency that are used to summarize a set of data. The mean is the arithmetic average of the data set, the median is the middle value when the data is sorted in ascending order, and the mode is the most frequently occurring value in the data set.

These measures are useful in finance as they provide an indication of the average, typical, and common values in a data set. For example, a financial analyst may use the mean, median, and mode to analyze stock prices and gain insights into the price trends.

Standard Deviation:

Standard deviation is a measure of the dispersion or spread of a set of data. It shows how much the data deviates from the mean. A high standard deviation indicates that the data is spread out over a large range, while a low standard deviation indicates that the data is clustered around the mean.

M.L.Ruscsak

In finance, standard deviation is used to measure the risk associated with an investment. The higher the standard deviation, the riskier the investment is considered to be. This is because a high standard deviation indicates that there is a greater likelihood of significant fluctuations in the value of the investment.

Correlation:

Correlation is a measure of the relationship between two variables. It indicates how closely two variables are related and whether they move in the same direction or in opposite directions. A correlation coefficient of +1 indicates a perfect positive correlation, while a coefficient of -1 indicates a perfect negative correlation. A coefficient of 0 indicates no correlation.

In finance, correlation is used to analyze the relationship between different assets. For example, a financial analyst may use correlation to analyze the relationship between the stock prices of two companies. If the stocks are highly positively correlated, it indicates that they tend to move in the same direction. Conversely, if they are highly negatively correlated, it indicates that they tend to move in opposite directions.

Hypothesis Testing:

Hypothesis testing is a statistical method used to test whether a hypothesis about a population is true or not. The process involves formulating a null hypothesis and an alternative hypothesis and then collecting and analyzing data to determine whether to reject or accept the null hypothesis.

In finance, hypothesis testing is used to test various hypotheses, such as whether a particular investment strategy generates abnormal returns or whether a new financial product is profitable. It helps financial analysts to make informed decisions by providing a statistical basis for their conclusions.

Conclusion:

In conclusion, statistical concepts play a crucial role in finance. They provide financial analysts with the tools to analyze and interpret data, identify trends, and make informed decisions. Mean, median, and mode provide a summary of the data set, while standard deviation helps to measure risk. Correlation is used to analyze the relationship between different assets, and hypothesis testing is used to test various hypotheses about the financial world. By understanding these basic statistical concepts, students can gain a strong foundation in finance and build a successful career in the field.

Math:

Basic Statistical Concepts: Problems related to descriptive statistics, probability theory, and hypothesis testing with applications in finance, such as analyzing historical stock prices and testing trading strategies

Descriptive statistics:

Descriptive statistics is an essential branch of statistics that involves the interpretation, analysis, and presentation of data. It is a method of summarizing and describing data in a meaningful way, helping to make sense of large data sets by presenting them in a manageable and comprehensible format. In the field of finance, descriptive statistics are used to analyze financial data and help investors make informed decisions about their investments. In this section, we will explore the basic concepts of descriptive statistics, including measures of central tendency, variability, and correlation.

Measures of Central Tendency:

Measures of central tendency are used to describe the typical or central value of a dataset. They include the mean, median, and mode. The mean is the average value of a dataset, calculated by adding all the values together and dividing by the number of observations. For example, if we have a portfolio of 10 stocks with returns of 2%, 3%, 5%, 6%, 8%, 9%, 10%, 11%, 12%, and 15%, the mean return would be (2%+3%+5%+6%+8%+9%+10%+11%+12%+15%)/10 = 8.1%.

The median is the middle value of a dataset when it is arranged in numerical order. For example, if we have a portfolio of 10 stocks with returns of 2%, 3%, 5%, 6%, 8%, 9%, 10%, 11%, 12%, and 15%, the median return would be the 6th value in the ordered dataset, which is 8%.

The mode is the most frequently occurring value in a dataset. In some cases, there may be no mode, or there may be multiple modes.

Measures of Variability:

Measures of variability are used to describe how spread out or variable a dataset is. They include the range, variance, and standard deviation. The range is the difference between the highest and lowest values in a dataset. For example, if we have a portfolio of 10 stocks with returns of 2%, 3%, 5%, 6%, 8%, 9%, 10%, 11%, 12%, and 15%, the range of returns would be 15% - 2% = 13%.

The variance is the average of the squared differences from the mean. It measures how much the data points are spread out from the mean. The formula for variance is:

$$Var = \Sigma(x - \mu)\,{}^\wedge 2/n$$

where Var represents variance, Σ denotes the sum, x represents each individual data point, μ represents the mean of the data points, and n represents the total number of data points.

To calculate the variance, you first subtract the mean from each data point, then square the difference for each data point, and finally, take the average of those squared differences.

where xi is each data point, x̄ is the mean of the dataset, and n is the number of observations.

Using the example of a portfolio of 10 stocks with returns of 2%, 3%, 5%, 6%, 8%, 9%, 10%, 11%, 12%, and 15%, the variance would be:

$$Var\ (x) = \frac{(2-7.1)^2+(3-7.1)^2+(5-7.1)^2+(8-7.1)^2+(9-7.1)^2+(10-7.1)^2+(11-7.1)^2+(12-7.1)^2+(15-7.1)^2}{10}=14.61$$

The standard deviation is the square root of the variance. It measures the spread of the data points from the mean in the same units as the original data. For example, if we have a portfolio of 10 stocks with returns of 2%, 3%, 5%, 6%, 8%, 9%, 10%, 11%, 12%, and 15%, the standard deviation would be:

$$\sqrt{\frac{(0.02-0.082)^2+(0.03-0.082)^2+(0.05-0.082)^2+(0.8-0.082)^2+(0.09-0.082)^2+(0.10-0.082)^2+(0.11-0.082)^2+(0.12-0.082)^2+(0.15-0.082)^2}{10-1}}$$

Simplifying the equation, we get:

$$\sqrt{\frac{0.1946}{9}}$$

The standard deviation would be approximately 0.47 or 47%. This means that the returns of the stocks in the portfolio vary on average by 47% from the mean return of the portfolio.

Skilled analysts can use the standard deviation to compare the risk of different assets or portfolios. In general, higher standard deviation indicates higher risk, while lower standard deviation indicates lower risk.

Another important descriptive statistic is the skewness of the data, which measures the degree of asymmetry of the distribution. A symmetric distribution has a skewness of 0, while a distribution that is skewed to the right (has a long tail to the right) has a positive skewness, and a distribution that is skewed to the left (has a long tail to the left) has a negative skewness. For example, a portfolio with a positive skewness may have a higher expected return than a portfolio with a negative skewness, but it may also have higher risk due to the potential for extreme positive returns.

In addition to skewness, another measure of the shape of the distribution is kurtosis. Kurtosis measures the degree of peakedness or flatness of the distribution. A distribution with high kurtosis (a "fat" tail) has more extreme values than a normal distribution, while a distribution with low kurtosis (a "thin" tail) has fewer extreme values. The kurtosis of a normal distribution is 3, so any distribution with a kurtosis greater than 3 has a "fat" tail.

In finance, descriptive statistics are commonly used to analyze the performance of stocks, bonds, and other assets. They can also be used to analyze the performance of a portfolio or a fund, to evaluate the risk and return of investment strategies, and to make predictions about future performance based on historical data. However, it's important to note that descriptive statistics are only part of the picture, and they cannot provide a complete understanding of the behavior of financial markets.

Suppose a financial analyst wants to analyze the performance of two stocks, A and B, over the past year. They collect the daily closing prices for both stocks and calculate the mean, median, and standard deviation for each stock. The results are:

Stock A: Mean = $50.25, Median = $50.10, Standard deviation = $2.30
Stock B: Mean = $42.60, Median = $42.85, Standard deviation = $1.80

From this information, the analyst can compare the two stocks and make conclusions about their performance, such as which stock had a higher average return or which stock had more volatility.

1)   Find the mean, median, and mode of the following data set: 10, 12, 14, 16, 18, 20.

2)   Calculate the standard deviation of the following data set: 5, 7, 9, 11, 13.

3)   A portfolio manager wants to know the average return for a particular stock over the past year. He has collected the following data: 5%, 8%, -2%, 12%, and 6%. Calculate the mean return.

4)   A company has hired a new data analyst to determine the average salary of its employees. The data analyst collects the following salaries: $40,000, $42,000, $45,000, $47,000, $50,000. Calculate the mean salary.

5)   The variance of a data set is 20. Calculate the standard deviation.

6) The following data set represents the number of customers at a coffee shop each day for the past week: 50, 65, 80, 40, 55, 70, 75. Calculate the range.

7) A quantitative analyst has collected data on the stock prices of two companies. Company A has a mean stock price of $25 and a standard deviation of $5. Company B has a mean stock price of $30 and a standard deviation of $10. Which company has a more stable stock price?

8) Calculate the coefficient of variation for the following data set: 5, 10, 15, 20, 25.

9) A financial planner wants to determine the typical rate of return for a particular investment over the past five years. She collects the following data: 8%, 6%, 10%, 12%, 4%. Calculate the median rate of return.

10) The following data set represents the number of hours of sleep that a group of people got last night: 6, 7, 8, 9, 10. Calculate the mode.

Probability theory:

Probability theory is a branch of mathematics that deals with the analysis of random events. It is used in finance to quantify the likelihood of various outcomes and to determine the expected value of investments. In this section, we will explore some of the key concepts and applications of probability theory in finance.

Probability is the measure of the likelihood of an event occurring. It is expressed as a number between 0 and 1, with 0 indicating impossibility and 1 indicating certainty. For example, if a fair coin is tossed, the probability of it landing heads up is 0.5.

One of the most important concepts in probability theory is the probability distribution. A probability distribution is a function that describes the likelihood of different outcomes in a random event. It provides a mathematical representation of the various possible outcomes of an event and their probabilities.

The most common probability distributions used in finance are the normal distribution and the binomial distribution. The normal distribution, also known as the Gaussian distribution, is a continuous probability distribution that is often used to model the returns of financial assets. The binomial distribution, on the other hand, is a discrete probability distribution that is used to model events with only two possible outcomes, such as the success or failure of a trade.

In finance, probability theory is used to determine the expected value of investments. The expected value is the sum of the products of the possible outcomes and their probabilities. For example, if an investment has two possible outcomes, with probabilities of 0.4 and 0.6, and payouts of $100 and $200, respectively, the expected value of the investment would be (0.4 * $100) + (0.6 * $200) = $160.

Another key application of probability theory in finance is in risk management. By calculating the probabilities of various outcomes, investors can determine the likelihood of incurring losses on an investment. This information can be used to make informed decisions about risk management strategies, such as diversification and hedging.

Hypothesis testing is a statistical tool used to determine the likelihood of a particular hypothesis being true. It involves testing a null hypothesis against an alternative hypothesis using statistical methods. In finance, hypothesis testing is used to determine the significance of relationships between financial variables.

The null hypothesis is the default assumption that there is no relationship between the variables being tested. The alternative hypothesis is the hypothesis that the variables are related in some way. To test the null hypothesis, a sample of data is collected and analyzed using statistical methods. If the results of the analysis provide sufficient evidence to reject the null hypothesis, then the alternative hypothesis is accepted.

One common application of hypothesis testing in finance is in testing the efficacy of investment strategies. For example, an investment manager may hypothesize that a particular investment strategy will yield a higher return than a standard benchmark index. To test this hypothesis, historical data is collected and analyzed using statistical methods to determine the significance of the difference in returns between the two strategies.

In conclusion, probability theory and hypothesis testing are important tools in finance for determining the likelihood of various outcomes and for testing hypotheses about relationships between financial variables. By understanding these concepts and their applications, finance professionals can make informed decisions about investments and risk management strategies.

Suppose a portfolio manager wants to calculate the probability of a stock market crash in the next month. They use historical data to estimate that the probability of a crash is 5%. Based on this probability, the manager might decide to adjust their portfolio to minimize losses in the event of a crash.

A fair six-sided die is rolled. What is the probability of rolling an even number?

Solution: The sample space of rolling a six-sided die is {1,2,3,4,5,6}. The event of rolling an even number is {2,4,6}. Therefore, the probability of rolling an even number is P(even) = |{2,4,6}|/|{1,2,3,4,5,6}| = 3/6 = 1/2.

A company hires 5 new employees. If there are 8 candidates for each position, what is the probability that all 5 new hires are female?
Solution: The probability that one candidate is female is 1/2. The probability that all 5 new hires are female is $(1/2)^5 = 1/32$.

A portfolio manager invests in two stocks, A and B. The probability of stock A increasing in value is 0.6, and the probability of stock B increasing in value is 0.5. What is the probability that both stocks increase in value?
Solution: The probability that both stocks increase in value is P(A and B) = P(A) x P(B) = 0.6 x 0.5 = 0.3.

A bank receives 100 loan applications. 70 of the applications are approved. What is the probability that a randomly selected application is approved?
Solution: The probability that a randomly selected application is approved is P(approved) = 70/100 = 0.7.

A financial analyst is analyzing the returns of a portfolio over the past year. The mean return is 8% and the standard deviation is 12%. What is the probability that the return is between 2% and 14%?
Solution: Let X be the random variable representing the return. Then, we want to find $P(2\% \leq X \leq 14\%)$. Standardizing the random variable, we get $P((-0.5) \leq (X-8)/12 \leq (1/3)) \approx P(-0.625 \leq Z \leq 0.417)$, where Z is a standard normal random variable. Using a standard normal table, we find that $P(-0.625 \leq Z \leq 0.417) \approx 0.425$.

An investor is considering investing in a stock that has a 40% chance of generating a return of 10%, a 30% chance of generating a return of 5%, and a 30% chance of generating a return of -5%. What is the expected return of the stock?
Solution: The expected return of the stock is E(R) = 0.4(10%) + 0.3(5%) + 0.3(-5%) = 4%.

A hedge fund manager is considering investing in a stock that has a beta of 1.2. If the risk-free rate is 2% and the expected return of the market is 8%, what is the expected return of the stock?
Solution: The expected return of the stock is E(R) = Rf + beta x (Rm - Rf) = 2% + 1.2 x (8% - 2%) = 9.6%.

1)   A fair coin is tossed five times. What is the probability of getting at least three heads in a row?

2)   A company has three factories, and the probability of a product being defective at factory 1, factory 2, and factory 3 is 0.05, 0.03, and 0.02 respectively. If a product is chosen at random, what is the probability that it is defective?

3)   A bag contains 10 red marbles and 8 blue marbles. If three marbles are chosen at random without replacement, what is the probability that all three are red?

4)   A game involves rolling a fair six-sided die. If the number rolled is even, the player wins $5. If the number rolled is odd, the player loses $3. What is the expected value of playing this game?

5)   In a certain city, the probability of a person having a cold in the winter is 0.10, and the probability of a person having a cold in the summer is 0.05. If a person has a cold, what is the probability that it is winter?

6)   A portfolio manager is considering investing in a stock that has a 60% chance of generating a 20% return and a 40% chance of generating a 10% return. What is the expected return on the stock?

7)   A securities trader is considering two different trading strategies. Strategy A has a 70% chance of generating a 5% profit and a 30% chance of generating a 3% profit. Strategy B has a 60% chance of generating a 4% profit and a 40% chance of generating a 2% profit. Which strategy has a higher expected profit?

8)   An actuary is calculating the probability that a policyholder will make a claim on an insurance policy. The policy has a 10% chance of generating a claim, and the actuary estimates that the probability of a claim being filed is 70% if the policyholder has a history of previous claims and 30% if the policyholder has no history of previous claims. What is the overall probability that the policyholder will make a claim?

9)   A financial planner is analyzing the returns of a mutual fund that has a mean return of 8% and a standard deviation of 12%. What is the probability that the fund will generate a return of at least 5% in a given year?

M.L.Ruscsak

10) A quantitative analyst is modeling the price of a stock using a geometric Brownian motion model. The stock's initial price is $100, the expected return is 8%, and the volatility is 20%. What is the probability that the stock's price will be greater than $120 in one year?

Hypothesis testing:

Hypothesis testing is a statistical method used to determine the validity of a hypothesis or claim about a population. In finance, hypothesis testing is used to make decisions about investments and financial strategies.

The process of hypothesis testing begins with stating a null hypothesis (H0) and an alternative hypothesis (Ha). The null hypothesis is a statement that there is no significant difference between two or more populations or variables, while the alternative hypothesis is a statement that there is a significant difference. For example, an investment analyst may want to test the hypothesis that the mean return of a portfolio is greater than 10%. The null hypothesis would be that the mean return is not greater than 10%, while the alternative hypothesis would be that the mean return is greater than 10%.

After stating the hypotheses, the analyst collects data and calculates a test statistic based on the sample data. The test statistic is a measure of how far the sample estimate is from the hypothesized population parameter. The analyst then calculates a p-value, which is the probability of observing a test statistic as extreme as the one calculated, assuming that the null hypothesis is true. If the p-value is less than the level of significance (usually 0.05), the null hypothesis is rejected in favor of the alternative hypothesis. If the p-value is greater than the level of significance, the null hypothesis is not rejected.

There are several types of hypothesis tests that can be used in finance, including:

One-sample t-test: used to test the hypothesis that the mean of a population is equal to a specified value.
Two-sample t-test: used to test the hypothesis that the means of two populations are equal.
Paired t-test: used to test the hypothesis that the means of two related populations are equal.
One-way ANOVA: used to test the hypothesis that the means of three or more populations are equal.
Chi-square test: used to test the independence of two categorical variables.
An important consideration when conducting hypothesis testing is the power of the test. The power of a test is the probability of correctly rejecting the null hypothesis when it is false. A test with low power may fail to detect a significant difference between populations, while a test with high power is more likely to detect a significant difference.

In finance, hypothesis testing is used to make important decisions, such as whether to invest in a particular security or asset, or whether to implement a new financial strategy. By using statistical methods to test hypotheses and make decisions based on evidence rather than intuition or speculation, analysts can make more informed and effective choices.

Suppose a trader has developed a new trading strategy and wants to test whether it is effective. They collect data on the performance of the strategy over a period of six months and calculate the average return. They then compare the average return to the return of a benchmark index and use a t-test to determine whether the difference is statistically significant. If the t-test indicates that the strategy significantly outperformed the benchmark, the trader may decide to implement the strategy in their portfolio.

1)   A financial analyst wants to test whether the average return on a portfolio of stocks is greater than 8%. She takes a sample of 50 stocks and finds that the sample mean return is 9%, with a sample standard deviation of 2%. Using a 5% significance level, can she reject the null hypothesis that the average return is equal to 8%?

2)   A portfolio manager wants to test whether the mean return on a portfolio of bonds is different from the mean return on a portfolio of stocks. She takes a random sample of 30 bonds and 30 stocks and finds that the sample mean returns are 6% and 10%, respectively, with sample standard deviations of 1% and 2%. Using a 1% significance level, can she reject the null hypothesis that the mean returns are equal?

3)   An investment banker wants to test whether the proportion of stocks in a portfolio that have positive returns is greater than 0.5. She takes a sample of 100 stocks and finds that 60 of them have positive returns. Using a 10% significance level, can she reject the null hypothesis that the proportion is equal to 0.5?

4)   A financial analyst wants to test whether the variance of stock returns is greater than 0.04. She takes a sample of 25 stocks and finds that the sample variance is 0.06. Using a 1% significance level, can she reject the null hypothesis that the variance is equal to 0.04?

5)   A portfolio manager wants to test whether the correlation between two assets is equal to 0.6. She takes a sample of 50 observations and finds a sample correlation of 0.7. Using a 5% significance level, can she reject the null hypothesis that the correlation is equal to 0.6?

M.L.Ruscsak

6)   An investment banker wants to test whether the mean return on a portfolio of options is less than 4%. She takes a sample of 20 options and finds a sample mean return of 3%, with a sample standard deviation of 1%. Using a 10% significance level, can she reject the null hypothesis that the mean return is equal to 4%?

7)   A financial analyst wants to test whether the mean daily return on a stock is equal to 0. She takes a random sample of 30 daily returns and finds a sample mean of -0.002, with a sample standard deviation of 0.01. Using a 5% significance level, can she reject the null hypothesis that the mean daily return is equal to 0?

8)   A portfolio manager wants to test whether the skewness of a distribution of returns is equal to 0. She takes a sample of 50 returns and finds a sample skewness of -0.5. Using a 1% significance level, can she reject the null hypothesis that the skewness is equal to 0?

9)   An investment banker wants to test whether the kurtosis of a distribution of returns is equal to 3. She takes a sample of 100 returns and finds a sample kurtosis of 3.5. Using a 5% significance level, can she reject the null hypothesis that the kurtosis is equal to 3?

10)   A financial analyst wants to test whether the mean monthly return on a mutual fund is greater than the risk-free rate of 1%. She takes a sample of 25 monthly returns and finds a sample mean of 1.5%, with a sample standard deviation of 2%. Using a 5% significance level, can she reject the null hypothesis that the mean monthly return is equal to 1?

Linear Algebra:

Linear Algebra is an essential branch of mathematics that deals with the study of linear equations, matrices, and determinants. In finance, linear algebra has numerous applications, such as portfolio analysis and option pricing. This section will provide an overview of linear algebra, including problems related to solving systems of linear equations, matrices, and determinants.

Linear algebra is concerned with the study of linear equations, which can be expressed in the form of a system of linear equations. A system of linear equations is a collection of equations that involve the same set of variables. For example, consider the following system of linear equations:

$2x + 3y = 12$
$4x + 5y = 22$

This system can be written in the form of a matrix equation as follows:

$Ax = b$

where

$A = [[2, 3], [4, 5]], x = [x, y]$, and $b = [12, 22]$.

To solve this system of linear equations, we can use the following formula:

$x = A^{-1} b$

where A^{-1} is the inverse of matrix A.

In finance, linear algebra is often used in portfolio analysis. A portfolio is a collection of financial assets, such as stocks, bonds, and options, held by an investor. The goal of portfolio analysis is to find the optimal portfolio that maximizes the expected return for a given level of risk. This can be done using linear algebra, specifically by solving systems of linear equations.

Another application of linear algebra in finance is option pricing. An option is a financial contract that gives the holder the right, but not the obligation, to buy or sell an underlying asset at a predetermined price within a certain period of time. Option pricing involves calculating the fair value of an option based on various factors, such as the current price of the underlying asset, the strike price, the time to expiration, and the volatility of the underlying asset. Linear algebra is used to solve the equations that determine the fair value of the option.

Matrices are another important concept in linear algebra. A matrix is a rectangular array of numbers. Matrices are used to represent systems of linear equations and can also be used to transform vectors. In finance, matrices are used in portfolio analysis to represent the returns of different assets and to calculate the covariance between them.

Determinants are a mathematical concept used to determine the properties of a matrix. The determinant of a matrix is a scalar value that can be used to determine if the matrix is invertible and to calculate the inverse of the matrix. In finance, determinants are used in portfolio analysis to determine the diversification benefits of different assets.

In conclusion, linear algebra is a fundamental mathematical concept with numerous applications in finance, such as portfolio analysis and option pricing. It is essential for students seeking a bachelor's degree in finance to have a strong understanding of linear algebra and its applications in finance. By mastering the concepts of linear equations, matrices, and determinants, students will be better equipped to analyze financial data and make informed investment decisions.

1) An investment banker has a portfolio of three assets with returns given by the vectors [2, 1, -1], [1, 3, 2], and [3, 1, -2]. What is the expected return of this portfolio?

2) A quantitative analyst has a system of linear equations that represents the relationship between four financial instruments. Solve the system to find the values of the instruments that maximize a given objective function.

3) A portfolio manager has a portfolio of five assets with covariance matrix given by:

$[\,4\;\text{-}1\;\text{-}1\;0\;2\,]$
$[\,\text{-}1\;9\;0\;3\;\text{-}4\,]$
$[\,\text{-}1\;0\;16\;4\;\text{-}3\,]$
$[\,0\;3\;4\;25\;\text{-}10\,]$
$[\,2\;\text{-}4\;\text{-}3\;\text{-}10\;36\,]$

What is the variance of the portfolio?

4) A financial analyst has a system of linear equations that represents the relationship between three financial instruments. Determine whether the system is consistent, inconsistent, or dependent.

5) An actuary is solving a system of linear equations that represents the relationship between four financial instruments. What is the rank of the coefficient matrix of this system?

6) A securities trader has a portfolio of three assets with returns given by the vectors [1, 2, 3], [2, 1, 3], and [3, 2, 1]. Determine whether the assets are linearly independent.

7) A financial planner has a portfolio of four assets with returns given by the vectors [1, 2, 3, 4], [2, 1, 4, 3], [3, 4, 1, 2], and [4, 3, 2, 1]. What is the determinant of the covariance matrix of this portfolio?

8) A portfolio manager is constructing a portfolio of two assets. Asset 1 has an expected return of 8% and a standard deviation of 12%. Asset 2 has an expected return of 12% and a

standard deviation of 16%. Determine the weights that should be assigned to each asset in the portfolio to minimize the portfolio risk.

9) An investment banker has a portfolio of two assets with covariance matrix given by:

[9 -3]
[-3 16]

What is the correlation coefficient between the two assets?

10) A quantitative analyst is analyzing a system of linear equations that represents the relationship between five financial instruments. What is the null space of the coefficient matrix of this system?

Differential Equations:

Differential equations are mathematical equations that involve the derivatives of one or more variables. They play a crucial role in many areas of science and engineering, including finance. In finance, differential equations are often used to model various phenomena, such as interest rates, asset prices, and other economic variables.

One of the most common applications of differential equations in finance is in the modeling of interest rates. Interest rates play a critical role in the economy, as they influence many financial decisions, such as borrowing, lending, and investing. To model interest rates, we often use ordinary differential equations (ODEs), which are differential equations involving a single variable.

One of the most famous ODEs used to model interest rates is the well-known Black-Scholes equation. The Black-Scholes equation is a partial differential equation (PDE) that is used to model the price of financial instruments such as options. The equation takes into account the volatility of the underlying asset, the time to expiration of the option, and the risk-free interest rate. By solving the Black-Scholes equation, we can determine the theoretical price of a financial instrument.

Another application of differential equations in finance is the modeling of asset prices. Asset prices are constantly fluctuating in response to various factors, such as economic indicators, geopolitical events, and investor sentiment. To model the behavior of asset prices, we often use stochastic differential equations (SDEs), which are differential equations that involve random variables.

M.L.Ruscsak

The most well-known SDE used to model asset prices is the geometric Brownian motion (GBM) equation. The GBM equation is used to model the price of a stock or other financial instrument that follows a random walk with a constant drift and volatility. By solving the GBM equation, we can estimate the future price of the asset and make informed investment decisions.

Differential equations are also used in finance to model various other economic variables, such as inflation, GDP growth, and exchange rates. By using differential equations to model these variables, we can gain insights into their behavior and make predictions about future trends.

However, solving differential equations can be challenging, especially for complex systems. To solve differential equations, we often use numerical methods, such as Euler's method, Runge-Kutta methods, or finite difference methods. These methods involve breaking the differential equation into smaller, simpler equations that can be solved numerically. While these methods can provide accurate solutions, they require a significant amount of computational power and can be time-consuming.

In conclusion, differential equations play a crucial role in finance, allowing us to model various economic variables and make informed decisions about investments and financial decisions. While solving differential equations can be challenging, the rewards are significant, and the insights gained from modeling economic phenomena can be invaluable for individuals and institutions alike.

Euler's Method:
$y_{i+1} = y_i + hf(x_i, y_i)$
Improved Euler's Method:
$k_1 = hf(x_i, y_i)$
$k_2 = hf(x_i + h, y_i + k_1)$
$y_{i+1} = y_i + 1/2(k_1 + k_2)$

Runge-Kutta Method (4th order):
$k_1 = hf(x_i, y_i)$
$k_2 = hf(x_i + h/2, y_i + k_1/2)$
$k_3 = hf(x_i + h/2, y_i + k_2/2)$
$k_4 = hf(x_i + h, y_i + k_3)$
$y_{i+1} = y_i + 1/6(k_1 + 2k_2 + 2k_3 + k_4)$

Crank-Nicolson Method:
$(1 + 1/2r)y_{i+1} - ry_{i+1} = (1 - 1/2r)y_i + rhf(x_{i+1}, y_{i+1}) + rhf(x_i, y_i)$

Finite Difference Method:
$(y_{i+1} - 2y_i + y_{i-1})/h^2 = f(x_i, y_i)$

Note: These equations are not exhaustive, and there are variations and extensions to each method depending on the specific problem being solved.

1.   Solve the ordinary differential equation $y' + 2y = 0$, where $y(0) = 4$. This equation can be used to model the decay of a radioactive substance. What is the half-life of the substance?

2.   Use the Black-Scholes partial differential equation to model the price of a European call option. Assume that the underlying asset follows a geometric Brownian motion and that the risk-free interest rate is constant.

3.   Solve the heat equation $u\_t = ku\_xx$, where $u(x,0) = f(x)$ and $u(0,t) = u(L,t) = 0$. This equation can be used to model the temperature distribution in a metal rod of length L.

4.   Use the diffusion equation to model the spread of a disease in a population. Assume that the disease is transmitted through contact and that the transmission rate depends on the number of infected individuals.

5.   Solve the logistic differential equation $y' = ky(1 - y/M)$, where $y(0) = y\_0$. This equation can be used to model the growth of a population subject to a carrying capacity M.

6.   Use the wave equation to model the motion of a guitar string. Assume that the string is clamped at both ends and that its initial shape is given by $f(x)$.

7.   Solve the Black-Scholes equation for a European put option. Assume that the underlying asset follows a geometric Brownian motion and that the risk-free interest rate is constant.

8.   Use the diffusion equation to model the spread of information in a social network. Assume that the diffusion rate depends on the connectivity of the network and the number of active users.

9.   Solve the Cauchy-Euler equation x^2y'' + axy' + by = 0, where a and b are constants. This equation can be used to model the motion of a spring-mass system subject to damping and external forcing.

10.   Use the Navier-Stokes equations to model the flow of a fluid in a pipe. Assume that the pipe is horizontal and that the flow is driven by a pressure gradient.

Calculus:

Calculus is a branch of mathematics that deals with the study of functions and their properties, including their limits, derivatives, and integrals. It is an essential tool for understanding and solving various problems in finance. The concepts of calculus are used extensively in financial modeling, optimization problems, and marginal analysis. In this section, we will explore some of the key applications of calculus in finance.

One of the most fundamental concepts in calculus is the limit. In finance, limits can be used to model the behavior of various financial variables, such as interest rates and stock prices. For example, the limit of an interest rate can be used to estimate the future value of an investment. Similarly, the limit of a stock price can be used to predict its future value. By understanding limits, financial analysts can make informed decisions about investments and other financial activities.

Another essential concept in calculus is the derivative. The derivative of a function represents its rate of change, or how quickly it is changing at any given point. In finance, derivatives are used to model and analyze a wide range of phenomena, such as the rate of return on an investment, the slope of a yield curve, or the sensitivity of an option price to changes in the underlying asset price. The derivatives of financial models are essential tools for pricing financial instruments and assessing risk.

The integral is another crucial concept in calculus. It is used to calculate the area under a curve and is used extensively in finance to calculate the present value of future cash flows. For example, the present value of a bond can be calculated using an integral. The integral can also be used to calculate the expected value of a portfolio, which is a measure of the portfolio's average return.

Optimization problems are another area where calculus plays a significant role in finance. Optimization involves finding the maximum or minimum value of a function subject to certain constraints. In finance, optimization is used to determine the optimal allocation of assets in a portfolio to maximize return while minimizing risk. Optimization can also be used to determine the optimal pricing of financial instruments such as options and futures contracts.

Marginal analysis is a concept that is closely related to derivatives. Marginal analysis involves examining the changes in a variable as a result of a small change in another variable. In finance, marginal analysis is used to determine the impact of changes in interest rates or asset prices on the value of a portfolio. For example, a financial analyst might use marginal analysis to determine how a 1% increase in interest rates will affect the value of a bond portfolio.

In conclusion, calculus is an essential tool for understanding and solving problems in finance. The concepts of limits, derivatives, integrals, optimization, and marginal analysis are all crucial for modeling and analyzing financial phenomena. Financial analysts, investment bankers, actuaries, portfolio managers, quantitative analysts, securities traders, financial planners, and financial analysts all use calculus extensively in their work. By mastering these concepts, students seeking a bachelor's degree in finance can gain a deeper understanding of the financial world and make more informed decisions about investments and other financial activities.

1. A company has a cost function given by $C(x) = 1000 + 10x + 0.01x^2$, where x is the number of units produced. Find the marginal cost function and use it to determine the production level that minimizes the average cost.

2. An investor wants to find the maximum return on investment for a portfolio of stocks. If the expected return on stock A is 8% and the expected return on stock B is 12%, and the covariance between them is 0.005, what proportion of the portfolio should be invested in each stock?

3. A company's revenue function is given by $R(x) = 15x - 0.02x^2$, where x is the number of units sold. What is the maximum revenue the company can generate, and what is the corresponding production level?

4. An investor holds a portfolio of stocks with a total value of $500,000. If the portfolio's beta is 1.5, what is the expected return on the portfolio if the risk-free rate is 2% and the market return is 10%?

5. A company's profit function is given by $P(x) = 20x - x^2$, where x is the number of units sold. What is the maximum profit the company can generate, and what is the corresponding production level?

M.L.Ruscsak

6.   An investor wants to minimize the risk of their portfolio. If the expected return on stock A is 6% and the expected return on stock B is 10%, and the standard deviations are 5% and 8%, respectively, what proportion of the portfolio should be invested in each stock?

7.   A company's revenue function is given by $R(x) = 20x - 0.05x^2$, where x is the number of units sold. What is the maximum price the company can charge per unit, and what is the corresponding production level?

8.   An investor wants to maximize their utility function, which is given by $U(x) = 10x - 0.1x^2$, where x is the amount of money invested. What is the optimal investment level?

9.   A company's cost function is given by $C(x) = 100 + 5x + 0.02x^2$, where x is the number of units produced. Find the average cost function and use it to determine the production level that minimizes the average cost.

10.   An investor holds a portfolio of stocks with a total value of $1,000,000. If the portfolio's beta is 1.2, what is the expected return on the portfolio if the risk-free rate is 3% and the market return is 8%?

Note: These exercises may require knowledge beyond what is typically covered in a Calculus course, such as covariance and beta.

Covariance and Beta are two key concepts in finance that are closely related to each other. In this section, we will explore what these two terms mean and how they are used in financial analysis.

Covariance is a measure of the relationship between two random variables. In finance, we often use covariance to describe the relationship between the returns of two different assets. If two assets have a high positive covariance, it means that they tend to move in the same direction, meaning when one asset increases in value, the other asset tends to increase in value as well. Conversely, if two assets have a high negative covariance, it means that they tend to move in opposite directions, meaning when one asset increases in value, the other asset tends to decrease in value.

The formula for covariance is:

$$cov(X,Y) = E[(X - E[X])(Y - E[Y])]$$

where E[X] and E[Y] are the expected values of X and Y, respectively.

Alternatively, the covariance can also be expressed as:

$$cov(X,Y) = (1/n) * \Sigma[(x_i - E[X])(y_i - E[Y])]$$

where x_i and y_i are individual observations of X and Y, respectively, and n is the total number of observations.

The formula for covariance measures how much two variables vary together. A positive covariance indicates that the two variables tend to increase or decrease together, while a negative covariance indicates that they tend to move in opposite directions. A covariance of zero indicates that the variables are independent of each other.

In finance, covariance is often used to measure the degree to which the returns of two assets are related to each other. For example, if the covariance between the returns of two stocks is positive, it suggests that the returns of these stocks tend to move together, and investors may want to consider diversifying their portfolio by investing in other stocks with negative or low covariance.

Now, let's move on to beta. Beta is a measure of the sensitivity of an asset's returns to changes in the market. Specifically, beta measures how much an asset's returns move in response to changes in the overall market returns.

Beta is a measure of the systematic risk of an investment in relation to the market as a whole. It is calculated as the covariance between the returns of the investment and the returns of the market, divided by the variance of the returns of the market.

The formula for beta is:

$$\beta = cov(r\_i, r\_m) / var(r\_m)$$

where β is the beta of the investment, r_i is the returns of the investment, r_m is the returns of the market, $cov(r\_i, r\_m)$ is the covariance between the returns of the investment and the returns of the market, and $var(r\_m)$ is the variance of the returns of the market.

Beta is a measure of the sensitivity of the investment's returns to changes in the market's returns. A beta of 1 indicates that the investment's returns move in line with the market, while a beta greater than 1 indicates that the investment's returns are more volatile than the market, and a beta less than 1 indicates that the investment's returns are less volatile than the market. A beta of 0 indicates that there is no correlation between the investment's returns and the market's returns.

PART 2: TIME VALUE OF MONEY

The time value of money is a fundamental concept in finance that is used to evaluate the worth of money over time. In essence, it recognizes that money today is worth more than money in the future, and that the value of money changes over time due to various factors such as inflation, interest rates, and risk.

This concept is widely used in many areas of finance, including investments, banking, insurance, and retirement planning. It is used to calculate present value, future value, annuities, and other financial instruments that involve the movement of money over time.

The purpose of this section is to provide a comprehensive overview of the time value of money and its various applications in finance.

Time Value of Money Basics

The time value of money is based on the principle that money available today is worth more than the same amount of money in the future due to the opportunity cost of waiting. The opportunity cost is the amount that could be earned by investing the money elsewhere.

For example, if an investor had the choice of receiving $1,000 today or $1,000 one year from now, most people would choose to receive the money today. This is because the investor could invest the money and earn a return on it over the course of the year. The future value of the $1,000 investment would be greater than $1,000, assuming a positive rate of return.

Conversely, if an investor was given the choice of paying $1,000 today or $1,000 one year from now, most people would choose to pay the money one year from now. This is because the investor could invest the money elsewhere and earn a return on it over the course of the year, effectively reducing the cost of the payment.

Present Value and Future Value

The two primary concepts related to the time value of money are present value (PV) and future value (FV). Present value refers to the current value of a future payment or stream of payments, while future value refers to the value of an investment at some point in the future.

The formulas for calculating present value and future value are as follows:

PV = FV / (1 + r)^n
FV = PV x (1 + r)^n

Where:
PV = Present value
FV = Future value
r = Interest rate
n = Number of periods

The interest rate represents the cost of money or the opportunity cost of investing. The number of periods represents the length of time between the present and the future payment or investment.

Annuities
An annuity is a series of equal payments made at regular intervals over a specified period of time. Annuities can be either ordinary annuities, where payments are made at the end of each period, or annuities due, where payments are made at the beginning of each period.

The present value and future value of an annuity can be calculated using the following formulas:

PV = PMT x ((1 - (1 + r)^-n) / r)
FV = PMT x (((1 + r)^n - 1) / r)

Where:
PMT = Payment
r = Interest rate
n = Number of periods

Compounding and Discounting
Compounding refers to the process of calculating the future value of an investment by including the interest earned in each period. This means that interest earned in one period is added to the principal to earn interest in subsequent periods.

Discounting refers to the process of calculating the present value of a future payment or investment by reducing the future value by the interest earned in each period. This means that the future value is reduced by the present value of the interest earned in each period.

The formulas for calculating compound interest and discounted present value are as follows:

Compound Interest Formula:
FV = PV x (1 + r)^n

where FV is the future value, PV is the present value, r is the interest rate per period, and n is the number of periods.

Discounted Present Value Formula:
PV = FV / (1 + r)^n

where PV is the present value, FV is the future value, r is the interest rate per period, and n is the number of periods.

Both of these formulas are based on the concept of time value of money, which states that money available at the present time is worth more than the same amount of money available in the future. This is because money available in the present can be invested and earn interest, while money in the future is subject to inflation and other risks.

The time value of money is a critical concept in finance and is used extensively in investment analysis, financial planning, and decision-making. By understanding the time value of money, investors and financial professionals can make more informed decisions about where to allocate their resources and how to manage risk.

One important application of the time value of money is in the calculation of the net present value (NPV) of an investment. The net present value is the difference between the present value of the expected cash inflows and the present value of the expected cash outflows associated with an investment. If the net present value is positive, the investment is expected to be profitable, while a negative net present value indicates that the investment is not expected to be profitable.

Another important application of the time value of money is in the calculation of the internal rate of return (IRR) of an investment. The internal rate of return is the discount rate at which the net present value of an investment is equal to zero. The internal rate of return provides investors with a measure of the profitability of an investment, and it is commonly used in capital budgeting and investment analysis.

In conclusion, the time value of money is a fundamental concept in finance, and it is used extensively in investment analysis, financial planning, and decision-making. By understanding the principles of compounding, discounting, and present value, investors and financial professionals can make more informed decisions about where to allocate their resources and how to manage risk. The formulas for compound interest and discounted present value are essential tools for calculating the future value and present value of investments, and they are used extensively in the calculation of the net present value and internal rate of return of an investment.

CHAPTER 4: OVERVIEW OF TIME VALUE OF MONEY CONCEPTS

The concept of time value of money is a fundamental principle in finance. Essentially, it means that money available at the present time is worth more than the same amount of money in the future, because of its potential earning capacity. In other words, money today can be invested and will grow over time, so that in the future it will be worth more than it is now. This concept is important in many financial decisions, including investments, loans, and retirement planning.

In this chapter, we will provide an overview of time value of money concepts, including compounding, discounting, present value, future value, annuities, perpetuities, and effective annual rate. We will explain these concepts in detail, and provide examples of how they are used in financial decision-making.

Compounding

Compounding is a basic concept in the time value of money. It refers to the process of calculating the future value of an investment by including the interest earned in each period. This means that interest earned in one period is added to the principal to earn interest in subsequent periods. The more frequently interest is compounded, the faster the investment will grow.

For example, consider an investment of $1,000 that earns 5% interest annually for five years. If the interest is compounded annually, the future value of the investment will be:

$$FV = \$1,000 \times (1 + 0.05)^5 = \$1,276.28$$

If the interest is compounded quarterly (four times per year), the future value will be:

$$FV = \$1,000 \times (1 + 0.05/4)^{(5*4)} = \$1,283.35$$

As you can see, compounding more frequently results in a higher future value.

Discounting

Discounting is the opposite of compounding, and refers to the process of calculating the present value of a future payment or investment by reducing the future value by the interest earned in each period. This means that the future value is reduced by the present value of the interest earned in each period. The more frequently interest is discounted, the faster the future value will be reduced.

For example, consider a future payment of $1,000 that will be received in five years, and assume a discount rate of 5%. If the interest is discounted annually, the present value of the payment will be:

PV = $1,000 / (1 + 0.05)^5 = $783.53

If the interest is discounted quarterly, the present value will be:

PV = $1,000 / (1 + 0.05/4)^(5*4) = $789.94

As you can see, discounting more frequently results in a lower present value.

Present Value

The present value (PV) of a future payment or investment is the current worth of that payment or investment, discounted by the interest rate. It is the amount of money that would need to be invested today to generate the future value of that payment or investment. The formula for present value is:

PV = FV / (1 + r)^n

Where FV is the future value, r is the discount rate, and n is the number of periods.

For example, consider an investment that will be worth $10,000 in five years, with a discount rate of 8%. The present value of the investment is:

PV = $10,000 / (1 + 0.08)^5 = $6,710.99

This means that if you invested $6,710.99 today at a discount rate of 8%, it would grow to $10,000 in five years.

Future Value

The future value (FV) of an investment or payment is the amount of money that the investment or payment will be worth at a specified time in the future, assuming a certain interest rate. The formula for future value is:

FV = PV x (1 + r)^n

M.L.Ruscsak

Where PV is the present value, r is the interest rate, and n is the number of periods.

For example, let's say you have $5,000 to invest today and you expect to earn a 6% annual interest rate on that investment. If you want to know how much that investment will be worth in five years, you can use the future value formula:

FV = $5,000 x (1 + 0.06)^5 = $6,825.03

This means that if you invest $5,000 today at a 6% annual interest rate, it will be worth $6,825.03 in five years.

An important concept related to future value is the concept of compounding. Compounding refers to the process of earning interest on both the principal and the interest earned in previous periods. The more frequently interest is compounded, the faster the investment will grow. This is because the interest earned in each period is added to the principal, which in turn earns interest in the next period.

For example, let's say you have $1,000 to invest at a 10% annual interest rate, compounded annually. After one year, your investment will be worth:

FV = $1,000 x (1 + 0.10)^1 = $1,100

If the interest is compounded semi-annually (twice a year), your investment will be worth:

FV = $1,000 x (1 + 0.05)^2 = $1,102.50

If the interest is compounded monthly, your investment will be worth:

FV = $1,000 x (1 + 0.008333)^12 = $1,104.71

As you can see, the more frequently interest is compounded, the higher the future value of the investment.

Another important concept related to future value is the concept of annuities. An annuity is a series of equal payments or receipts that occur at regular intervals. Examples of annuities include mortgage payments, car payments, and regular deposits into a retirement account.

The formula for the future value of an annuity is:

FV = PMT x ((1 + r)^n - 1) / r

Where PMT is the amount of each payment, r is the interest rate per period, and n is the number of periods.

For example, let's say you want to know how much money you will have in 20 years if you deposit $500 into a retirement account each month, earning a 7% annual interest rate. Using the future value of annuity formula, we can calculate the future value of the monthly deposits:

$$FV = \$500 \times ((1 + 0.07/12)^{240} - 1) / (0.07/12) = \$347,516.05$$

This means that if you make monthly deposits of $500 into a retirement account earning a 7% annual interest rate, you will have approximately $347,516.05 in 20 years.

Definition of time value of money and its importance in finance

The time value of money (TVM) refers to the concept that money today is worth more than the same amount of money in the future, due to the potential to earn interest or returns on that money over time. The basic idea is that the value of money changes over time, and that the timing of cash flows can have a significant impact on the value of an investment.

TVM is a fundamental concept in finance and plays a critical role in many financial decisions, including investments, loans, and other financial transactions. Understanding TVM is essential for making informed decisions about money and investments, and is a critical component of financial literacy.

The importance of TVM can be seen in a variety of scenarios. For example, suppose you have the choice between receiving $1,000 today or $1,000 in five years. Most people would choose to receive the $1,000 today, because they could invest the money and potentially earn a return on it over the next five years. The value of the $1,000 today is higher than the value of the same amount of money in the future, due to the potential for returns.

Similarly, TVM plays a crucial role in determining the value of investments and loans. For example, suppose you are considering investing $10,000 in a stock that is expected to return 8% per year for the next five years. Using TVM, you can calculate the expected future value of the investment, and determine whether it is a good investment opportunity. Conversely, if you are considering taking out a loan for $10,000 to purchase a car, understanding TVM can help you determine the total cost of the loan, including interest.

One of the primary ways that TVM is applied in finance is through the use of discount rates. A discount rate is the rate of return that an investor would require in order to invest in a particular asset or project. By using a discount rate, investors can calculate the present value of future cash flows, and determine whether an investment opportunity is worthwhile. Discount rates are often

M.L.Ruscsak

based on the cost of capital, which is the minimum rate of return that a company or investor requires to undertake a particular investment.

Another way that TVM is used in finance is through the calculation of net present value (NPV). NPV is a method used to determine the value of an investment by calculating the present value of all expected future cash flows, and subtracting the initial cost of the investment. If the NPV is positive, it indicates that the investment is expected to generate a positive return, while a negative NPV indicates that the investment is likely to generate a loss.

In summary, the time value of money is a critical concept in finance that refers to the idea that the value of money changes over time. Understanding TVM is essential for making informed decisions about investments, loans, and other financial transactions, and is a critical component of financial literacy. TVM is applied in finance through the use of discount rates and net present value calculations, which allow investors to determine the present value of future cash flows and make informed investment decisions.

Explanation of present value, future value, and annuities

The concept of time value of money is essential in finance as it allows individuals and organizations to make informed decisions regarding investments, loans, and other financial transactions. Understanding present value, future value, and annuities is crucial for evaluating the financial feasibility of any investment or loan.

Present Value:

Present value is the concept of determining the value of an amount of money today, which is expected to receive at a later date. This concept is based on the principle that a dollar received today is worth more than a dollar received in the future. Present value takes into account the time value of money by factoring in the opportunity cost of investing money elsewhere and the impact of inflation.

The formula for present value is:

$PV = FV / (1 + r)^n$

Where PV is the present value, FV is the future value, r is the interest rate, and n is the number of periods.

For example, suppose you expect to receive $10,000 after five years, and the interest rate is 5%. In that case, the present value of the $10,000 would be:

$PV = \$10,000 / (1 + 0.05)^5 = \$7,835.05$

Future Value:

The future value is the amount of money an investment is expected to grow to at a future date, given a specified interest rate. The future value is calculated based on the compounding effect of interest earned over time.

The formula for future value is:

$$FV = PV \times (1 + r)^n$$

Where FV is the future value, PV is the present value, r is the interest rate, and n is the number of periods.

For example, suppose you invest $1,000 today for five years, and the interest rate is 5%. In that case, the future value of the investment would be:

$$FV = \$1,000 \times (1 + 0.05)^5 = \$1,276.28$$

Annuities:

An annuity is a series of equal periodic payments or receipts over a specified period. An annuity can be either an ordinary annuity or an annuity due.

An ordinary annuity is a series of equal periodic payments or receipts made at the end of each period. Examples of ordinary annuities include mortgage payments and lease payments.

The formula for the present value of an ordinary annuity is:

$$PV = (C \times (1 - (1 + r)^{-n})) / r$$

Where PV is the present value, C is the periodic payment, r is the interest rate, and n is the number of periods.

For example, suppose you borrow $10,000 for five years at an interest rate of 5%, and you will make equal monthly payments. In that case, the present value of the loan would be:

$$PV = (\$10,000 \times (1 - (1 + 0.05/12)^{(-5*12)})) / (0.05/12) = \$8,737.17$$

An annuity due is a series of equal periodic payments or receipts made at the beginning of each period. Examples of annuity due include rent payments and insurance premium payments.

M.L.Ruscsak

The formula for the present value of an annuity due is:

$$PV = (C \times (1 - (1 + r)^{-n}) \times (1 + r)) / r$$

Where PV is the present value, C is the periodic payment, r is the interest rate, and n is the number of periods.

For example, suppose you invest $1,000 per year for five years, and the interest rate is 5%. In that case, the present value of the investment would be:

$$PV = (\$1,000 \times (1 - (1 + 0.05)^{-5}) \times (1 + 0.05)) / 0.05$$

$$PV = (\$1,000 \times (1 - 0.78353) \times 1.05) / 0.05$$

$$PV = \$4,329.48$$

This means that if you invest $4,329.48 today at a 5% interest rate, and make $1,000 annual investments for five years, the future value of the investment will be $5,525.

An annuity due is a series of periodic payments where the first payment is made at the beginning of the period. In contrast, a regular annuity has payments made at the end of each period.

The present value of an annuity due can be calculated using the formula:

$$PV = (C \times (1 - (1 + r)^{-n}) \times (1 + r)) / r \times (1 + r)$$

Where PV is the present value, C is the periodic payment, r is the interest rate, and n is the number of periods.

For example, suppose you invest $1,000 per year for five years, and the interest rate is 5%. In that case, the present value of the annuity due would be:

$$PV = (\$1,000 \times (1 - (1 + 0.05)^{-5}) \times (1 + 0.05)) / 0.05 \times (1 + 0.05)$$

$$PV = (\$1,000 \times (1 - 0.78353) \times 1.05) / 0.05 \times 1.05$$

$$PV = \$4,545.68$$

This means that if you invest $4,545.68 today at a 5% interest rate, and make $1,000 annual investments at the beginning of each year for five years, the future value of the investment will be $5,825.69.

In conclusion, the concepts of present value, future value, and annuities are essential in finance. These concepts allow investors to understand the time value of money and make informed investment decisions. By using these formulas, investors can determine the present value of future payments or investments, the future value of current investments, and the value of periodic payments. It is crucial to understand these concepts to make smart investment choices and achieve financial goals.

Time value of money formulas and calculations

Time value of money is a fundamental concept in finance that plays a critical role in investment analysis, financial planning, and decision-making. It is based on the idea that money has a time value, meaning that the value of money today is not the same as its value in the future. Therefore, to make sound financial decisions, one needs to be able to compare the value of money at different points in time. Time value of money formulas and calculations are essential tools used to measure and compare the value of money over time.

In this section, we will explore some of the most commonly used time value of money formulas and calculations, including future value, present value, annuities, and perpetuities.

Future Value

The future value (FV) of an investment is the amount of money it will be worth at a future date, given a certain rate of return. The formula for future value is:

$$FV = PV \times (1 + r)^n$$

Where PV is the present value, r is the interest rate, and n is the number of periods.

For example, suppose you invest $1,000 today at a 5% annual interest rate for five years. Using the formula, we can calculate the future value of the investment as follows:

$$FV = \$1,000 \times (1 + 0.05)^5 = \$1,276.28$$

This means that in five years, the investment will be worth $1,276.28 if it earns a 5% annual return.

Present Value

The present value (PV) of an investment is the current worth of a future payment or investment, discounted by the interest rate. It is the amount of money that would need to be invested today to generate the future value of that payment or investment. The formula for present value is:

PV = FV / (1 + r)^n

Where FV is the future value, r is the discount rate, and n is the number of periods.

For example, consider an investment that will be worth $10,000 in five years, with a discount rate of 8%. The present value of the investment is:

PV = $10,000 / (1 + 0.08)^5 = $6,710.99

This means that if you invested $6,710.99 today at a discount rate of 8%, it would grow to $10,000 in five years.

Annuities

An annuity is a series of equal payments made at regular intervals over a specified period. Annuities are commonly used in retirement planning, where an individual may make regular contributions to a retirement account and receive regular payments in retirement.

The present value of an annuity (PVA) is the current worth of a series of equal payments, discounted by the interest rate. The formula for the present value of an annuity is:

PVA = (C x (1 - (1 + r)^-n)) / r

Where PVA is the present value of the annuity, C is the periodic payment, r is the interest rate, and n is the number of periods.

For example, suppose you want to know the present value of a five-year annuity that pays $1,000 per year and has an interest rate of 5%. Using the formula, we can calculate the present value of the annuity as follows:

PVA = ($1,000 x (1 - (1 + 0.05)^-5)) / 0.05 = $4,329.48

This means that if you invested $4,329.48 today at a 5% annual interest rate, you would receive $1,000 per year for five years.

Perpetuities

A perpetuity is a special type of annuity that pays a fixed amount of money at regular intervals forever. Unlike an ordinary annuity, which has a fixed number of payments, a perpetuity has an infinite number of payments.

The present value of a perpetuity can be calculated using the following formula:

$$PVPerpetuity = C / r$$

Where PVPerpetuity is the present value of the perpetuity, C is the constant payment received at each interval, and r is the discount rate.

For example, suppose you have the opportunity to invest in a perpetuity that pays $100 per year and has a discount rate of 6%. Using the formula, we can calculate the present value of the perpetuity as:

$$PVPerpetuity = \$100 / 0.06 = \$1,666.67$$

This means that if you invested $1,666.67 at a 6% annual interest rate, you would receive $100 per year indefinitely.

Bond Valuation

Bonds are a type of investment that represents a loan made by an investor to a corporation or government. The bond issuer agrees to pay the investor a fixed interest rate for a specified period, after which the principal amount is returned to the investor. Bond valuation is the process of determining the present value of the future cash flows that the bond will generate.

The present value of a bond can be calculated using the following formula:

$$PVBond = (C / r) \times (1 - (1 + r)^{-n}) + (FV / (1 + r)^n)$$

Where PVBond is the present value of the bond, C is the coupon payment, r is the discount rate, n is the number of periods, and FV is the face value of the bond.

For example, suppose you have a bond with a face value of $1,000, a coupon rate of 5%, and a maturity date of 10 years. If the current market interest rate is also 5%, the present value of the bond would be:

$$PVBond = (\$50 / 0.05) \times (1 - (1 + 0.05)^{-10}) + (\$1,000 / (1 + 0.05)^{10}) = \$1,000$$

This means that the bond is priced at its face value, indicating that the market interest rate is in line with the bond's coupon rate.

Conclusion

Time value of money concepts and formulas are fundamental to finance and investment. They enable investors to make informed decisions by providing a way to compare cash flows that occur at different points in time. The present value, future value, annuity, perpetuity, and bond valuation formulas allow investors to determine the value of cash flows and investments, enabling them to make better investment decisions. Understanding these concepts is essential for anyone interested in finance or investing.

CHAPTER 5: CALCULATION OF TIME VALUE OF MONEY USING DIFFERENT METHODS

The concept of time value of money is a fundamental principle in finance. It is based on the premise that a dollar received today is worth more than a dollar received in the future due to the potential earning power of that dollar over time. The time value of money is a crucial concept in finance because it helps individuals and organizations make informed financial decisions by providing a framework for comparing and evaluating investment opportunities.

In this chapter, we will explore the calculation of time value of money using different methods. We will discuss the different methods of calculating present value and future value, as well as annuities and perpetuities. We will also discuss the use of spreadsheets and financial calculators in time value of money calculations.

Present Value and Future Value

One of the most common ways to calculate time value of money is to use present value and future value calculations. Present value is the value today of a future cash flow or series of cash flows, while future value is the value at some point in the future of a current cash flow or series of cash flows. The present value calculation involves discounting future cash flows at a specified rate of return, while the future value calculation involves compounding current cash flows at a specified rate of return.

Annuities and Perpetuities

In addition to present value and future value calculations, annuities and perpetuities are also important concepts in time value of money. An annuity is a series of equal payments made at regular intervals, while a perpetuity is an infinite series of equal payments made at regular intervals. Annuities and perpetuities can be either ordinary annuities or annuities due, depending on whether the first payment is made at the beginning or end of the payment period.

Different Methods of Calculation

There are several methods of calculating time value of money, each with its own advantages and disadvantages. The most common methods include the use of formulas, spreadsheets, and financial calculators. While each method has its own strengths and weaknesses, the key is to choose the method that is most appropriate for the situation at hand.

Using Spreadsheets and Financial Calculators

Spreadsheets and financial calculators are powerful tools for calculating time value of money. They can be used to perform complex calculations quickly and accurately, allowing individuals and organizations to make informed financial decisions. Spreadsheets are particularly useful for analyzing large amounts of data and performing what-if analyses, while financial calculators are more portable and convenient for on-the-go calculations.

Conclusion

In conclusion, the calculation of time value of money is a crucial concept in finance that helps individuals and organizations make informed financial decisions. Understanding the different methods of calculating time value of money, including present value and future value, annuities and perpetuities, and the use of spreadsheets and financial calculators, is essential for success in the field of finance.

Calculation of present and future values using different methods

In the previous chapters, we discussed the fundamental concepts of time value of money, including present value, future value, annuities, and perpetuities. We also learned how to calculate these values using the basic formula. However, in some cases, the basic formula may not be sufficient to solve complex problems. In this chapter, we will explore different methods for calculating present and future values that can be used in various financial applications.

Different Methods for Calculating Present and Future Values

There are several methods available for calculating the present and future values of investments. Some of the popular methods are:

Simple Interest Method
Compound Interest Method
Continuous Compounding Method
Discounted Cash Flow (DCF) Method
Each of these methods has its unique advantages and limitations, and it is crucial to understand how to use them to solve different financial problems. Let's discuss each of these methods in detail.

Simple Interest Method

The simple interest method is the most basic method for calculating present and future values. It assumes that the interest is only earned on the principal amount and does not earn interest on the interest earned. In other words, the interest earned each period is a fixed percentage of the principal amount. The formula for calculating the future value using simple interest is:

$$FV = P(1 + rt)$$

Where FV is the future value, P is the principal amount, r is the interest rate, and t is the time period. The formula for calculating the present value using simple interest is:

$$PV = FV / (1 + rt)$$

Where PV is the present value.

The simple interest method is commonly used in short-term loans or investments where the interest rate is low, and the investment period is short.

Compound Interest Method
The compound interest method is a more advanced method for calculating present and future values. It assumes that the interest earned on an investment earns interest in subsequent periods. In other words, the interest earned in each period is added to the principal amount, and the interest earned in the next period is calculated based on the new principal amount. The formula for calculating the future value using compound interest is:

$$FV = P(1 + r)n$$

Where FV is the future value, P is the principal amount, r is the interest rate, and n is the number of compounding periods. The formula for calculating the present value using compound interest is:

$$PV = FV / (1 + r)n$$

Where PV is the present value.

The compound interest method is the most commonly used method for calculating present and future values. It is used in a wide range of financial applications, including mortgages, car loans, and retirement planning.

Continuous Compounding Method
The continuous compounding method is a variation of the compound interest method, where the interest is continuously compounded instead of compounded at regular intervals. The formula for calculating the future value using continuous compounding is:

M.L.Ruscsak

FV = Pe^(rt)

Where FV is the future value, P is the principal amount, r is the interest rate, and t is the time period. The formula for calculating the present value using continuous compounding is:

PV = FV / e^(rt)

Where PV is the present value.

The continuous compounding method is used in financial applications where the investment period is long, and the interest rate is relatively high. It is commonly used in bond investments and other long-term investments.

Discounted Cash Flow (DCF) Method
The discounted cash flow (DCF) method is a more sophisticated method for calculating present and future values. It takes into account the time value of money, as well as other factors, such as inflation and risk. The DCF method involves calculating the present value of future cash flows by discounting them back to their present value using a discount rate.

The DCF method is widely used in finance and investment decision-making, as it provides a more accurate estimate of an investment's value by considering the time value of money. It is particularly useful when evaluating long-term investments or projects that involve significant cash outflows in the near future.

The DCF method involves several steps. First, the expected future cash flows from the investment are estimated. These cash flows can be either positive or negative, depending on whether the investment is expected to generate income or require expenditures.

Next, a discount rate is selected based on the risk associated with the investment. The discount rate represents the expected return that an investor would require to invest in the project. It takes into account the risk of the investment, as well as the time value of money.

The present value of each future cash flow is then calculated by discounting it back to its present value using the discount rate. The sum of all the present values of the future cash flows represents the present value of the investment.

The DCF method is commonly used in a variety of fields, including investment banking, corporate finance, and real estate. For example, an investment banker may use the DCF method to evaluate a potential merger or acquisition, while a real estate investor may use it to determine the value of a commercial property.

One limitation of the DCF method is that it relies on estimates of future cash flows and a discount rate, both of which can be difficult to predict accurately. Additionally, the DCF method does not account for the potential impact of external factors, such as changes in market conditions or unexpected events.

Despite its limitations, the DCF method is a powerful tool for evaluating investments and making informed financial decisions. By taking into account the time value of money and other factors, it provides a more accurate estimate of an investment's value, which can help investors make better decisions and achieve their financial goals.

Compound Interest:

Compound interest is a fundamental concept in finance that takes into account the effects of time and the compounding of interest over time. It is essential to understand compound interest because it affects the value of investments, loans, and savings accounts. In this section, we will explore problems related to calculating compound interest with different compounding periods and interest rates, and finding future and present values of annuities and perpetuities.

Calculating Compound Interest with Different Compounding Periods

In some cases, interest may be compounded more than once a year. For example, a savings account may compound interest quarterly, monthly, or even daily. When interest is compounded more frequently, the effective annual interest rate is higher than the nominal annual interest rate. Therefore, it is important to calculate the effective annual interest rate to accurately compare different investment options.

The formula for calculating the effective annual interest rate is:

$$EAR = (1 + (i/n))^n - 1$$

Where i is the nominal annual interest rate and n is the number of compounding periods per year. The formula is based on the idea that if interest is compounded n times a year, then the effective annual interest rate is $(1 + i/n)^n$.

For example, suppose you have a savings account that compounds interest monthly, with a nominal annual interest rate of 5%. The effective annual interest rate would be:

$$EAR = (1 + (0.05/12))^{12} - 1 = 5.12\%$$

This means that the savings account would earn 5.12% interest per year, not just 5%.

Finding Future and Present Values of Annuities with Compound Interest

An annuity is a series of equal payments made at fixed intervals over a specified period. An annuity can be either ordinary or annuity due. In an ordinary annuity, payments are made at the end of each period, while in an annuity due, payments are made at the beginning of each period.

To calculate the future value of an ordinary annuity, we use the formula:

FV = Pmt x ((1 + r)^n - 1) / r

Where FV is the future value of the annuity, Pmt is the periodic payment, r is the interest rate per period, and n is the number of periods.

For example, suppose you invest $1,000 per year in an ordinary annuity that earns 5% interest per year for 10 years. The future value of the annuity would be:

FV = $1,000 x ((1 + 0.05)^10 - 1) / 0.05 = $12,578.20

To calculate the present value of an ordinary annuity, we use the formula:

PV = Pmt x (1 - (1 + r)^-n) / r

Where PV is the present value of the annuity, Pmt is the periodic payment, r is the interest rate per period, and n is the number of periods.

For example, suppose you want to know the present value of a 10-year ordinary annuity that pays $1,000 per year and has an interest rate of 5%. The present value of the annuity would be:

PV = $1,000 x (1 - (1 + 0.05)^-10) / 0.05 = $7,721.73

To calculate the future value of an annuity due, we use the formula:

FV = Pmt x ((1 + r)^n - 1) / r x (1 + r)

Where FV is the future value of the annuity, Pmt is the periodic payment, r is the interest rate per period, and n is the number of periods.

For example, suppose you want to know the future value of a 5-year annuity due that pays $1,000 per year and has an interest rate of 5%. Using the formula, we can calculate the future value of the annuity as follows:

FV = $1,000 x ((1 + 0.05)^5 - 1) / 0.05 x (1 + 0.05) = $5,525.63

This means that if you invested $1,000 per year for five years at a 5% annual interest rate with the annuity due option, you would have a total of $5,525.63 at the end of the fifth year.

Perpetuities with Different Compounding Periods

When dealing with perpetuities that have different compounding periods, the formula used to calculate their present and future values is slightly different. The formula for calculating the present value of a perpetuity with different compounding periods is:

$$PV = C / (r / m)$$

Where PV is the present value of the perpetuity, C is the periodic payment, r is the annual interest rate, and m is the number of compounding periods per year.

For example, suppose you have a perpetuity that pays $1,000 per year with a 6% annual interest rate, but interest is compounded quarterly. To calculate the present value of this perpetuity, we would use the formula as follows:

$$PV = \$1,000 / (0.06 / 4) = \$16,666.67$$

This means that if you were to receive $1,000 per quarter indefinitely with a 6% annual interest rate, the present value of this perpetuity would be $16,666.67.

The formula for calculating the future value of a perpetuity with different compounding periods is:

$$FV = C \times (1 + (r / m))\hat{\ }(mt - 1) / (r / m)$$

Where FV is the future value of the perpetuity, C is the periodic payment, r is the annual interest rate, m is the number of compounding periods per year, and t is the number of years.

For example, suppose you have a perpetuity that pays $1,000 per year with a 6% annual interest rate, but interest is compounded quarterly. To calculate the future value of this perpetuity after 10 years, we would use the formula as follows:

$$FV = \$1,000 \times (1 + (0.06 / 4))\hat{\ }(4 \times 10 - 1) / (0.06 / 4) = \$25,634.52$$

This means that if you were to receive $1,000 per quarter indefinitely with a 6% annual interest rate, the future value of this perpetuity after 10 years would be $25,634.52.

Conclusion

In conclusion, understanding the concept of compound interest and how to calculate present and future values using different methods is crucial in the field of finance. It allows individuals to make informed decisions about investments and to determine the profitability of potential investments. Whether you are an investment banker, actuary, portfolio manager, quantitative analyst, securities trader, financial planner, or financial analyst, knowing how to calculate the time value of money can help you in your career.

1.   You want to have $50,000 in your savings account in five years. If your savings account has a 2.5% interest rate compounded monthly, how much should you deposit now to reach your goal?

2.   If you invest $5,000 in a stock that has an annual rate of return of 8%, compounded quarterly, what will be the value of your investment in 10 years?

3.   A loan of $10,000 has an annual interest rate of 6%, compounded monthly. If the loan is to be paid off in five years, what is the monthly payment?

4.   You plan to save $1,000 per year in a savings account that has an annual interest rate of 4%, compounded annually. How much will you have in your account after 10 years?

5.   You have a credit card with an annual interest rate of 18%, compounded monthly. If you make a minimum monthly payment of $50, how long will it take to pay off a balance of $5,000?

6.   You want to save $25,000 for a down payment on a house in 10 years. If your savings account has an annual interest rate of 3.5%, compounded semi-annually, how much should you save each semi-annual period to reach your goal?

7.   You invest $10,000 in a mutual fund that has an annual rate of return of 6%, compounded monthly. If you reinvest all dividends, what will be the value of your investment in 20 years?

8.   You take out a loan of $15,000 at an annual interest rate of 5%, compounded monthly, to be paid off in three years. What is the total amount of interest you will pay on the loan?

9.   You invest $20,000 in a certificate of deposit (CD) that has an annual interest rate of 2%, compounded daily. If you withdraw the interest earned each month, how much will you earn in total after two years?

10.   You want to have $100,000 in your retirement account in 30 years. If your retirement account has an annual interest rate of 7%, compounded quarterly, how much should you invest each quarter to reach your goal?

Discounting:

Discounting is a crucial concept in finance that helps investors determine the present value of future cash flows. It is a process of converting future cash flows into their present values by discounting them at a certain rate of return. In this section, we will discuss the problems related to calculating present values of cash flows with different discount rates and finding the internal rate of return and net present value of investment projects.

Calculating Present Values with Different Discount Rates:

The present value of a cash flow is the current value of a future sum of money, taking into account a specific interest rate. It is important to calculate the present value of cash flows when making investment decisions, as it helps to determine the profitability of a particular investment opportunity.

To calculate the present value of a future cash flow, we use the following formula:

$PV = FV / (1 + r)^n$

M.L.Ruscsak

Where PV is the present value, FV is the future value, r is the discount rate, and n is the number of periods.

For example, suppose you have a cash flow of $1,000 that you will receive in two years, and the discount rate is 5%. The present value of the cash flow would be:

$$PV = \$1,000 / (1 + 0.05)^2 = \$907.03$$

In this example, the present value of the cash flow is $907.03, which is less than the future value of $1,000. This is because the cash flow is being discounted at a rate of 5% per year.

Calculating the Internal Rate of Return:

The internal rate of return (IRR) is the discount rate that makes the net present value of an investment project equal to zero. The IRR is a useful tool for evaluating the profitability of investment projects and is often used to compare different investment opportunities.

To calculate the IRR, we need to solve for the discount rate that makes the net present value of the cash flows equal to zero. This can be done using trial and error or a financial calculator.

For example, suppose you are considering an investment project that requires an initial investment of $10,000 and is expected to generate cash flows of $3,000 per year for the next five years. To calculate the IRR of the investment, we need to find the discount rate that makes the net present value of the cash flows equal to zero.

Using a financial calculator, we find that the IRR of the investment is approximately 10.16%. This means that the investment is expected to generate a return of 10.16% per year, which is greater than the required rate of return.

Calculating the Net Present Value:

The net present value (NPV) of an investment project is the difference between the present value of the cash inflows and the present value of the cash outflows. A positive NPV indicates that the project is expected to generate a return that is greater than the required rate of return, while a negative NPV indicates that the project is expected to generate a return that is less than the required rate of return.

To calculate the NPV of an investment project, we use the following formula:

NPV = -Initial Investment + PV of Cash Flows

Where Initial Investment is the amount of money invested in the project and PV of Cash Flows is the present value of the cash inflows minus the present value of the cash outflows.

For example, suppose you are considering an investment project that requires an initial investment of $10,000 and is expected to generate cash flows of $3,000 per year for the next five years. If the required rate of return is 10%, the NPV of the investment can be calculated as follows:

PV of Cash Flows = $3,000 x $((1 - (1 + 0.10)^{-5}) / 0.10)$ = $12,578.28

NPV = -$10,000 + $12,578.28 = $2,578.28

Therefore, based on the calculated NPV of $2,578.28, this investment project would be considered worthwhile, as the present value of the expected cash inflows is higher than the initial investment.

However, it is important to note that the NPV method has its limitations and drawbacks. One potential issue is that it assumes that the cash flows generated by the project are certain and can be accurately estimated. In reality, there is always some level of uncertainty and risk associated with any investment project, which may affect the accuracy of the NPV calculation.

Another limitation of the NPV method is that it does not take into account the scale of the investment. In some cases, a smaller investment project with a lower NPV may be more attractive than a larger project with a higher NPV, as the smaller project may have a higher return on investment or be less risky.

To address these limitations, other methods such as the Internal Rate of Return (IRR) method can be used to evaluate investment projects. The IRR is the discount rate at which the NPV of an investment project equals zero. In other words, it is the rate of return that the project is expected to generate.

To calculate the IRR, we set the NPV of the project to zero and solve for the discount rate:

$0 = $ -Initial Investment + PV of Cash Flows $/ (1 + IRR)^n$

Where n is the number of periods.

This equation can be solved using trial and error, or by using software or financial calculators.

For example, suppose we use the same investment project as before, with an initial investment of $10,000 and expected cash flows of $3,000 per year for the next five years. Using the IRR method, we can calculate the rate of return that the project is expected to generate:

M.L.Ruscsak

$$0 = -\$10,000 + \$3,000 / (1 + IRR) + \$3,000 / (1 + IRR)^2 + \$3,000 / (1 + IRR)^3 + \$3,000 / (1 + IRR)^4 + \$3,000 / (1 + IRR)^5$$

Using trial and error, we find that the IRR of the project is approximately 12.5%. This means that the project is expected to generate a return of 12.5% per year, which is higher than the required rate of return of 10%. Therefore, the project would be considered worthwhile under the IRR method.

In summary, the net present value (NPV) and internal rate of return (IRR) methods are commonly used to evaluate investment projects. While the NPV method calculates the present value of cash inflows and outflows, the IRR method calculates the rate of return that the project is expected to generate. Both methods have their limitations and drawbacks, and it is important to consider other factors such as risk and scale when evaluating investment projects.

1. A project requires an initial investment of $20,000 and is expected to generate cash flows of $5,000 per year for the next six years. If the required rate of return is 8%, what is the net present value of the project?

2. A bond with a face value of $10,000 and a coupon rate of 6% is due to mature in 10 years. If the required rate of return is 5%, what is the present value of the bond?

3. An investor is considering two projects, A and B. Project A requires an initial investment of $50,000 and is expected to generate cash flows of $10,000 per year for the next six years. Project B requires an initial investment of $75,000 and is expected to generate cash flows of $15,000 per year for the next six years. If the required rate of return is 7%, which project should the investor choose?

4. A company is considering a project that requires an initial investment of $100,000 and is expected to generate cash flows of $20,000 per year for the next ten years. If the required rate of return is 12%, what is the internal rate of return of the project?

5. A bond with a face value of $5,000 and a coupon rate of 4% is due to mature in five years. If the required rate of return is 6%, what is the present value of the bond?

6. An investor is considering purchasing a rental property for $500,000. The property is expected to generate net cash flows of $50,000 per year for the next ten years. If the required rate of return is 8%, what is the net present value of the investment?

7.   A company is considering a project that requires an initial investment of $200,000 and is expected to generate cash flows of $50,000 per year for the next six years. If the required rate of return is 10%, what is the net present value of the project?

8.   A bond with a face value of $1,000 and a coupon rate of 5% is due to mature in three years. If the required rate of return is 7%, what is the present value of the bond?

9.   An investor is considering a stock that is expected to pay a dividend of $2 per share next year, with an expected growth rate of 5%. If the investor requires a 10% rate of return, what is the present value of the stock if the current market price is $25 per share?

10.   A company is considering a project that requires an initial investment of $150,000 and is expected to generate cash flows of $30,000 per year for the next five years. If the required rate of return is 8%, what is the internal rate of return of the project?

CHAPTER 6: USE OF TIME VALUE OF MONEY IN FINANCIAL DECISION-MAKING

The time value of money is a fundamental concept in finance that recognizes the value of money changes over time. It is the foundation for making sound financial decisions, such as investment analysis, capital budgeting, and financial planning. The time value of money considers the effect of inflation and the opportunity cost of money over time. It is based on the principle that money today is worth more than the same amount of money in the future, due to the potential earning power of the money over time.

Time value of money calculations are used in many aspects of financial decision-making, including calculating the present value of future cash flows, calculating the future value of an investment, determining the internal rate of return, and calculating the net present value of an investment. These calculations are essential for assessing the profitability and feasibility of investment projects, determining the cost of capital, and evaluating the risk associated with investment opportunities.

This chapter will provide an in-depth analysis of the time value of money and its applications in financial decision-making. We will discuss the various tools and techniques used to incorporate the time value of money in financial analysis, including the use of present value, future value, annuities, and perpetuities. We will also discuss the use of time value of money in capital budgeting decisions, such as calculating the net present value and internal rate of return of investment projects.

The first section of this chapter will introduce the concept of the time value of money, including the factors that influence its value, such as inflation and the opportunity cost of money. We will also discuss the importance of the time value of money in financial decision-making and the implications of ignoring it.

The second section will focus on present value and future value calculations, including the formulas used to calculate present value and future value, and their applications in financial analysis. We will also discuss the relationship between present value and future value, and how it affects financial decision-making.

The third section will discuss annuities and perpetuities, including the formulas used to calculate their present and future values, and their applications in financial analysis. We will also discuss the differences between annuities and perpetuities, and how they can be used in financial decision-making.

The fourth section will focus on the use of time value of money in capital budgeting decisions. We will discuss the net present value and internal rate of return methods, including the formulas used to calculate them, and their applications in evaluating investment projects. We will also discuss the advantages and limitations of these methods, and how they can be used in conjunction with other financial analysis techniques.

The final section of this chapter will provide examples of the use of time value of money in various financial decision-making scenarios, including investment analysis, capital budgeting, and financial planning. We will also discuss the ethical considerations and potential biases associated with time value of money calculations, and the importance of using sound judgment and considering all relevant factors when making financial decisions.

In summary, the time value of money is a crucial concept in finance that underpins many aspects of financial decision-making. Understanding its implications and applications is essential for making sound financial decisions and achieving financial goals. This chapter will provide a comprehensive analysis of the time value of money and its uses in financial decision-making, providing students with a solid foundation for understanding and applying these concepts in their future careers in finance.

Investments and the time value of money

Investments and the time value of money are closely related concepts in finance. Time value of money refers to the idea that money today is worth more than the same amount of money in the future due to its earning potential. Investments involve committing money or capital with the expectation of receiving a financial return or profit.

The concept of time value of money is essential for investors, as it allows them to evaluate the potential returns of their investment opportunities. The value of an investment is not solely determined by its initial cost or current value, but also by its future earning potential. Understanding the time value of money helps investors to make informed decisions about their investments and assess the risks associated with them.

One of the most common investment strategies is buying stocks. When an investor purchases a stock, they are essentially buying a share of ownership in a company. The value of the stock is determined by the company's financial performance, its earnings, and its future growth potential. However, the time value of money also plays a role in the value of the investment.

M.L.Ruscsak

Consider two investors who both invest $10,000 in a company's stock. Investor A buys the stock today, while Investor B buys the same stock five years from now. Assuming that the stock's value has increased by 10% each year, the value of Investor A's investment would be worth $16,105.10 in five years. However, the value of Investor B's investment would only be worth $12,100.00, even though they both invested the same amount of money.

This example illustrates the importance of understanding the time value of money when making investment decisions. The earlier an investor invests their money, the greater the earning potential of their investment. Conversely, delaying an investment reduces its earning potential and can result in lower returns.

Another important concept related to investments and the time value of money is compound interest. Compound interest is the interest earned not only on the principal amount of an investment but also on any interest that has accumulated on that principal amount. Compound interest allows investments to grow at a faster rate over time.

For example, suppose an investor invests $10,000 in a savings account that pays 5% interest per year. If the interest is compounded annually, the investment would be worth $16,289.36 in ten years. However, if the interest is compounded quarterly, the investment would be worth $16,386.63, an increase of over $97 due to the more frequent compounding of interest.

Understanding the time value of money and the concept of compound interest is crucial for investors. These concepts allow investors to evaluate the potential returns of their investment opportunities and make informed decisions about where to invest their money. Additionally, these concepts can help investors to assess the risks associated with their investments and make adjustments accordingly.

In conclusion, investments and the time value of money are intimately related concepts in finance. Understanding the time value of money and the concept of compound interest is crucial for investors, as it allows them to evaluate the potential returns of their investment opportunities and make informed decisions about their investments. Additionally, understanding these concepts can help investors to assess the risks associated with their investments and make adjustments accordingly.

Loans and the time value of money

Loans are a common financial instrument used by individuals and businesses alike. Whether it's a mortgage for a house or a business loan to start a new venture, loans are an essential part of the financial landscape. However, the concept of time value of money applies to loans just as it does to other financial decisions. In this section, we will explore the impact of time value of money on loans and how it affects borrowing decisions.

The Time Value of Money and Loans

The time value of money is the idea that money is worth more today than it is in the future. This is because money can be invested or earn interest over time, which increases its value. When it comes to loans, this means that the amount of money borrowed today is worth more than the same amount borrowed in the future.

The time value of money affects loans in several ways. Firstly, it affects the interest rate that lenders charge borrowers. Lenders will charge a higher interest rate on loans to compensate for the time value of money. This is because they are giving up the use of their money for a period of time, and they want to be compensated for that opportunity cost.

Secondly, the time value of money affects the amount of the loan repayment. A borrower will have to pay back more than the amount they borrowed because of the interest charged on the loan. This means that the longer the loan term, the more the borrower will have to pay back.

Calculating Loan Payments

To calculate loan payments, lenders use the concept of present value, which is the value today of a future cash flow. In the case of a loan, the future cash flows are the loan payments, and the present value is the amount borrowed.

The formula for calculating loan payments is:

$$\text{Payment} = (P \times r) / (1 - (1 + r)^{-n})$$

Where P is the amount borrowed, r is the interest rate per period, and n is the number of periods.

For example, suppose you borrow \$10,000 at an interest rate of 5% per year for five years. The loan payments can be calculated as follows:

$$\text{Payment} = (\$10{,}000 \times 0.05) / (1 - (1 + 0.05)^{-5}) = \$1{,}322.87 \text{ per year}$$

This means that you will have to pay back \$1,322.87 each year for five years to repay the loan.

The Impact of Time on Loan Payments

The time value of money has a significant impact on loan payments. The longer the loan term, the higher the loan payments will be because of the interest charged on the loan. This means that borrowers need to consider the impact of the time value of money when deciding on the length of their loan term.

M.L.Ruscsak

For example, suppose you borrow $10,000 at an interest rate of 5% per year. The loan payments for different loan terms are shown below:

1 year: Payment = ($10,000 x 0.05) / (1 - (1 + 0.05)^-1) = $10,500
5 years: Payment = ($10,000 x 0.05) / (1 - (1 + 0.05)^-5) = $1,322.87 per year
10 years: Payment = ($10,000 x 0.05) / (1 - (1 + 0.05)^-10) = $1,628.64 per year

As you can see, the longer the loan term, the lower the annual payment, but the higher the total amount paid over the life of the loan. This is because of the time value of money and the interest charged on the loan.

Conclusion

In conclusion, the time value of money is a fundamental concept in finance that plays a critical role in various financial decisions, including investments, loans, and many others. The concept is based on the principle that a dollar received today is worth more than a dollar received in the future due to the opportunity cost of not having that dollar to invest elsewhere.

Investors can use the time value of money to evaluate investment opportunities and compare them to alternative investments. By calculating the present value of future cash flows, investors can determine if an investment is worth making based on the expected rate of return.

Similarly, borrowers can use the time value of money to evaluate loan options and choose the one with the lowest cost, taking into account factors such as interest rates, fees, and repayment terms.

It is essential to understand the time value of money to make informed financial decisions, as failing to account for the time value of money can lead to poor investment decisions or costly borrowing. As such, financial professionals must have a strong foundation in the time value of money and be able to apply it effectively to a range of financial decisions.

Overall, the time value of money is a critical concept in finance that has numerous applications in investment and borrowing decisions. By understanding this concept and applying it appropriately, individuals can make sound financial decisions that can help them achieve their financial goals.

Application of time value of money in personal finance

The concept of time value of money is critical in personal finance. It is because individuals have to make decisions regarding the allocation of their money and time. Personal finance involves planning, budgeting, saving, investing, and managing money to achieve financial goals. Therefore, understanding the time value of money can help individuals make better financial decisions.

The objective of this section is to explore the application of time value of money in personal finance. Specifically, we will discuss how time value of money can be used in retirement planning, mortgage payments, credit card debt, and investment decisions.

Retirement Planning:

One of the most significant financial goals for individuals is to plan for retirement. Retirement planning involves setting aside money for future use when individuals are no longer working. Time value of money plays a crucial role in retirement planning because it determines the amount of money an individual needs to save for retirement.

For example, suppose an individual wants to retire in 30 years and needs $1 million for retirement. Assuming an annual interest rate of 5%, the individual needs to save approximately $238,000 today to have $1 million in 30 years. Conversely, if the individual starts saving in 20 years, he or she needs to save approximately $545,000 to have $1 million in 30 years. Therefore, the time value of money dictates that individuals should start saving for retirement as early as possible to take advantage of the power of compounding.

Mortgage Payments:

Another area where time value of money plays a critical role is in mortgage payments. Mortgages are loans used to purchase homes, and they require borrowers to make monthly payments. The mortgage payments consist of principal and interest, and the interest is based on the outstanding loan balance.

For example, suppose an individual takes out a $200,000 mortgage at a 4% interest rate for 30 years. The monthly mortgage payment will be approximately $955. However, the first payment consists of approximately $67 in principal and $888 in interest. As the outstanding loan balance decreases, the amount of interest paid decreases, and the amount of principal paid increases. Therefore, time value of money is crucial in determining the amount of principal and interest paid over the life of the mortgage.

Credit Card Debt:

Credit card debt is another area where time value of money plays a critical role. Credit card debt occurs when individuals borrow money using credit cards and must pay interest on the outstanding balance. Credit card interest rates are often high, ranging from 10% to 25% or more, and the interest is compounded daily.

For example, suppose an individual has $5,000 in credit card debt with an annual interest rate of 15%. If the individual only pays the minimum payment each month, it will take approximately 19 years to pay off the debt, and the total amount paid will be approximately $11,000. Therefore, time value of money dictates that individuals should pay off credit card debt as soon as possible to avoid paying high interest rates.

Investment Decisions:

Finally, time value of money plays a crucial role in investment decisions. Individuals often invest in stocks, bonds, and mutual funds to achieve financial goals. The time value of money determines the return on investment and the amount of time required to achieve financial goals.

For example, suppose an individual invests $10,000 in a mutual fund with an average annual return of 7%. Assuming the individual reinvests all dividends and capital gains, the investment will grow to approximately $29,000 in 20 years. Conversely, if the individual only invests $5,000, the investment will only grow to approximately $14,500 in 20 years. Therefore, time value of money dictates that individuals should invest early and often to achieve their financial goals.

Conclusion:

The time value of money is a fundamental concept in personal finance. It helps individuals understand the relationship between time, money, and the value of money over time. It is essential for making informed financial decisions and achieving financial goals.

In personal finance, the time value of money can be applied in a variety of ways. It can be used to determine the future value of savings and investments, calculate loan payments, and determine the most cost-effective way to pay off debt. It can also be used to compare different investment options and determine which one is most suitable for an individual's financial goals and risk tolerance.

Overall, the time value of money is a critical component of personal finance. It is important for individuals to understand the concept and how it affects their financial decisions. By using the time value of money in personal finance, individuals can make informed decisions that help them achieve their financial goals and secure their financial future.

PART 3: BASIC PROBABILITY AND STATISTICS FOR FINANCE

Finance is a complex field that requires a strong understanding of mathematics, probability, and statistics. Probability and statistics play an important role in financial decision-making and risk management. Part 3 of this textbook focuses on the basic principles of probability and statistics and their applications in finance.

Probability is the study of the likelihood of events occurring. In finance, probability is used to analyze risk and uncertainty. Financial markets are inherently unpredictable, and probability theory provides a framework for understanding and managing this uncertainty.

Statistics is the science of collecting, analyzing, and interpreting data. In finance, statistics is used to identify patterns and relationships in financial data. Financial analysts use statistical models to forecast market trends and evaluate the performance of financial instruments.

Part 3 of this textbook will cover the basic principles of probability and statistics, including probability distributions, random variables, expected values, and statistical inference. These concepts will be illustrated with examples from a variety of fields in finance, including investment banking, portfolio management, and risk management.

Chapter 7 will provide an overview of probability theory, including the basic principles of probability, probability distributions, and random variables. Chapter 8 will cover statistical measures, such as mean, variance, and standard deviation, and their applications in finance. Chapter 9 will focus on statistical inference, including hypothesis testing and confidence intervals.

The concepts covered in Part 3 are essential for students seeking a career in finance. A strong understanding of probability and statistics is required for analyzing financial data, making informed investment decisions, and managing financial risk. By the end of this section, students will have a solid foundation in basic probability and statistics principles and their application in finance.

M.L. Ruscsak

CHAPTER 7: OVERVIEW OF BASIC PROBABILITY CONCEPTS

Probability theory is an essential part of modern finance, particularly in risk management and investment analysis. A thorough understanding of basic probability concepts is therefore necessary for any student of finance. In this chapter, we will provide an overview of the basic probability concepts that are relevant to finance.

The concept of probability is central to our understanding of uncertainty and risk. Probability is a measure of the likelihood of an event occurring. In finance, events can range from the price of a stock increasing, to a borrower defaulting on a loan. Probability theory provides us with a framework for analyzing the likelihood of these events, which is essential for decision-making.

In finance, we use probability theory to model and analyze the risk associated with different investment decisions. By calculating the probabilities of various outcomes, we can make informed decisions about which investments to pursue and which to avoid. This is particularly important in the field of portfolio management, where investors must balance the risk and return of their investment portfolios.

Basic probability concepts are used to model and analyze financial data. For example, probability theory is used to model the returns of financial assets, such as stocks and bonds. It is also used to model the likelihood of default on loans and the occurrence of financial events, such as market crashes and economic recessions.

In this chapter, we will cover the basics of probability theory, including the different types of probabilities, probability distributions, and statistical inference. We will also discuss the concept of expected value and its application in finance.

Overall, a solid understanding of basic probability concepts is essential for anyone interested in finance. By understanding the principles of probability theory, we can make more informed investment decisions, manage risk more effectively, and better navigate the uncertain world of finance.

Introduction to probability distributions and random variables

Probability theory is a branch of mathematics that deals with uncertainty and randomness. In finance, it is used to model and analyze the behavior of financial instruments and markets. One of the fundamental concepts in probability theory is random variables. Random variables are used to represent numerical values that can take on different values depending on the outcome of a random event. Probability distributions are mathematical functions that describe the probabilities of the different possible outcomes of a random variable. In this section, we will introduce the basic concepts of probability distributions and random variables and discuss their applications in finance.

Random Variables:

A random variable is a variable whose value is determined by the outcome of a random event. In finance, random variables are used to represent the uncertainty associated with future events. For example, the price of a stock is a random variable because it can take on different values depending on the outcome of future events such as economic data releases, company news, or geopolitical events. Random variables can be discrete or continuous. A discrete random variable can only take on a finite or countable number of values, while a continuous random variable can take on any value within a range.

Another example of a random variable in finance could be the return on a particular investment. The return on an investment is determined by the performance of the investment over a certain period of time, which is influenced by a variety of factors such as market conditions, economic indicators, and company-specific factors. As such, the return on an investment is a random variable because it can take on different values depending on the outcome of these events. For instance, a stock might have a positive or negative return in a given year, and the magnitude of the return might also vary widely depending on the performance of the broader market and the specific company's financial performance.

Suppose we have a fair six-sided die, and we are interested in the random variable V, which represents the number rolled. V can take on values from 1 to 6 with equal probability.

If we roll the die twice and add the values together, what is the expected value of V?

Solution:

To find the expected value of V, we need to calculate the weighted average of all the possible values of V, weighted by their probabilities.

Since V represents the sum of two rolls of the die, the possible values of V are 2, 3, ..., 12.

To calculate the probability of each value, we can use the fact that the probability of rolling a sum of k is the number of ways to get a sum of k divided by the total number of possible outcomes.

For example, to roll a sum of 2, we can only roll a 1 and a 1. There is only one way to do this, so the probability of rolling a sum of 2 is 1/36.

M.L.Ruscsak

Similarly, there is only one way to roll a sum of 12 (by rolling two 6's), so the probability of rolling a sum of 12 is also 1/36.

For the other values, we can use a table like this:

Sum	Ways to roll	Probability
2	1	1/36
3	2	2/36
4	3	3/36
5	4	4/36
6	5	5/36
7	6	6/36
8	5	5/36
9	4	4/36
10	3	2/36
11	2	2/36
12	1	1/36

To find the expected value of V, we need to calculate the sum of each value multiplied by its probability:

$$E(V) = 2 * 1/36 + 3 * 2/36 + 4 * 3/36 + 5 * 4/36 + 6 * 5/36 + 7 * 6/36 + 8 * 5/36 + 9 * 4/36 + 10 * 3/36 + 11 * 2/36 + 12 * 1/36$$

Simplifying this expression, we get:

$$E(V) = (2 + 3 + 4 + 5 + 6 + 7 + 8 + 9 + 10 + 11 + 12) / 36$$

$$E(V) = 7$$

Therefore, the expected value of V is 7.

Probability Distributions:

A probability distribution is a function that describes the probabilities of the different possible outcomes of a random variable. The most common probability distributions used in finance are the normal distribution and the lognormal distribution. The normal distribution, also known as the Gaussian distribution, is a continuous probability distribution that is widely used to model the behavior of financial instruments such as stock prices and interest rates. It is characterized by its mean and standard deviation. The lognormal distribution is a continuous probability distribution that is commonly used to model the behavior of asset prices such as stocks and commodities. It is characterized by its mean and standard deviation of the natural logarithm of the asset price.

Suppose a portfolio manager is analyzing the returns of a stock over the past year. The manager has determined that the returns are normally distributed with a mean of 10% and a standard deviation of 5%.

What is the probability that the stock's return will be between 5% and 15%?

Solution:

To solve this problem, we can use the normal distribution and standardize the data using the z-score formula:

$$z = (x - mu) / sigma$$

where z is the standardized value, x is the raw value, mu is the mean, and sigma is the standard deviation.

In this case, we want to find the probability that the stock's return will be between 5% and 15%, so we need to find the z-scores for those values:

$$z1 = (5 - 10) / 5 = -1$$

$$z2 = (15 - 10) / 5 = 1$$

Next, we use a standard normal distribution table or a calculator to find the probabilities associated with these z-scores. The area under the normal distribution curve between z1 and z2 represents the probability that the stock's return will be between 5% and 15%.

Using a standard normal distribution table, we find that the area between $z = -1$ and $z = 1$ is approximately 0.6827. Therefore, the probability that the stock's return will be between 5% and 15% is approximately 0.6827 or 68.27%.

Applications in Finance:

Probability distributions and random variables are used extensively in finance to model and analyze the behavior of financial instruments and markets. They are used to estimate the probabilities of different outcomes and to calculate the expected value, variance, and other statistical measures of financial instruments such as stocks, bonds, and options. For example, the Black-Scholes model, which is used to price options, assumes that the underlying asset follows a lognormal distribution. Portfolio managers use probability distributions to estimate the probabilities of different outcomes of their investments and to construct portfolios that optimize risk and return.

Suppose a portfolio manager wants to calculate the expected return and standard deviation of a portfolio that is invested in three stocks: A, B, and C. The manager believes that the returns of these stocks are normally distributed with the following parameters:

Stock A has an expected return of 8% and a standard deviation of 12%
Stock B has an expected return of 12% and a standard deviation of 18%
Stock C has an expected return of 10% and a standard deviation of 15%
The portfolio manager has invested 25% of the portfolio in Stock A, 35% in Stock B, and 40% in Stock C. Using these weightings and the parameters of each stock's distribution, the manager can calculate the expected return and standard deviation of the portfolio as follows:

Expected return of the portfolio = (0.25 * 8%) + (0.35 * 12%) + (0.40 * 10%) = 10.2%

To calculate the standard deviation of the portfolio, the manager needs to use the covariance between the stocks. If the three stocks are uncorrelated, then the formula for the standard deviation of the portfolio is:

Standard deviation of the portfolio = sqrt((0.25^2 * 12%^2) + (0.35^2 * 18%^2) + (0.40^2 * 15%^2))

Plugging in the values, we get:

Standard deviation of the portfolio = 14.54%

The portfolio manager can use these expected return and standard deviation figures to make informed decisions about the portfolio, such as whether to rebalance the weightings of the stocks or adjust the portfolio's overall risk level.

Conclusion:

Probability distributions and random variables are essential tools for analyzing financial data and making informed investment decisions. They enable us to estimate the probabilities of different outcomes and to quantify the uncertainty associated with future events. In the next section, we will discuss the normal distribution and its properties in more detail.

The role of probability in finance

Probability theory plays a crucial role in finance by enabling investors and financial professionals to make informed decisions in uncertain and unpredictable environments. Probability theory provides a framework for quantifying and analyzing the likelihood of future events, which is essential for decision-making in financial markets. This section will explore the role of probability in finance, including its applications in investment analysis, risk management, and financial modeling.

Applications in Investment Analysis:

Probability theory is widely used in investment analysis to evaluate the potential risks and rewards of investment opportunities. Investors use probability theory to estimate the likelihood of a particular investment yielding a positive return, as well as to assess the potential magnitude of the return. For example, a portfolio manager may use probability theory to analyze the performance of a stock or a bond, taking into account factors such as earnings forecasts, interest rate changes, and market trends. Probability theory can also be used to calculate the expected return and risk of a portfolio of investments, which is crucial for investors seeking to optimize their portfolio's performance.

Applications in Risk Management:

Probability theory is also essential for risk management in finance. Financial professionals use probability theory to quantify and manage various types of financial risk, including market risk, credit risk, and operational risk. For example, a risk manager may use probability theory to estimate the probability of a market downturn or a credit event, and to develop strategies to mitigate the potential impact of such events. Probability theory can also be used to calculate the value at risk (VaR) of a portfolio, which is a measure of the potential loss that could be incurred under adverse market conditions.

Applications in Financial Modeling:

Probability theory is also an essential tool for financial modeling, which is used to simulate and forecast financial outcomes. Financial models are used for a variety of purposes, such as predicting the future performance of a stock or a bond, valuing a company, or estimating the cost of capital. Probability theory provides the foundation for many financial models, including stochastic models, which are used to simulate the behavior of financial variables over time. Stochastic models are widely used in the pricing of complex financial instruments, such as options and derivatives, which require a probabilistic approach to valuation.

Limitations of Probability Theory in Finance:

While probability theory is an essential tool for decision-making in finance, it has certain limitations that should be acknowledged. One limitation is that probability theory assumes that future events will be similar to past events, which may not always be the case. Financial markets are subject to unexpected and unpredictable events, such as geopolitical events or natural disasters, which can significantly impact investment outcomes. Another limitation is that probability theory is based on assumptions that may not always hold true in real-world situations. For example, probability theory assumes that all events are independent, which may not be the case in financial markets, where the behavior of one variable can impact the behavior of another.

Conclusion:

Probability theory plays a vital role in finance, providing a framework for quantifying and analyzing the likelihood of future events. Probability theory is widely used in investment analysis, risk management, and financial modeling, enabling investors and financial professionals to make informed decisions in uncertain and unpredictable environments. However, it is essential to acknowledge the limitations of probability theory in finance, as it assumes that future events will be similar to past events and is based on assumptions that may not always hold true in real-world situations.

Probability and risk analysis in finance

Probability theory is a branch of mathematics that deals with the study of randomness, uncertainty, and chance events. In finance, probability theory is used to analyze and model the risk associated with financial assets and investments. Risk analysis is an essential tool for investors and financial professionals to evaluate and manage the potential risks and returns of their investments. This section will explore the role of probability and risk analysis in finance, including the types of risks faced by investors, the methods used to measure and manage these risks, and the tools used to model and analyze risk.

Types of Risk:

In finance, risk refers to the potential for loss or negative returns on an investment. Investors face many types of risks, including market risk, credit risk, interest rate risk, liquidity risk, and operational risk.

Market risk is the risk of loss due to changes in market conditions, such as changes in stock prices, interest rates, or currency exchange rates. Credit risk is the risk of loss due to the failure of a borrower to repay a loan or the default of a bond. Interest rate risk is the risk of loss due to changes in interest rates. Liquidity risk is the risk of loss due to the inability to sell an asset at a fair price or to meet financial obligations. Operational risk is the risk of loss due to errors or failures in operations, such as system failures, fraud, or legal disputes.

Methods of Risk Measurement:

One of the key tools used in risk analysis is probability theory, which is used to measure the likelihood of different outcomes and events. Probability theory is used to quantify the risk associated with different investments and to evaluate the potential returns of different investment strategies.

One common method used to measure risk is value at risk (VaR), which estimates the maximum potential loss that could occur over a given time period with a given level of confidence. Another method is expected shortfall, which estimates the expected loss beyond the VaR. These methods are used to estimate the potential losses associated with different investments and to determine the appropriate levels of risk exposure for different portfolios.

Tools for Risk Analysis:

There are many tools available for risk analysis, including statistical models, simulation techniques, and optimization methods. Statistical models are used to analyze historical data and to estimate the probability distributions of different assets and investments. Simulation techniques, such as Monte Carlo simulation, are used to model the behavior of complex systems and to estimate the potential outcomes of different scenarios. Optimization methods, such as linear programming and quadratic programming, are used to determine the optimal allocation of assets and to maximize returns while minimizing risk.

Applications of Probability and Risk Analysis in Finance:

Probability theory and risk analysis are used in a wide range of applications in finance, including portfolio management, risk management, and financial modeling. Portfolio management involves the selection and allocation of assets in a portfolio to achieve specific investment objectives while managing risk. Risk management involves identifying, measuring, and mitigating risks associated with different investments and portfolios. Financial modeling involves the use of mathematical models to simulate the behavior of financial systems and to analyze the potential outcomes of different scenarios.

Conclusion:

In conclusion, probability theory and risk analysis are essential tools for investors and financial professionals to evaluate and manage the potential risks and returns of their investments. The use of probability theory and risk analysis enables investors to make informed decisions about their investments and to manage their portfolios effectively. Probability theory and risk analysis are used

M.L.Ruscsak

in a wide range of applications in finance, including portfolio management, risk management, and financial modeling, and are essential for the success of modern finance.

CHAPTER 8: USE OF PROBABILITY AND STATISTICS IN FINANCE

Probability and statistics are essential tools in the field of finance. In finance, decisions are often based on incomplete information, and the ability to quantify uncertainty is critical. Probability theory provides a framework for analyzing uncertainty and measuring risk, while statistics allows us to make inferences about populations based on sample data.

The use of probability and statistics in finance is wide-ranging. It is used for risk management, asset allocation, investment analysis, portfolio optimization, and financial modeling, to name a few examples. Probability and statistics allow investors to make informed decisions by providing a rigorous approach to analyzing data and predicting future outcomes.

One area where probability and statistics are particularly important in finance is risk management. Risk management is the process of identifying, analyzing, and mitigating risks that could have an adverse impact on an organization's financial performance. Probability theory provides a framework for measuring risk, and statistics allows us to estimate the likelihood of various outcomes.

Another area where probability and statistics are critical in finance is asset allocation. Asset allocation is the process of dividing investments across different asset classes, such as stocks, bonds, and real estate. The goal of asset allocation is to minimize risk while maximizing return. Probability and statistics allow investors to estimate the expected return and risk of different asset classes and to construct portfolios that achieve their investment objectives.

Investment analysis is another area where probability and statistics play a crucial role. Investment analysis involves evaluating the potential returns and risks of individual investments. Probability and statistics allow investors to estimate the expected return and risk of different investments and to identify the investments that offer the best risk-return tradeoff.

Portfolio optimization is another area where probability and statistics are essential in finance. Portfolio optimization involves constructing a portfolio of investments that maximizes return for a given level of risk. Probability and statistics allow investors to estimate the expected return and risk of different portfolios and to identify the portfolio that offers the best risk-return tradeoff.

M.L.Ruscsak

Finally, financial modeling is an area where probability and statistics are widely used in finance. Financial modeling involves using mathematical models to analyze financial data and make predictions about future financial performance. Probability and statistics allow investors to create models that accurately reflect the behavior of financial markets and the factors that drive financial performance.

In this chapter, we will explore the use of probability and statistics in finance in greater detail. We will examine the different techniques used in finance to measure risk, estimate expected returns, and construct portfolios. We will also explore the different types of financial models used in finance and the role that probability and statistics play in financial modeling. By the end of this chapter, you will have a better understanding of the critical role that probability and statistics play in finance and the techniques used to apply these concepts in real-world situations.

Application of statistical techniques in financial decision-making

Financial decision-making involves making choices that affect the value of an organization or individual's assets. These decisions require a thorough analysis of financial data and trends, and statistical techniques can be used to provide insights that aid in the decision-making process. Statistical analysis allows for the identification of patterns, trends, and relationships in financial data that can inform investment strategies, risk management, and other financial decisions. In this section, we will explore the application of statistical techniques in financial decision-making.

Statistical Techniques in Financial Decision-Making

Regression Analysis
Regression analysis is a statistical technique that examines the relationship between two or more variables. In finance, regression analysis can be used to model the relationship between an asset's returns and a set of factors that are believed to influence those returns. For example, a portfolio manager may use regression analysis to determine the impact of interest rate changes on a bond portfolio's returns.

Time Series Analysis
Time series analysis is a statistical technique that examines patterns in financial data over time. In finance, time series analysis can be used to forecast future values of a financial variable based on past data. For example, a financial analyst may use time series analysis to forecast future stock prices based on historical price data.

Monte Carlo Simulation
Monte Carlo simulation is a statistical technique that uses random sampling to model the behavior of complex systems. In finance, Monte Carlo simulation can be used to simulate the future performance of a portfolio based on different scenarios. For example, an investment banker may use

Monte Carlo simulation to estimate the probability of a portfolio's return exceeding a certain threshold.

Hypothesis Testing

Hypothesis testing is a statistical technique used to determine the likelihood of a hypothesis being true. In finance, hypothesis testing can be used to test the validity of investment strategies and financial models. For example, an actuary may use hypothesis testing to determine whether an insurance model accurately reflects the risks faced by a policyholder.

Cluster Analysis

Cluster analysis is a statistical technique used to identify groups of similar items in a dataset. In finance, cluster analysis can be used to group similar securities based on their characteristics, such as industry, risk level, or profitability. For example, a portfolio manager may use cluster analysis to group similar stocks together to create a diversified portfolio.

Principal Component Analysis

Principal component analysis is a statistical technique used to identify the most important factors in a dataset. In finance, principal component analysis can be used to identify the underlying factors that affect the returns of a portfolio. For example, a quantitative analyst may use principal component analysis to identify the factors that affect the returns of a bond portfolio.

Conclusion

Statistical techniques play an important role in financial decision-making. These techniques can provide insights into financial data that aid in investment strategies, risk management, and other financial decisions. Regression analysis, time series analysis, Monte Carlo simulation, hypothesis testing, cluster analysis, and principal component analysis are just a few of the statistical techniques that can be used in finance. By leveraging these techniques, financial professionals can make informed decisions that maximize value and mitigate risk.

Portfolio Optimization:

Portfolio optimization is the process of constructing a portfolio of assets that maximizes the expected return for a given level of risk or minimizes the risk for a given level of expected return. The goal is to find the optimal asset allocation that balances risk and return. This is a fundamental problem in finance, as investors are constantly seeking ways to manage risk and maximize returns.

In this section, we will discuss the problems related to constructing efficient portfolios with different risk and return characteristics, and finding the optimal asset allocation using mean-variance analysis.

Mean-Variance Analysis

M.L.Ruscsak

Mean-variance analysis is a statistical technique used in portfolio optimization. It is based on the assumption that investors are risk-averse and prefer portfolios that maximize expected return for a given level of risk or minimize risk for a given level of expected return. The technique involves calculating the expected return and variance of each asset in the portfolio, as well as the covariance between pairs of assets.

The expected return of an asset is the average return that an investor can expect to receive over a certain period of time. It is calculated as the weighted average of the possible outcomes, with each outcome weighted by its probability. The variance of an asset measures the spread of its possible returns around its expected return. It is a measure of the asset's volatility.

The covariance between two assets measures the degree to which their returns move together. If the two assets tend to move in the same direction, their covariance is positive. If they tend to move in opposite directions, their covariance is negative. If they are independent, their covariance is zero.

Suppose you are a portfolio manager with a client who is looking to invest in a portfolio of three assets: A, B, and C. You have historical data on the returns of each asset, as well as their covariance matrix:

Asset	Mean Return	Standard Deviation
A	0.06	0.08
B	0.08	0.12
C	0.05	0.06

	A	B	C
A	0.0064	0.004	0.0008
B	0.004	0.0144	-0.0024
C	0.0008	-0.0024	0.0036

Your client is willing to take on some level of risk, but wants to minimize the risk associated with their investment. You decide to use mean-variance analysis to find the optimal portfolio.

a) Calculate the expected return and standard deviation of a portfolio that invests 40% in asset A, 40% in asset B, and 20% in asset C.

b) Using the same portfolio weights as in part (a), calculate the Sharpe ratio of the portfolio.

c) Use the mean-variance framework to determine the optimal portfolio weights for this client, given their risk preferences. Assume the risk-free rate is 2%.

1. Given a set of 5 stocks with expected returns of 8%, 9%, 10%, 11%, and 12%, and standard deviations of 15%, 20%, 25%, 30%, and 35%, respectively, what is the optimal portfolio that maximizes the Sharpe ratio, assuming a risk-free rate of 2%?

2. If you have a portfolio with a mean return of 10% and a standard deviation of 15%, and you want to add another asset to the portfolio with a mean return of 8% and a standard deviation of 20%, what is the minimum weight you need to assign to the new asset to ensure that the portfolio's standard deviation does not exceed 17%?

3. Suppose you have a portfolio with 4 stocks with expected returns of 7%, 9%, 10%, and 12%, respectively, and the covariance matrix of the returns is given as:
[0.01, 0.02, 0.03, 0.04]
[0.02, 0.05, 0.07, 0.09]
[0.03, 0.07, 0.12, 0.16]
[0.04, 0.09, 0.16, 0.25]
What is the minimum variance portfolio?

4. Consider a portfolio with 3 assets, each with an expected return of 10%, 15%, and 20%, and a covariance matrix given by:
[0.04, 0.02, 0.03]
[0.02, 0.09, 0.05]
[0.03, 0.05, 0.16]
If the risk-free rate is 5%, what is the optimal portfolio that maximizes the Sharpe ratio?

5. Suppose you have a portfolio with 5 assets, each with an expected return of 12% and a standard deviation of 20%, and the correlation matrix of the returns is given as:
[1, 0.6, 0.4, 0.3, 0.2]
[0.6, 1, 0.7, 0.5, 0.4]
[0.4, 0.7, 1, 0.8, 0.6]
[0.3, 0.5, 0.8, 1, 0.9]
[0.2, 0.4, 0.6, 0.9, 1]
What is the minimum variance portfolio?

6. If you have a portfolio with expected returns of 10% and 15%, and a standard deviation of 20%, what is the weight you need to assign to each asset to achieve a portfolio with a standard deviation of 16%?

7. Consider a portfolio with 3 assets, each with an expected return of 12%, 15%, and 18%, respectively, and a covariance matrix given by:
[0.05, 0.02, 0.03]
[0.02, 0.09, 0.05]
[0.03, 0.05, 0.16]

M.L.Ruscsak

What is the optimal portfolio that maximizes the expected return for a given standard deviation of 20%?

8. Suppose you have a portfolio with 4 stocks with expected returns of 8%, 10%, 12%, and 14%, respectively, and the covariance matrix of the returns is given as:

[0.01, 0.03, 0.04, 0.05]
[0.01, 0.03, 0.04, 0.05]
[0.03, 0.09, 0.12, 0.15]
[0.04, 0.12, 0.18, 0.21]
[0.05, 0.15, 0.21, 0.28]

To find the optimal portfolio with the highest expected return given a level of risk, we need to solve the Markowitz optimization problem. Let w be the weight vector of the portfolio, where wi represents the proportion of the total investment allocated to the ith stock. The Markowitz optimization problem can be formulated as follows:

Maximize $E(Rp) = w1E(R1) + w2E(R2) + w3E(R3) + w4E(R4)$

Subject to:

$w1 + w2 + w3 + w4 = 1$ (sum of weights must be equal to 1)
$w1, w2, w3, w4 \geq 0$ (weights must be non-negative)
$w^T \Sigma w \leq \sigma 2$ (portfolio variance must be less than or equal to a given level of risk, σ)
where Σ is the covariance matrix of the returns.

We can solve this problem using quadratic programming techniques. In this particular case, let's assume that we want to find the optimal portfolio with a risk level of $\sigma = 0.10$. The problem can be solved using software such as MATLAB, R, or Python. The optimal weights and expected return can be calculated as follows:

w = [0.004, 0.333, 0.463, 0.200] (weights for each stock)
$E(Rp) = 11.32\%$ (expected return of the portfolio)

Thus, the optimal portfolio consists of 0.4% of stock 1, 33.3% of stock 2, 46.3% of stock 3, and 20% of stock 4, with an expected return of 11.32% and a risk level of 0.10.

Efficient Portfolios

An efficient portfolio is a portfolio that offers the highest expected return for a given level of risk or the lowest risk for a given level of expected return. It is achieved by combining assets in a way that maximizes the expected return while minimizing the variance. This is done by solving the mean-variance optimization problem.

The mean-variance optimization problem involves finding the optimal asset allocation that minimizes the portfolio variance for a given level of expected return or maximizes the expected return for a given level of portfolio variance. The optimal asset allocation is found by solving a system of equations known as the Markowitz optimization problem.

Suppose an investor has a portfolio consisting of three assets: Asset A, Asset B, and Asset C. The expected returns and standard deviations of each asset are given in the table below:

Asset	Expected Return	Standard Deviation
A	10%	20%
B	15%	30%
C	20%	40%

The investor wants to construct an efficient portfolio with a target expected return of 16%. What should be the weight of each asset in the portfolio?

To solve this problem, we can use mean-variance analysis and the efficient frontier. We can first calculate the expected return and variance of all possible portfolios with different weight combinations of the three assets. We can then plot the portfolios on the risk-return plane and find the efficient frontier, which represents the set of portfolios that offer the highest expected return for a given level of risk.

To construct an efficient portfolio with a target expected return of 16%, we can find the point on the efficient frontier that corresponds to an expected return of 16%. We can then read off the weights of each asset from the corresponding portfolio. These weights will represent the optimal allocation that achieves the target expected return while minimizing the portfolio's risk.

This problem illustrates the importance of efficient portfolio construction in finance and the use of mean-variance analysis to optimize portfolio allocation.

1. Given a portfolio with two stocks A and B, where stock A has a standard deviation of 0.1 and expected return of 10%, and stock B has a standard deviation of 0.15 and expected return of 15%, what is the minimum variance portfolio that can be constructed with these two stocks?

2. Suppose there are three stocks in a portfolio with the following expected returns and standard deviations: Stock A has an expected return of 8% and a standard deviation of 0.05; Stock B has an expected return of 10% and a standard deviation of 0.06; and Stock C has an expected return of 12% and a standard deviation of 0.08. What is the efficient frontier for this portfolio?

M.L.Ruscsak

3. Given a portfolio with three stocks and the following information: Stock A has a standard deviation of 0.15 and expected return of 12%; Stock B has a standard deviation of 0.1 and expected return of 10%; and Stock C has a standard deviation of 0.05 and expected return of 8%. What is the minimum variance portfolio that can be constructed with these three stocks?

4. Suppose there are two stocks in a portfolio with the following expected returns and standard deviations: Stock A has an expected return of 12% and a standard deviation of 0.1, while Stock B has an expected return of 10% and a standard deviation of 0.08. What is the expected return and standard deviation of the optimal portfolio with a 50/50 allocation to both stocks?

5. Given a portfolio with four stocks and the following information: Stock A has a standard deviation of 0.12 and expected return of 15%; Stock B has a standard deviation of 0.08 and expected return of 12%; Stock C has a standard deviation of 0.05 and expected return of 10%; and Stock D has a standard deviation of 0.06 and expected return of 11%. What is the weight of each stock in the optimal portfolio that has the highest Sharpe ratio?

6. Suppose there are four stocks in a portfolio with the following expected returns and standard deviations: Stock A has an expected return of 8% and a standard deviation of 0.07; Stock B has an expected return of 10% and a standard deviation of 0.1; Stock C has an expected return of 12% and a standard deviation of 0.15; and Stock D has an expected return of 14% and a standard deviation of 0.2. What is the optimal portfolio with a target expected return of 12%?

7. Given a portfolio with three stocks and the following information: Stock A has a standard deviation of 0.1 and expected return of 8%; Stock B has a standard deviation of 0.12 and expected return of 10%; and Stock C has a standard deviation of 0.15 and expected return of 12%. What is the efficient frontier for this portfolio?

8. Suppose there are two stocks in a portfolio with the following expected returns and standard deviations: Stock A has an expected return of 15% and a standard deviation of 0.1, while Stock B has an expected return of 10% and a standard deviation of 0.08. What is the expected return and standard deviation of the optimal portfolio with a 75/25 allocation to Stock A and Stock B, respectively?

9. Given a portfolio with three stocks and the following information: Stock A has a standard deviation of 0.12 and expected return of 10%; Stock B has a standard deviation of 0.15 and expected return of 12%;

Markowitz Optimization Problem

The Markowitz optimization problem is a mathematical formulation of the mean-variance optimization problem. It is named after Harry Markowitz, who introduced the concept of efficient portfolios in 1952. The problem involves finding the optimal asset allocation that minimizes the portfolio variance for a given level of expected return or maximizes the expected return for a given level of portfolio variance.

The optimal asset allocation is found by solving a system of equations that take into account the expected returns, variances, and covariances of the assets in the portfolio. The solution involves calculating the portfolio weights for each asset in the portfolio. These weights represent the proportion of the total investment that should be allocated to each asset.

Suppose we have three assets with the following characteristics:

Asset	Expected Return	Standard Deviation
A	0.08	0.15
B	0.10	0.20
C	0.12	0.25

Assume there is no correlation among the assets.

Suppose the investor wants to create a portfolio with a target expected return of 10% while minimizing the portfolio's variance.

The Markowitz optimization problem can be formulated as:

Minimize $w'\Sigma w$

Subject to:

$w'A = 0.1$
$w'1 = 1$

Where:

w is a vector of weights representing the proportion of each asset in the portfolio
A is a vector of expected returns for each asset
Σ is the covariance matrix of the assets
1 is a vector of ones
Solve for the optimal weights of each asset in the portfolio.

Applications of Portfolio Optimization

Portfolio optimization has numerous applications in finance. It is used by investment managers, hedge funds, and other financial institutions to construct portfolios that meet specific investment objectives. The technique is also used in the construction of index funds and exchange-traded funds (ETFs).

One of the major applications of portfolio optimization is in asset allocation. Asset allocation involves dividing an investment portfolio among different asset categories, such as stocks, bonds, and cash. The goal is to balance risk and return by allocating assets to different categories based on their risk and return characteristics.

Another application of portfolio optimization is in risk management. Portfolio optimization can be used to construct portfolios that minimize the risk of losses during market downturns. This is achieved by constructing portfolios that are diversified across different asset classes and that have low correlations with each other.

Sure, here's a math problem related to applications of portfolio optimization:

Suppose a portfolio manager is constructing a portfolio with $10 million to invest in four stocks: Stock A, Stock B, Stock C, and Stock D. The expected returns and standard deviations of the four stocks are:

Stock A: expected return of 8% and standard deviation of 20%
Stock B: expected return of 10% and standard deviation of 25%
Stock C: expected return of 12% and standard deviation of 30%
Stock D: expected return of 15% and standard deviation of 35%

The portfolio manager wants to construct an efficient portfolio that has a target expected return of 11% and a target standard deviation of 25%. Using Markowitz optimization, what should be the weights of each stock in the portfolio?

(Note: The weights should sum up to 1)

Conclusion

Portfolio optimization is a fundamental problem in finance. It involves constructing portfolios that balance risk and return by choosing the optimal asset allocation. The use of statistical techniques such as mean-variance analysis, efficient frontier analysis, and Monte Carlo simulations have allowed investors to make informed decisions about their investments and construct portfolios that meet their objectives.

In this section, we have discussed the various problems related to constructing efficient portfolios with different risk and return characteristics, and finding the optimal asset allocation using mean-variance analysis. We have also highlighted the importance of diversification and low correlation in risk management.

It is important to note that portfolio optimization is not a one-time process, but rather an ongoing process that requires continuous monitoring and adjustment to changing market conditions and investment objectives. Additionally, it is important to recognize that portfolio optimization is not a guarantee against losses and that all investments carry a certain level of risk.

Overall, portfolio optimization is a powerful tool in the hands of investors, allowing them to make informed decisions about their investments and construct portfolios that meet their objectives. By using statistical techniques and diversification, investors can minimize risk and maximize returns, ultimately leading to a successful investment portfolio.

1. Find the optimal portfolio weights for a portfolio consisting of 3 assets with expected returns of 5%, 8%, and 12%, respectively, and a covariance matrix given as [0.01, 0.02, 0.03; 0.02, 0.04, 0.05; 0.03, 0.05, 0.09].

2. Consider a portfolio consisting of 4 assets with expected returns of 7%, 9%, 11%, and 13%, respectively. The covariance matrix of the returns is given as [0.01, 0.02, 0.03, 0.04; 0.02, 0.04, 0.05, 0.06; 0.03, 0.05, 0.06, 0.07; 0.04, 0.06, 0.07, 0.09]. Find the efficient frontier and the optimal portfolio for a given risk level.

3. Suppose you have a portfolio consisting of 5 stocks with expected returns of 8%, 10%, 12%, 14%, and 16%, respectively. The covariance matrix of the returns is given as [0.01, 0.02, 0.03, 0.04, 0.05; 0.02, 0.04, 0.05, 0.06, 0.07; 0.03, 0.05, 0.07, 0.08, 0.09; 0.04, 0.06, 0.08, 0.10, 0.11; 0.05, 0.07, 0.09, 0.11, 0.13]. Find the minimum variance portfolio and the efficient frontier.

4. Consider a portfolio consisting of 3 assets with expected returns of 6%, 8%, and 10%, respectively, and a covariance matrix given as [0.02, 0.03, 0.04; 0.03, 0.06, 0.07; 0.04, 0.07, 0.10]. Find the expected return, variance, and standard deviation of the optimal portfolio.

5. Suppose you have a portfolio consisting of 4 assets with expected returns of 7%, 9%, 11%, and 13%, respectively. The covariance matrix of the returns is given as [0.01, 0.02, 0.03, 0.04; 0.02, 0.04, 0.05, 0.06; 0.03, 0.05, 0.06, 0.07; 0.04, 0.06, 0.07, 0.08]. Find the efficient frontier and the optimal portfolio for a given return level.

6. Consider a portfolio consisting of 5 assets with expected returns of 8%, 10%, 12%, 14%, and 16%, respectively, and a covariance matrix given as [0.01, 0.02, 0.03, 0.04, 0.05; 0.02, 0.04, 0.05, 0.06, 0.07; 0.03, 0.05, 0.07, 0.08, 0.09; 0.04, 0.06, 0.08, 0.10,

Risk Analysis:

Risk analysis is a critical component of financial decision-making, as it helps individuals and institutions to identify, measure, and manage the risks associated with their investments. In this section, we will explore the different problems related to measuring and managing risk in finance, and the various risk measures that are commonly used for this purpose.

Measuring Risk in Finance

In finance, risk refers to the potential loss that an investor may incur on their investment. There are several ways to measure risk, including standard deviation, value-at-risk (VaR), and expected shortfall.

Standard deviation is a commonly used measure of risk that measures the degree of dispersion of returns around their average. It is calculated by taking the square root of the variance of returns, which is the average of the squared differences between each return and the average return. A higher standard deviation indicates a higher level of risk.

Value-at-risk (VaR) is a measure of the maximum loss that a portfolio may incur over a specified time period, at a given level of confidence. VaR is calculated by estimating the distribution of returns of the portfolio, and then determining the loss that would occur at a specific level of confidence, typically 95% or 99%. VaR is a popular measure of risk used by risk managers and portfolio managers, as it provides a clear estimate of the potential loss that may be incurred.

Expected shortfall, also known as conditional value-at-risk, is a risk measure that estimates the average loss that may occur in the tail of the distribution of returns, beyond the VaR threshold. It is a more conservative measure of risk than VaR, as it takes into account the possibility of extreme losses.

Managing Risk in Finance

Once risks have been identified and measured, the next step is to manage them effectively. There are several ways to manage risk in finance, including diversification, hedging, and insurance.

Diversification is the process of investing in a variety of assets that have low correlations with each other, in order to reduce the overall risk of the portfolio. By diversifying across different asset classes, such as stocks, bonds, and real estate, investors can reduce the risk of losing money during market downturns.

Hedging is a strategy that involves taking a position in a security or derivative that will offset the risk of an existing investment. For example, an investor who owns a portfolio of stocks may hedge against a market downturn by buying put options on a stock index.

Insurance is another way to manage risk in finance, as it provides protection against unexpected events that may cause financial losses. For example, an investor may purchase insurance against losses due to natural disasters or other catastrophic events.

Conclusion

Risk analysis is a critical component of financial decision-making, as it helps investors to identify, measure, and manage the risks associated with their investments. By using a variety of risk measures and management strategies, investors can build portfolios that balance risk and return, and achieve their financial goals. Understanding the problems related to measuring and managing risk is essential for anyone looking to succeed in the field of finance.

Suppose you are a portfolio manager and you are trying to evaluate the risk of a particular asset in your portfolio. The asset has an expected return of 10% and a standard deviation of 5%. You want to calculate the value-at-risk (VaR) of the asset at a 95% confidence level. What is the VaR of the asset?

To solve this problem, we first need to calculate the asset's expected return and standard deviation. We can then use the following formula to calculate the VaR at a 95% confidence level:

VaR = expected return - z * standard deviation

where z is the number of standard deviations from the mean corresponding to the desired confidence level. For a 95% confidence level, z = 1.645.

Using the given values, we can calculate the VaR as follows:

Expected return = 10%
Standard deviation = 5%
z = 1.645

M.L.Ruscsak

VaR = 10% - 1.645 * 5% = 1.28%

Therefore, the VaR of the asset at a 95% confidence level is 1.28%.

1. Suppose you have a portfolio of 5 stocks with the following returns: 6%, 9%, 12%, 15%, and 18%. Calculate the standard deviation of the portfolio returns if the weights of the stocks are 20%, 30%, 15%, 25%, and 10%, respectively.

2. A portfolio manager wants to construct a portfolio with a maximum expected shortfall of 5%. The portfolio consists of 3 stocks with expected returns of 8%, 10%, and 12%, and the covariance matrix of the returns is given as:
[0.02, 0.03, 0.04]
[0.03, 0.06, 0.05]
[0.04, 0.05, 0.08]
What is the optimal asset allocation for the portfolio?

3. A financial analyst is analyzing the performance of a mutual fund. The fund has a standard deviation of 12% and an average return of 8%. What is the probability that the fund's return will be less than 5%?

4. An investor is considering two stocks with expected returns of 10% and 12%, respectively. The stocks have a correlation coefficient of 0.6. What is the variance of a portfolio consisting of 50% of each stock?

5. A portfolio consists of 4 stocks with expected returns of 8%, 9%, 10%, and 11%, and the covariance matrix of the returns is given as:
[0.01, 0.02, 0.03, 0.04]
[0.02, 0.05, 0.06, 0.07]
[0.03, 0.06, 0.08, 0.09]
[0.04, 0.07, 0.09, 0.1]
What is the value-at-risk (VaR) at the 5% significance level?

6. A portfolio manager wants to construct a portfolio with a maximum VaR of 6%. The portfolio consists of 3 stocks with expected returns of 8%, 10%, and 12%, and the covariance matrix of the returns is given as:
[0.02, 0.03, 0.04]
[0.03, 0.06, 0.05]
[0.04, 0.05, 0.08]
What is the optimal asset allocation for the portfolio?

7. An investment banker is analyzing the performance of a bond fund. The fund has a 10-year average return of 7.5% and a standard deviation of 1.5%. What is the 95% confidence interval for the fund's average return?

8. A portfolio consists of 3 stocks with expected returns of 8%, 10%, and 12%, and the covariance matrix of the returns is given as:
[0.02, 0.03, 0.04]
[0.03, 0.06, 0.05]
[0.04, 0.05, 0.08]
What is the expected shortfall of the portfolio at the 5% significance level?

9. An actuary is calculating the premium for a life insurance policy. The policy has a death benefit of $500,000 and the probability of death in the next year is 0.02. If the actuary wants to make a profit of $10,000 on the policy, what is the premium?

10. A portfolio consists of 4 stocks with expected returns of 8%, 9%, 10%, and 11%, and the covariance matrix of the returns is given as:

[0.01, 0.02, 0.03, 0.04]
[0.02, 0.05, 0.07, 0.09]
[0.03, 0.07, 0.11, 0.15]
[0.04, 0.09, 0.15, 0.21]

Suppose we want to construct a portfolio with a target expected return of 9.5%. What is the minimum variance of the portfolio?

To solve this problem, we can use the formula for the minimum variance portfolio:

w = (1 / (e^T * V^-1 * e)) * V^-1 * e

where w is the vector of weights, e is a vector of ones, and V is the covariance matrix of the returns.

First, we need to calculate the vector e and the matrix V^-1:

e = [1, 1, 1, 1]

V^-1 =
[54.1667, -156.2500, 90.6250, - 10.4167]
[-156.2500, 625.0000,-468.7500, 78.1250]
[90.6250, -468.7500, 421.8750,- 78.1250]
[- 10.4167, 78.1250,- 78.1250, 19.7917]

Next, we need to calculate e^T * V^-1 * e:

e^T * V^-1 * e = 0.013542

Finally, we can calculate the minimum variance portfolio weights:

w = (1 / (e^T * V^-1 * e)) * V^-1 * e
w = [0.064, 0.211, 0.346, 0.379]

Therefore, the minimum variance portfolio has weights of 6.4% in the first stock, 21.1% in the second stock, 34.6% in the third stock, and 37.9% in the fourth stock. The variance of the portfolio can be calculated as:

variance = w^T * V * w
variance = 0.0157 or 1.57%

Hypothesis Testing:

Hypothesis testing is a statistical method used to make inferences about the population based on a sample of data. In finance, hypothesis testing is often used to make decisions about financial data, such as whether a stock's mean return is significantly different from zero or whether two assets are significantly correlated. In this section, we will discuss the principles of hypothesis testing and how it can be applied to financial data.

Principles of Hypothesis Testing

Hypothesis testing involves the following steps:

Formulate the null hypothesis: The null hypothesis is a statement that assumes that there is no significant difference between the population parameter and the hypothesized value. For example, if we want to test whether the mean return of a stock is significantly different from zero, the null hypothesis would be that the mean return is equal to zero.

Formulate the alternative hypothesis: The alternative hypothesis is a statement that contradicts the null hypothesis. In our example, the alternative hypothesis would be that the mean return is not equal to zero.

Choose a significance level: The significance level is the probability of rejecting the null hypothesis when it is true. A commonly used significance level is 0.05, which means that we are willing to accept a 5% chance of making a Type I error (rejecting the null hypothesis when it is true).

Collect data and calculate the test statistic: The test statistic is a measure of how far the sample estimate is from the hypothesized value. In our example, the test statistic would be the t-statistic, which is calculated as the difference between the sample mean and the hypothesized value, divided by the standard error of the mean.

Calculate the p-value: The p-value is the probability of observing a test statistic as extreme or more extreme than the one observed, assuming that the null hypothesis is true.

Make a decision: If the p-value is less than the significance level, we reject the null hypothesis in favor of the alternative hypothesis. If the p-value is greater than the significance level, we fail to reject the null hypothesis.

Applications in Finance

Hypothesis testing is widely used in finance to test statistical hypotheses about financial data. For example, it can be used to test whether the mean return of a stock is significantly different from zero, whether the correlation between two assets is significantly different from zero, or whether a regression coefficient is significantly different from zero.

One common application of hypothesis testing in finance is in the analysis of investment strategies. For example, suppose we want to test whether a certain investment strategy outperforms the market. We could formulate the null hypothesis as "the strategy has the same return as the market" and the alternative hypothesis as "the strategy has a higher return than the market." We could then collect data on the returns of the strategy and the market and use hypothesis testing to determine whether the strategy outperforms the market.

Another application of hypothesis testing in finance is in the analysis of financial risk. For example, we may want to test whether the standard deviation of the returns of a portfolio is significantly different from a certain value. We could formulate the null hypothesis as "the standard deviation is equal to the hypothesized value" and the alternative hypothesis as "the standard deviation is not equal to the hypothesized value." We could then collect data on the returns of the portfolio and use hypothesis testing to determine whether the portfolio has a significantly different standard deviation than the hypothesized value.

Conclusion

Hypothesis testing is a powerful statistical tool that can be used to make inferences about financial data. By formulating null and alternative hypotheses, choosing a significance level, and calculating test statistics and p-values, we can test whether our assumptions about financial data are supported by the evidence. Hypothesis testing is widely used in finance to make decisions about investments, risk management, and other financial operations.

One common application of hypothesis testing in finance is testing the mean return of a stock. Investors may want to know whether the mean return of a stock is significantly different from zero, which can inform their decision to buy or sell the stock. Another example is testing the correlation between two assets, which can inform the construction of a diversified portfolio.

It's important to note that hypothesis testing is not without limitations and potential pitfalls. For example, using a significance level of 0.05 may result in a Type I error, or a false positive, 5% of the time. Additionally, hypothesis testing assumes that the data follows a normal distribution and that the sample size is large enough for the Central Limit Theorem to apply.

Overall, hypothesis testing is a valuable tool in finance for making evidence-based decisions and testing assumptions about financial data. By understanding the underlying principles and potential limitations of hypothesis testing, professionals in the finance industry can make informed decisions and manage risk effectively.

Suppose an investment manager wants to test whether a particular stock has a mean monthly return of at least 1%. She takes a random sample of 50 monthly returns and finds that the sample mean return is 0.8% with a sample standard deviation of 2%. Assume the monthly returns are normally distributed.

a) State the null and alternative hypotheses for this test.
b) Calculate the test statistic.
c) Determine the p-value for this test using a significance level of 0.05.
d) Based on your results, should the investment manager reject or fail to reject the null hypothesis at the 5% significance level? What conclusion can be drawn?

(Note: This is a one-sample t-test with a null hypothesis of $\mu = 1\%$ and an alternative hypothesis of $\mu > 1\%$, where μ is the population mean monthly return of the stock.)

1. A financial analyst wants to test if the mean daily return of a stock is greater than 1%. She collects a sample of 50 daily returns and calculates a sample mean of 1.5% with a standard deviation of 2%. Test the hypothesis at a 5% significance level.

2. A portfolio manager wants to test if there is a significant correlation between the daily returns of two assets. She collects a sample of 100 daily returns for each asset and calculates a sample correlation of 0.6. Test the hypothesis at a 10% significance level.

3. An investment banker wants to test if the mean weekly return of a stock index is less than 0.5%. She collects a sample of 25 weekly returns and calculates a sample mean of 0.3% with a standard deviation of 1%. Test the hypothesis at a 1% significance level.

4. A financial planner wants to test if there is a significant difference in the mean monthly returns of two investment portfolios. She collects a sample of 20 monthly returns for each portfolio and calculates a sample mean difference of 0.2% with a standard deviation of 0.5%. Test the hypothesis at a 5% significance level.

5. A quantitative analyst wants to test if the mean annual return of a mutual fund is equal to 8%. He collects a sample of 30 annual returns and calculates a sample mean of 7.5% with a standard deviation of 1.5%. Test the hypothesis at a 1% significance level.

6. An actuary wants to test if the variance of daily returns of a stock is greater than 0.02. She collects a sample of 200 daily returns and calculates a sample variance of 0.025. Test the hypothesis at a 5% significance level.

7. A securities trader wants to test if the skewness of weekly returns of a stock is significantly different from zero. He collects a sample of 50 weekly returns and calculates a sample skewness of -0.2. Test the hypothesis at a 10% significance level.

8. A financial analyst wants to test if the mean monthly return of a bond index is greater than 0.3%. She collects a sample of 15 monthly returns and calculates a sample mean of 0.4% with a standard deviation of 0.2%. Test the hypothesis at a 5% significance level.

9. A portfolio manager wants to test if the correlation between the monthly returns of two assets is significantly different from 0.8. She collects a sample of 50 monthly returns for each asset and calculates a sample correlation of 0.7. Test the hypothesis at a 5% significance level.

10. An investment banker wants to test if the mean daily return of a stock is equal to 0.75%. She collects a sample of 40 daily returns and calculates a sample mean of 0.8% with a standard deviation of 1%. Test the hypothesis at a 10% significance level.

CHAPTER 9: REVIEW OF STATISTICAL TECHNIQUES COMMONLY USED IN FINANCE

Finance is a discipline that involves the management of financial resources, such as money, investments, and assets, in order to achieve financial objectives. One of the key challenges in finance is dealing with uncertainty and risk. Statistical techniques are essential tools for measuring and managing risk, as well as for making informed financial decisions.

This chapter provides a review of statistical techniques commonly used in finance. It covers a range of statistical methods, including descriptive statistics, probability theory, hypothesis testing, regression analysis, and time series analysis. These techniques are used for a variety of purposes in finance, such as portfolio optimization, risk management, and financial forecasting.

Descriptive statistics is a branch of statistics that deals with summarizing and analyzing data. It involves measures such as mean, median, mode, variance, standard deviation, and correlation. These measures provide insights into the distribution and relationships between variables in financial data.

Probability theory is a fundamental concept in finance, as it provides a framework for measuring uncertainty and risk. It involves calculating the likelihood of events occurring based on the available information. Probability theory is used to model financial instruments such as stocks, bonds, options, and derivatives.

Hypothesis testing is a statistical method used to test assumptions about financial data. It involves formulating a null hypothesis, choosing a significance level, and calculating test statistics and p-values. Hypothesis testing is used to make inferences about financial data, such as the mean return of a stock or the correlation between two assets.

Regression analysis is a statistical method used to model the relationship between two or more variables. It involves fitting a mathematical model to the data, and using it to predict future values. Regression analysis is used in finance for various purposes, such as forecasting stock prices, estimating asset returns, and identifying the factors that influence financial outcomes.

Time series analysis is a statistical method used to analyze time series data, which is data that is collected over time. It involves modeling the data to identify trends, seasonality, and other patterns. Time series analysis is used in finance for various purposes, such as forecasting financial returns, analyzing economic indicators, and monitoring market trends.

In conclusion, statistical techniques are essential tools for understanding and managing financial data. The review of statistical techniques provided in this chapter will provide students with a solid foundation for understanding and analyzing financial data. By applying these techniques, students will be able to make informed financial decisions and manage risk effectively.

Regression analysis and its applications in finance

Regression analysis is a statistical technique that is commonly used in finance to analyze relationships between variables. It is a powerful tool that allows us to estimate the effect of one variable on another, and to identify the key factors that drive financial outcomes. Regression analysis has a wide range of applications in finance, including asset pricing, risk management, and portfolio management.

This chapter provides an overview of regression analysis and its applications in finance. We will begin by defining regression analysis and discussing its basic principles. We will then explore some of the key applications of regression analysis in finance, including asset pricing models, risk management models, and portfolio management models. Finally, we will discuss some of the challenges and limitations of regression analysis in finance.

What is Regression Analysis?

Regression analysis is a statistical technique that is used to analyze the relationship between two or more variables. It is based on the assumption that there is a linear relationship between the variables, which means that the change in one variable is proportional to the change in the other variable.

The basic idea behind regression analysis is to estimate the slope and intercept of a line that best fits the data. This line is known as the regression line or the line of best fit. The slope of the line represents the change in the dependent variable for every one-unit change in the independent variable, while the intercept represents the value of the dependent variable when the independent variable is equal to zero.

There are two main types of regression analysis: simple regression and multiple regression. Simple regression involves the analysis of the relationship between two variables, while multiple regression involves the analysis of the relationship between three or more variables.

Applications of Regression Analysis in Finance

M.L.Ruscsak

Asset Pricing Models

One of the key applications of regression analysis in finance is in the development of asset pricing models. Asset pricing models are used to determine the fair value of financial assets, such as stocks and bonds, based on their underlying characteristics and the risk and return characteristics of the market as a whole.

The most well-known asset pricing model is the Capital Asset Pricing Model (CAPM). The CAPM is a simple regression model that relates the expected return of an asset to its systematic risk, as measured by the beta coefficient. The beta coefficient measures the sensitivity of an asset's returns to changes in the market returns.

Risk Management Models

Another important application of regression analysis in finance is in the development of risk management models. Risk management models are used to measure and manage the risk of financial investments, such as stocks and bonds.

One of the most widely used risk management models is Value at Risk (VaR). VaR is a statistical technique that estimates the maximum loss that a portfolio is likely to experience over a given time period, at a given level of confidence. VaR is based on a regression analysis of historical returns, and provides a measure of the downside risk of a portfolio.

Portfolio Management Models

Regression analysis is also widely used in portfolio management, which involves the selection and management of a group of financial assets that are designed to achieve a specific investment objective.

One of the most popular portfolio management models is the Markowitz Portfolio Theory. This model is based on a regression analysis of historical returns, and is used to identify the optimal mix of assets that will provide the highest expected return for a given level of risk.

Challenges and Limitations of Regression Analysis in Finance

Despite its many benefits, regression analysis has several limitations when it comes to its applications in finance. One of the key challenges is the need for large amounts of high-quality data. Regression analysis is highly dependent on the quality and quantity of data, and small sample sizes or incomplete data can lead to inaccurate results.

Another challenge is the assumption of linearity. Regression analysis assumes that there is a linear relationship between the variables being analyzed, which may not always be the case in finance. Nonlinear relationships can lead to inaccurate predictions and biased results. To address this challenge, analysts can use techniques such as polynomial regression, which allows for the fitting of nonlinear relationships.

One application of regression analysis in finance is in the valuation of stocks. Analysts can use regression analysis to estimate the relationship between a stock's price and its fundamental factors, such as earnings per share, price-to-earnings ratio, and book value. This relationship can then be used to estimate the intrinsic value of the stock and determine whether it is overvalued or undervalued.

Another application of regression analysis in finance is in the evaluation of portfolio performance. By regressing a portfolio's returns against a benchmark index, analysts can determine the portfolio's alpha, which measures the portfolio's excess returns relative to the benchmark. This information can then be used to evaluate the performance of the portfolio manager and make adjustments to the portfolio's holdings.

Regression analysis can also be used in financial forecasting, such as predicting future interest rates or stock prices. By regressing historical data against economic or market indicators, analysts can create models to make predictions about future trends.

In addition to its applications in finance, regression analysis has also been used in other fields, such as marketing, psychology, and sports analytics. For example, regression analysis can be used to study the relationship between a company's advertising budget and its sales, or the relationship between a student's study habits and their academic performance.

In conclusion, regression analysis is a powerful statistical tool that has numerous applications in finance and other fields. By analyzing the relationship between variables, regression analysis can provide insights into the factors that drive financial performance and can be used to make predictions and inform decision-making. However, it is important to carefully consider the assumptions and limitations of regression analysis and to use appropriate techniques to address any challenges that may arise.

Hypothesis testing and its applications in finance

Hypothesis testing is a statistical technique used in finance to test assumptions about financial data. In the financial world, it is common to make predictions or assumptions about market trends, stock prices, and economic indicators. Hypothesis testing provides a way to test these assumptions using statistical evidence.

In this section, we will provide an in-depth analysis of hypothesis testing and its applications in finance. We will start by defining hypothesis testing, its types, and its significance in finance. Next, we will explain the process of hypothesis testing, including the formulation of null and alternative hypotheses, the selection of significance levels, and the calculation of test statistics and p-values. We will also discuss the interpretation of results and the potential sources of error in hypothesis testing. Finally, we will explore the applications of hypothesis testing in finance, including its use in asset pricing, risk management, and financial modeling.

Definition and Types of Hypothesis Testing

Hypothesis testing is a statistical technique used to test a hypothesis or assumption about a population or a data set. The process involves formulating a null hypothesis, which represents the assumption being tested, and an alternative hypothesis, which represents the opposite of the null hypothesis. The null hypothesis is usually assumed to be true until proven otherwise, while the alternative hypothesis represents the researcher's theory or hypothesis.

There are two types of hypothesis testing: one-tailed and two-tailed tests. A one-tailed test is used when the alternative hypothesis is directional, meaning it predicts the direction of the difference between the sample mean and the population mean. For example, a one-tailed test could be used to test the hypothesis that a stock's return is higher than the market average. A two-tailed test is used when the alternative hypothesis is non-directional, meaning it predicts that there is a difference between the sample mean and the population mean but does not specify the direction. For example, a two-tailed test could be used to test the hypothesis that a stock's return is different from the market average.

The significance level, or alpha, is the probability of rejecting the null hypothesis when it is actually true. It is usually set at 0.05 or 0.01, indicating a 5% or 1% chance of rejecting the null hypothesis when it is actually true.

Process of Hypothesis Testing

The process of hypothesis testing involves several steps, including the formulation of null and alternative hypotheses, the selection of a significance level, and the calculation of test statistics and p-values.

Formulation of Null and Alternative Hypotheses

The first step in hypothesis testing is to formulate a null hypothesis and an alternative hypothesis. The null hypothesis represents the assumption being tested, while the alternative hypothesis represents the opposite of the null hypothesis. For example, if we are testing the hypothesis that a stock's return is higher than the market average, the null hypothesis would be that the stock's return is equal to or lower than the market average, while the alternative hypothesis would be that the stock's return is higher than the market average.

Selection of Significance Level

The significance level, or alpha, is the probability of rejecting the null hypothesis when it is actually true. It is usually set at 0.05 or 0.01, indicating a 5% or 1% chance of rejecting the null hypothesis when it is actually true. The choice of significance level depends on the researcher's risk tolerance and the consequences of making a Type I error (rejecting the null hypothesis when it is actually true).

Calculation of Test Statistics and P-values

The next step is to calculate a test statistic and a p-value. The test statistic is a measure of how far the sample mean deviates from the null hypothesis. The p-value is the probability of obtaining a test statistic as extreme or more extreme than the one calculated, assuming that the null hypothesis is true. The smaller the p-value, the stronger the evidence against the null hypothesis.

There are different test statistics and methods for calculating p-values, depending on the type of hypothesis being tested, the sample size, and the distribution of the data. In finance, some commonly used test statistics and methods include:

Z-test: A z-test is used to test a hypothesis about a population mean when the population standard deviation is known. The test statistic is calculated as the difference between the sample mean and the hypothesized population mean, divided by the standard error of the mean. The p-value is then calculated using the standard normal distribution.

T-test: A t-test is used to test a hypothesis about a population mean when the population standard deviation is unknown and must be estimated from the sample data. The test statistic is calculated as the difference between the sample mean and the hypothesized population mean, divided by the standard error of the mean. The p-value is then calculated using the t-distribution.

Chi-square test: A chi-square test is used to test a hypothesis about the distribution of categorical data. The test statistic is calculated as the sum of the squared differences between the observed and expected frequencies, divided by the expected frequencies. The p-value is then calculated using the chi-square distribution.

F-test: An F-test is used to test a hypothesis about the equality of variances between two populations. The test statistic is calculated as the ratio of the sample variances, and the p-value is then calculated using the F-distribution.

ANOVA: Analysis of variance (ANOVA) is used to test a hypothesis about the equality of means between two or more populations. ANOVA calculates an F-test statistic and a p-value to determine if there is a significant difference between the means.

Once the test statistic and p-value have been calculated, we can compare the p-value to the chosen significance level (alpha) to determine whether to reject or fail to reject the null hypothesis. If the p-value is less than alpha, we reject the null hypothesis and conclude that there is significant evidence to support the alternative hypothesis. If the p-value is greater than alpha, we fail to reject the null hypothesis and conclude that there is insufficient evidence to support the alternative hypothesis.

Applications of Hypothesis Testing in Finance

Hypothesis testing is widely used in finance to make inferences about financial data and to inform investment decisions. Some common applications of hypothesis testing in finance include:

Testing the efficacy of investment strategies: Hypothesis testing can be used to test the effectiveness of different investment strategies, such as value investing, momentum investing, and growth investing. By formulating a null hypothesis that the strategy has no effect on returns and an alternative hypothesis that the strategy does have an effect on returns, we can test whether the strategy is statistically significant.

Assessing market efficiency: Hypothesis testing can be used to test the efficiency of financial markets, such as the stock market or the bond market. By formulating a null hypothesis that the market is efficient and an alternative hypothesis that the market is not efficient, we can test whether there are any exploitable market inefficiencies.

Evaluating financial models: Hypothesis testing can be used to evaluate the validity of financial models, such as the capital asset pricing model (CAPM) or the Black-Scholes model. By formulating a null hypothesis that the model is valid and an alternative hypothesis that the model is not valid, we can test whether the model accurately reflects the behavior of financial assets.

Risk management: Hypothesis testing can be used to test the validity of risk management strategies, such as value at risk (VaR) or conditional value at risk (CVaR). VaR and CVaR are commonly used measures of risk that estimate the potential loss of an investment over a given time period with a certain degree of confidence. Hypothesis testing can be used to determine whether these measures are accurate and whether they are useful in managing risk.

For example, a portfolio manager may use VaR to estimate the potential loss of a portfolio over a 10-day time period with a 95% confidence level. The manager can then use hypothesis testing to determine whether the estimated VaR accurately reflects the potential risk of the portfolio. If the VaR estimate is found to be inaccurate, the manager can adjust the risk management strategy accordingly to better protect the portfolio from potential losses.

Another example is the use of hypothesis testing in testing the effectiveness of a hedging strategy. Hedging is a risk management technique used to offset potential losses by taking a position in a related asset. Hypothesis testing can be used to test the effectiveness of a hedging strategy by comparing the returns of the hedged portfolio to those of an unhedged portfolio. If the hedged portfolio is found to have significantly lower risk and higher returns, the hedging strategy can be considered effective.

Overall, hypothesis testing is an important tool in risk management as it allows investors to make informed decisions about their portfolios and minimize potential losses. By testing the validity of risk management strategies and analyzing their effectiveness, investors can better manage their risk exposure and achieve their financial goals.

Overview of other statistical techniques used in finance

While regression analysis and hypothesis testing are two widely used statistical techniques in finance, there are several others that are commonly used as well. These techniques help finance professionals to better understand and analyze financial data, make more informed decisions, and mitigate risks. In this section, we will provide an overview of some of the other statistical techniques used in finance.

Time-series analysis
Time-series analysis is a statistical technique used to analyze trends, patterns, and changes in data over time. In finance, time-series analysis is commonly used to analyze stock prices, interest rates, and economic indicators. By analyzing historical data, financial professionals can make informed predictions about future trends, which can help them make better investment decisions.

Monte Carlo simulation
Monte Carlo simulation is a statistical technique used to simulate possible outcomes of a complex system. In finance, Monte Carlo simulation is commonly used to model and analyze financial risk. By simulating various outcomes of a portfolio under different market conditions, financial professionals can better understand the risks associated with different investment strategies.

Cluster analysis
Cluster analysis is a statistical technique used to group data points into clusters based on similarities or dissimilarities. In finance, cluster analysis is commonly used to analyze market trends and identify patterns in financial data. By identifying these patterns, financial professionals can make more informed decisions about investment strategies and risk management.

Principal component analysis
Principal component analysis is a statistical technique used to reduce the dimensionality of data by identifying the most important features or variables. In finance, principal component analysis is commonly used to analyze the relationships between different assets in a portfolio. By identifying the most important factors that influence portfolio performance, financial professionals can make more informed investment decisions.

M.L.Ruscsak

Decision tree analysis

Decision tree analysis is a statistical technique used to analyze complex decision-making processes. In finance, decision tree analysis is commonly used to analyze investment decisions and risk management strategies. By simulating various outcomes of a decision under different scenarios, financial professionals can make more informed decisions about investment strategies and risk management.

Neural networks

Neural networks are a type of artificial intelligence algorithm that are commonly used in finance to analyze and predict market trends. By analyzing historical data, neural networks can identify patterns and relationships between different variables. These patterns can then be used to make predictions about future market trends and inform investment decisions.

Bayesian analysis

Bayesian analysis is a statistical technique used to update probability estimates based on new data. In finance, Bayesian analysis is commonly used to analyze investment decisions and risk management strategies. By updating probability estimates based on new market data, financial professionals can make more informed decisions about investment strategies and risk management.

Conclusion

In conclusion, there are several statistical techniques used in finance beyond regression analysis and hypothesis testing. These techniques help financial professionals to better understand and analyze financial data, make more informed decisions, and mitigate risks. By leveraging these statistical techniques, financial professionals can gain a competitive advantage in the market and achieve better investment outcomes.

PART 4: CALCULUS FOR FINANCE

Calculus is a branch of mathematics that deals with the study of rates of change and their application to various problems. In finance, calculus plays a vital role in understanding and analyzing the behavior of financial systems, such as stock markets and interest rates. Calculus is also used to derive and solve complex financial models, such as options pricing models and portfolio optimization models.

This section provides an overview of the calculus concepts used in finance and their applications. It covers topics such as derivatives, integrals, differential equations, optimization, and partial derivatives, among others. These topics are essential in understanding various financial models and how they are used in finance.

One of the main concepts in calculus is derivatives. Derivatives measure the rate at which a function changes with respect to its input variable. In finance, derivatives are used to calculate the rate of change of financial instruments such as stocks, bonds, and options. The concept of derivatives is also used in risk management to calculate the sensitivity of a financial instrument to changes in market conditions.

Another important concept in calculus is integrals. Integrals are used to calculate the area under a curve and can be used to calculate various financial measures, such as the present value of future cash flows. In finance, integrals are also used to calculate the expected value of a financial instrument and the expected return on an investment.

Differential equations are also a fundamental concept in calculus. They are used to describe the behavior of dynamic systems and can be used to model financial systems, such as the behavior of interest rates over time. Differential equations are also used to model options pricing models and portfolio optimization models.

Optimization is another crucial concept in calculus. It is used to find the optimal solution to a problem, such as maximizing profit or minimizing risk. In finance, optimization is used to construct portfolios that maximize returns while minimizing risk. Optimization techniques are also used in option pricing models to find the optimal exercise price and in hedging strategies to minimize risk.

M.L.Ruscsak

Partial derivatives are also an important concept in calculus. They are used to measure the rate of change of a function with respect to two or more input variables. In finance, partial derivatives are used to calculate the sensitivity of a financial instrument to changes in multiple market conditions. This information is used in risk management to construct effective hedging strategies.

In conclusion, calculus is a vital tool for understanding and analyzing financial systems. This section provides an overview of the calculus concepts used in finance and their applications. A thorough understanding of these concepts is essential for anyone seeking a career in finance, as they are used in a wide range of financial models and calculations.

CHAPTER 10: OPTIMIZATION AND MARGINAL ANALYSIS

Chapter 10 of our finance textbook delves into the topic of optimization and marginal analysis, which are crucial concepts in the field of finance. Optimization is the process of maximizing or minimizing a certain objective function subject to certain constraints. Marginal analysis, on the other hand, is the study of how changes in one variable affect the changes in another variable.

Optimization techniques are widely used in finance to maximize profits or minimize costs, subject to various constraints such as limited resources, legal and regulatory requirements, and risk management. For example, investment managers use optimization to build portfolios that maximize returns while minimizing risks. This involves selecting a mix of assets that can provide the desired return while diversifying risks across different asset classes.

Marginal analysis, on the other hand, is useful in understanding how changes in market conditions or policy changes affect financial decisions. It is commonly used in pricing decisions, where firms need to balance the costs of production with the demand for their products.

In this chapter, we will explore the various optimization techniques used in finance, such as linear programming, quadratic programming, and nonlinear programming. We will also examine the use of marginal analysis in financial decision-making, such as pricing decisions and portfolio management.

We will start with a basic understanding of optimization techniques and gradually move towards more advanced topics such as Lagrange multipliers, convexity, and nonlinear optimization. We will also cover the applications of optimization techniques in finance, such as portfolio optimization, option pricing, and risk management.

Throughout this chapter, we will use real-world examples from various fields such as investment banking, actuarial science, portfolio management, quantitative analysis, securities trading, financial planning, and financial analysis. This will help students to understand the practical applications of optimization and marginal analysis in finance.

By the end of this chapter, students will have a solid understanding of the key optimization techniques used in finance and how to apply them in real-world financial decision-making. They will also be equipped with the tools to perform marginal analysis and make informed financial decisions based on changes in market conditions or policy changes.

Introduction to optimization and marginal analysis

Optimization is a fundamental concept in mathematics and economics, and it is used extensively in finance. The goal of optimization is to find the optimal solution to a problem given certain constraints. Optimization can be used to maximize profits, minimize costs, and achieve other objectives.

Marginal analysis is a related concept that is used to determine the impact of a small change in a variable on the overall outcome. Marginal analysis is useful in determining the optimal level of a variable, such as production or investment, given a set of constraints.

In this chapter, we will introduce the basics of optimization and marginal analysis and explore their applications in finance. We will discuss how optimization can be used to determine the optimal portfolio allocation and risk management strategy. We will also examine how marginal analysis can be used to determine the optimal level of investment and pricing strategies.

Optimization

Optimization is the process of finding the best solution to a problem given certain constraints. In finance, optimization is used to determine the optimal portfolio allocation and risk management strategy. The goal of portfolio optimization is to maximize returns while minimizing risk.

The basic idea behind portfolio optimization is to find the combination of assets that provides the highest expected return for a given level of risk. This can be achieved by using techniques such as mean-variance analysis, which seeks to minimize portfolio risk for a given level of expected return.

In order to perform portfolio optimization, it is necessary to have a set of assets to choose from and a set of constraints that limit the portfolio composition. These constraints may include limitations on the maximum allocation to a particular asset class or sector, as well as other regulatory or ethical constraints.

One important consideration in portfolio optimization is the concept of diversification. Diversification involves investing in a variety of assets in order to spread risk and reduce the impact of any one asset on the overall portfolio. By diversifying across asset classes and sectors, investors can reduce their exposure to any one asset or sector and minimize the overall risk of the portfolio.

Marginal Analysis

Marginal analysis is a method used to determine the impact of a small change in a variable on the overall outcome. Marginal analysis is used in finance to determine the optimal level of investment and pricing strategies.

The basic idea behind marginal analysis is to examine the impact of a small change in a variable on the overall outcome. This can be done by calculating the marginal effect of a change in a variable on the overall outcome, such as profit or revenue.

In finance, marginal analysis is used to determine the optimal level of investment in a particular asset or project. By calculating the marginal return on investment for each additional unit of investment, investors can determine the optimal level of investment that maximizes returns.

Marginal analysis is also used in pricing strategies. By examining the marginal cost of production for each additional unit of output, companies can determine the optimal price to charge for their products. This can help companies maximize profits and achieve their business objectives.

Conclusion

Optimization and marginal analysis are important concepts in finance that are used to determine the optimal portfolio allocation, risk management strategy, and pricing strategy. These concepts are essential for investors and companies to make informed decisions and achieve their financial objectives.

By understanding the principles of optimization and marginal analysis, investors and companies can make better decisions and achieve better outcomes. In the following sections, we will explore the different techniques and methods used in optimization and marginal analysis and their applications in finance.

Optimization techniques for financial applications, including unconstrained optimization, constrained optimization, and Lagrange multipliers

Optimization is a powerful tool in finance that can help investors and financial professionals make more informed decisions. It involves finding the optimal solution to a problem, which often means maximizing profits, minimizing risk, or achieving some other objective. In this section, we will explore various optimization techniques used in finance, including unconstrained optimization, constrained optimization, and Lagrange multipliers.

Unconstrained Optimization:
Unconstrained optimization refers to finding the maximum or minimum of a function without any restrictions on the variables. This is useful in finance when trying to maximize profits or minimize risk. One common method for unconstrained optimization is the gradient descent algorithm. This algorithm iteratively updates the variables in the direction of the steepest descent of the function until a minimum or maximum is found.

Constrained Optimization:

M.L.Ruscsak

Constrained optimization is used when there are restrictions on the variables in the optimization problem. In finance, these constraints could represent budget constraints, regulatory requirements, or risk limits. One common method for constrained optimization is the linear programming (LP) algorithm. LP involves finding the optimal solution to a linear equation subject to linear constraints.

Lagrange Multipliers:
Lagrange multipliers are a method for solving optimization problems with constraints. This method involves adding a term to the original objective function that accounts for the constraint. The Lagrange multiplier is a parameter that determines the sensitivity of the objective function to the constraint. In finance, this method can be used to find the optimal portfolio allocation subject to constraints such as budget or risk limits.

One example of optimization in finance is portfolio optimization, where investors seek to allocate their funds across different assets in a way that maximizes returns while minimizing risk. Portfolio optimization is a complex optimization problem that involves several variables and constraints. The objective function could be the expected return on the portfolio, while the constraints could be budget constraints or risk limits.

Another example is the use of optimization in asset pricing models. In finance, asset pricing models are used to determine the fair price of an asset based on various factors such as interest rates, economic growth, and market volatility. Optimization can be used to determine the values of the parameters in the asset pricing model that best fit the available data.

In conclusion, optimization is a powerful tool in finance that can help investors and financial professionals make more informed decisions. Unconstrained optimization, constrained optimization, and Lagrange multipliers are common methods used in financial applications. By understanding and applying these optimization techniques, investors and financial professionals can better manage their portfolios, minimize risk, and maximize returns.

Marginal analysis and its application in finance, including marginal cost, revenue, and profit

Marginal analysis is a powerful tool used in finance to help determine the impact of changes in production, sales, and other factors on overall profitability. Marginal analysis involves studying the incremental changes in cost, revenue, and profit that result from changes in production levels, prices, or other factors. By analyzing these marginal changes, businesses can make more informed decisions about how to allocate resources, set prices, and manage their overall operations. In this section, we will explore the concept of marginal analysis in depth, including its application in finance, specifically in terms of marginal cost, revenue, and profit.

Marginal Cost:

Marginal cost is the additional cost incurred for producing one more unit of a good or service. In other words, it is the cost of producing an additional unit of output. Marginal cost is important in finance because it helps businesses determine the optimal level of production, where the marginal cost equals the marginal revenue.

For example, let's say a company produces widgets at a total cost of $100, and it produces 10 widgets. The marginal cost of producing the 11th widget is $12. If the company sells each widget for $15, the marginal revenue of producing the 11th widget is $15. In this case, the marginal revenue is greater than the marginal cost, indicating that the company should continue producing widgets until the marginal revenue equals the marginal cost. This is the point of profit maximization.

Marginal Revenue:

Marginal revenue is the additional revenue earned from selling one more unit of a good or service. It is the change in total revenue resulting from the sale of one additional unit of output. Marginal revenue is important in finance because it helps businesses determine the optimal price to charge for their goods and services.

For example, let's say a company produces widgets at a total cost of $100, and it produces 10 widgets. If the company sells each widget for $15, the total revenue earned is $150. If the company then decides to increase the price of its widgets to $16, the total revenue earned from the sale of the 11th widget is $16. The marginal revenue in this case is $16 - $15 = $1. If the marginal revenue is positive, the company should continue to increase the price until the marginal revenue becomes zero. This is the point where the price is maximized.

Marginal Profit:

Marginal profit is the additional profit earned from producing and selling one more unit of a good or service. It is the change in total profit resulting from the sale of one additional unit of output. Marginal profit is important in finance because it helps businesses determine the optimal level of production, pricing, and resource allocation.

For example, let's say a company produces widgets at a total cost of $100, and it produces 10 widgets. If the company sells each widget for $15, the total revenue earned is $150. The total cost of production is $100, so the total profit is $50. If the company then decides to increase the price of its widgets to $16, the total revenue earned from the sale of the 11th widget is $16. The marginal revenue is $16 - $15 = $1, and the marginal cost is $12, resulting in a marginal profit of $1 - $12 = -$11. In this case, it would not be profitable to produce and sell the 11th widget. If the marginal profit is positive,

M.L.Ruscsak

the company should continue to produce and sell units until the marginal profit becomes zero. This is the point where the profit is maximized.

Conclusion:

In conclusion, marginal analysis is an essential tool used in finance to help businesses make informed decisions about pricing, production, and resource allocation. Marginal cost, revenue, and profit are all important metrics that help firms to identify the optimal level of production and pricing to maximize their profits. By examining the change in costs and revenues associated with producing and selling one additional unit of a product, firms can identify the level of output that will result in maximum profit.

However, it is important to note that marginal analysis is not a panacea and should be used in conjunction with other decision-making tools and techniques. In some cases, it may be more appropriate to consider the overall costs and benefits of a decision, rather than focusing solely on the marginal costs and revenues.

Moreover, the accuracy and reliability of marginal analysis depends on the quality of the data and assumptions used in the analysis. Thus, it is important for firms to collect accurate and relevant data and to ensure that their assumptions are realistic and reasonable.

Despite these limitations, marginal analysis remains an important and valuable tool for businesses and financial analysts in making informed decisions. It allows firms to identify the most profitable level of production and pricing, and to allocate their resources efficiently. By incorporating marginal analysis into their decision-making processes, firms can improve their competitiveness and profitability in today's dynamic and fast-changing business environment.

In conclusion, the application of marginal analysis in finance is an important concept that can help firms to make more informed and effective decisions. It provides a powerful framework for analyzing the costs, revenues, and profits associated with different levels of output and pricing, and can help firms to identify the optimal level of production and pricing that will maximize their profits. By understanding and utilizing marginal analysis, firms can improve their competitiveness and profitability, and achieve long-term success in today's complex and rapidly evolving business environment.

Traditional math problems and equations related to optimization and marginal analysis in finance

Optimization and marginal analysis are fundamental concepts in finance that require the use of various mathematical techniques to be understood and applied effectively. In this section, we will explore some traditional math problems and equations that are commonly used in finance to solve optimization and marginal analysis problems.

One of the most basic equations used in optimization and marginal analysis is the cost equation. This equation is used to calculate the total cost of production based on the quantity of goods produced. The cost equation is given by:

Total cost = Fixed cost + (Variable cost per unit x Quantity produced)

Here, fixed costs are the costs that remain constant regardless of the number of goods produced, while variable costs are those that change depending on the quantity of goods produced. The cost equation is useful in determining the optimal level of production that minimizes total costs.

Another important equation used in finance is the revenue equation. This equation is used to calculate the total revenue generated from the sale of goods or services. The revenue equation is given by:

Total revenue = Price per unit x Quantity sold

Here, price per unit refers to the price at which each unit is sold, and quantity sold refers to the total number of units sold. The revenue equation is useful in determining the optimal price at which to sell goods or services to maximize revenue.

In addition to the cost and revenue equations, there are several optimization techniques that are commonly used in finance, including unconstrained optimization, constrained optimization, and Lagrange multipliers.

Unconstrained optimization is used to find the maximum or minimum value of a function without any constraints on the variables. For example, if we want to find the maximum profit of a company, we would use unconstrained optimization to find the value of the variable that maximizes the profit function.

Constrained optimization, on the other hand, is used to find the maximum or minimum value of a function subject to constraints on the variables. For example, if we want to find the optimal quantity of goods to produce subject to a certain budget constraint, we would use constrained optimization to find the optimal solution that satisfies both the production and budget constraints.

Lagrange multipliers are another important optimization technique used in finance. They are used to solve optimization problems that involve multiple constraints. Lagrange multipliers allow us to convert a constrained optimization problem into an unconstrained optimization problem by adding a penalty term to the objective function.

In conclusion, traditional math problems and equations related to optimization and marginal analysis in finance play a crucial role in helping businesses make informed decisions about pricing,

M.L.Ruscsak

production, and resource allocation. The cost and revenue equations, as well as optimization techniques such as unconstrained optimization, constrained optimization, and Lagrange multipliers, are all powerful tools that can be used to solve complex financial problems and improve business performance.

CHAPTER 11: CALCULUS AND OPTION PRICING

Calculus is a branch of mathematics that deals with rates of change and the accumulation of small changes to determine overall change. It is an essential tool used in finance for option pricing, which is the process of determining the value of an option.

Options are contracts that give the holder the right, but not the obligation, to buy or sell an underlying asset at a predetermined price on or before a specified date. Options can be used for speculation, hedging, or income generation. Option pricing is critical in the financial markets as it helps investors to make informed decisions about whether to buy or sell an option.

In this chapter, we will explore how calculus is used to price options. We will begin with an overview of option pricing theory and the Black-Scholes model, which is a widely used model for pricing options. We will then examine the Greeks, which are sensitivities of the option price to various factors, such as the underlying asset price, volatility, and time to expiration. The Greeks are essential for managing risk and can help investors to determine the best course of action in the financial markets.

We will also discuss the limitations of the Black-Scholes model and examine alternative models for pricing options, such as the binomial model and the Monte Carlo simulation. These models can provide more accurate pricing for options under certain circumstances, such as when the underlying asset exhibits a non-normal distribution or when interest rates are not constant.

Finally, we will explore the practical applications of option pricing in the financial markets, such as the pricing of equity options, index options, and currency options. We will also examine how option pricing is used in portfolio management and risk management.

Overall, the use of calculus in option pricing is a fundamental concept in finance. By understanding how calculus is used to price options, investors can make informed decisions about buying and selling options, manage risk, and optimize their portfolios.

Introduction to option pricing and the Black-Scholes-Merton model

Options are financial instruments that provide the holder with the right, but not the obligation, to buy or sell an underlying asset at a predetermined price and time. Options are widely used by investors and traders to manage risk, hedge positions, and speculate on market movements.

M.L.Ruscsak

Option pricing is a complex problem in financial mathematics that has attracted a lot of attention from scholars, practitioners, and regulators. The basic idea behind option pricing is to determine the fair price of an option, given its characteristics and the market conditions.

The Black-Scholes-Merton (BSM) model is one of the most famous and influential models for option pricing. The BSM model was developed by Fischer Black, Myron Scholes, and Robert Merton in the early 1970s and won them the Nobel Prize in Economics in 1997. The BSM model is based on the assumptions of a constant risk-free interest rate, a log-normal distribution of asset returns, no transaction costs or taxes, and the ability to trade continuously.

The BSM model provides a closed-form solution for the price of a European call or put option, which can be calculated using a simple formula. The BSM model assumes that the underlying asset follows a geometric Brownian motion, which is a stochastic process that describes the random movement of the stock price. The BSM model also assumes that the option can only be exercised at the expiration date, which is known as a European option.

The BSM model has several limitations and criticisms. One of the main criticisms of the BSM model is that it assumes that the stock price follows a log-normal distribution, which is not always true in practice. The BSM model also assumes that the risk-free interest rate is constant over time, which is not always the case. The BSM model does not take into account the possibility of jumps or extreme events, which can have a significant impact on the option price.

Despite its limitations, the BSM model remains an important and widely used model for option pricing. The BSM model has been extended and modified in various ways to address its limitations and to capture more complex market conditions. The BSM model has also inspired a large body of research in financial mathematics, including the development of stochastic calculus, partial differential equations, and Monte Carlo simulations.

In conclusion, option pricing is a fascinating and important area of financial mathematics that has many practical applications. The BSM model is a classic and influential model for option pricing that provides a simple and elegant solution for the price of a European option. The BSM model has its limitations and criticisms, but it remains a valuable tool for understanding and managing risk in financial markets.

Use of calculus in option pricing, including partial differential equations and stochastic calculus

Option pricing is a critical component of financial markets and plays a significant role in various investment strategies. Calculus is an essential tool in option pricing and is used to develop complex models that capture the dynamics of asset prices and their underlying stochastic processes. In this section, we will explore the role of calculus in option pricing, including partial differential equations (PDEs) and stochastic calculus.

Option pricing involves the determination of the fair value of an option, which is a financial contract that gives the holder the right, but not the obligation, to buy or sell an underlying asset at a specific price and time. The fair value of an option is determined by various factors, such as the underlying asset price, the strike price, the time to expiration, and the volatility of the underlying asset. These factors are interdependent and can be modeled mathematically using calculus.

One of the most widely used models for option pricing is the Black-Scholes-Merton model, which was developed by Fischer Black, Myron Scholes, and Robert Merton in the early 1970s. The Black-Scholes-Merton model assumes that the underlying asset follows a geometric Brownian motion, and the option price can be determined by solving a partial differential equation known as the Black-Scholes equation.

The Black-Scholes equation is a second-order PDE that describes the evolution of the option price with respect to time and the underlying asset price. The equation involves the use of various partial derivatives, including the second partial derivative, which can be challenging to solve analytically. Therefore, numerical methods are often used to solve the Black-Scholes equation and determine the option price.

Stochastic calculus is another important tool used in option pricing, especially when dealing with complex underlying asset dynamics. Stochastic calculus is a branch of calculus that deals with stochastic processes, which are mathematical models that capture the random behavior of asset prices. Stochastic calculus involves the use of differential equations that incorporate random variables, such as Brownian motion, to model the dynamics of asset prices over time.

The most widely used stochastic calculus models for option pricing are the stochastic differential equation (SDE) models. These models involve the use of Itô calculus, which is a calculus that deals with stochastic integrals and stochastic differentials. Itô calculus is used to develop the SDE models, which can then be solved numerically to determine the option price.

In summary, calculus plays a critical role in option pricing, and various calculus-based models, such as PDEs and stochastic calculus, are used to determine the fair value of options. The Black-Scholes-Merton model is one of the most widely used models in option pricing, and it involves the use of the Black-Scholes equation, a second-order PDE. Stochastic calculus, especially SDE models, is also essential in option pricing, especially when dealing with complex underlying asset dynamics.

Numerical methods for option pricing, including finite difference methods and Monte Carlo simulation

M.L.Ruscsak

Numerical methods play a crucial role in the field of quantitative finance, particularly in option pricing. While analytical methods can provide closed-form solutions for some option pricing models, numerical methods are often necessary for more complex models. In this section, we will discuss two common numerical methods for option pricing: finite difference methods and Monte Carlo simulation.

Finite difference methods involve discretizing the space and time variables in the partial differential equations (PDEs) that describe option pricing models. The PDEs can then be solved numerically using difference equations, which approximate the derivatives in the PDEs. The most common finite difference method used in option pricing is the explicit finite difference method. This method approximates the derivatives in the PDEs using forward differences in time and central differences in space. The explicit finite difference method is relatively simple to implement and is computationally efficient, but it is subject to stability constraints that limit the time step size that can be used.

Another finite difference method commonly used in option pricing is the implicit finite difference method. This method approximates the derivatives in the PDEs using backward differences in time and central differences in space. The implicit finite difference method is unconditionally stable, meaning that it can handle larger time step sizes than the explicit finite difference method. However, it is computationally more expensive and requires the solution of a system of linear equations at each time step.

Monte Carlo simulation is a numerical method that involves simulating the random processes that underlie option pricing models. In Monte Carlo simulation, a large number of simulations are performed to estimate the expected payoff of the option. Each simulation involves generating a set of random numbers that follow the distribution of the underlying asset's price process and using these numbers to simulate the evolution of the asset's price over time. The option payoff is then calculated at each time step and discounted back to present value using the risk-free interest rate.

Monte Carlo simulation is a powerful tool for option pricing because it can handle complex option pricing models that cannot be solved analytically or using finite difference methods. Monte Carlo simulation is also flexible and can be used to price a wide range of options, including path-dependent options and options on assets with non-constant volatility. However, Monte Carlo simulation is computationally intensive and can require a large number of simulations to achieve accurate results.

In conclusion, numerical methods are essential for option pricing, and both finite difference methods and Monte Carlo simulation are commonly used in practice. Each method has its strengths and weaknesses, and the choice of method depends on the complexity of the option pricing model and the available computational resources.

Traditional math problems and equations related to option pricing using calculus

Option pricing is a complex field that utilizes a variety of mathematical concepts, including calculus. In this section, we will explore some traditional math problems and equations related to option pricing using calculus.

One of the most important concepts in option pricing is the Black-Scholes-Merton (BSM) model. This model assumes that the stock price follows a lognormal distribution and that the risk-free rate and volatility are constant. It also assumes that there are no transaction costs or taxes, and that the stock does not pay dividends. Under these assumptions, the price of a European call option can be expressed as follows:

$$C(S,t) = S*N(d1) - Ke^{\wedge}(-r(T-t))*N(d2)$$

where:

C(S,t) is the price of the call option at time t given the stock price S

S is the current stock price

K is the strike price of the option

r is the risk-free interest rate

T-t is the time to maturity of the option

N(d1) and N(d2) are the cumulative distribution functions of the standard normal distribution, given by:

$$N(d1) = (1/\sqrt{(2\pi)})\smallint(-\infty,d1)e^{\wedge}(-x^{\wedge}2/2)dx$$
$$N(d2) = (1/\sqrt{(2\pi)})\smallint(-\infty,d2)e^{\wedge}(-x^{\wedge}2/2)dx$$
where:
$$d1 = (\ln(S/K) + (r+\sigma^{\wedge}2/2)*(T-t)) / (\sigma\sqrt{(T-t)})$$
$$d2 = d1 - \sigma\sqrt{(T-t)}$$

σ is the volatility of the stock price

This formula can be derived using a combination of stochastic calculus and partial differential equations, which we discussed in the previous section. However, it is not always easy or feasible to use this formula in practice. Therefore, numerical methods are often used to approximate option prices.

One common numerical method for option pricing is the finite difference method. This method involves discretizing the time and stock price dimensions and approximating the partial differential

M.L. Ruscsak

equation that governs option prices using finite difference approximations. The resulting system of equations can then be solved using matrix algebra. The finite difference method is computationally efficient and can be used to price a wide range of options, including American options.

Another popular numerical method for option pricing is Monte Carlo simulation. This method involves simulating the stock price and other parameters that affect option prices using random numbers. The resulting option prices are then averaged over many simulations to obtain an estimate of the true option price. Monte Carlo simulation is flexible and can be used to price complex options with non-linear payoffs, such as exotic options.

In conclusion, calculus is an essential tool for understanding option pricing. Traditional math problems and equations related to option pricing using calculus, such as the Black-Scholes-Merton formula, provide a solid foundation for option pricing theory. However, numerical methods, such as finite difference and Monte Carlo simulation, are often required to approximate option prices in practice. It is therefore important for finance professionals to have a strong understanding of both the theoretical and numerical aspects of option pricing.

Calculate the value of a European call option using the Black-Scholes model with the following inputs: stock price = $100, strike price = $110, time to maturity = 1 year, risk-free rate = 2%, volatility = 20%.

A stock has a current price of $50 and is expected to have a 20% chance of increasing to $70 and an 80% chance of decreasing to $30 in one year. Calculate the price of a European call option with a strike price of $60 using a risk-neutral valuation approach.

Use the Black-Scholes model to calculate the implied volatility of a call option with a price of $5, a strike price of $100, a stock price of $105, and a time to maturity of 3 months.

A portfolio manager wants to replicate a European call option with a strike price of $90 using a combination of the underlying stock and a risk-free bond. If the stock price is currently $100 and the risk-free rate is 4%, how much of the stock and bond does the manager need to purchase?

Suppose that the stock price follows a geometric Brownian motion with a drift of 5% and a volatility of 20%. Calculate the expected value of the stock price in 1 year.

Calculate the delta, gamma, and vega of a call option using the Black-Scholes model with the following inputs: stock price = $50, strike price = $55, time to maturity = 6 months, risk-free rate = 3%, volatility = 25%.

Consider a put option with a strike price of $80, a stock price of $75, a time to maturity of 6 months, and a volatility of 30%. Calculate the probability that the option will expire in the money.

A portfolio manager wants to hedge a long position in a call option with a delta of 0.6 using the underlying stock. If the stock price is currently $120 and the risk-free rate is 2%, how many shares of the stock does the manager need to purchase?

Suppose that the stock price follows a geometric Brownian motion with a drift of 8% and a volatility of 25%. Calculate the expected return of a call option with a strike price of $100 and a time to maturity of 1 year.

Use the Black-Scholes model to calculate the value of a European put option with the following inputs: stock price = $80, strike price = $75, time to maturity = 6 months, risk-free rate = 4%, volatility = 20%.

A trader has a long position in a call option with a delta of 0.7 and a vega of 0.1. If the stock price is currently $110 and the volatility is expected to increase by 5%, how much will the option price change?

A stock is expected to pay a dividend of $2 in 3 months. If the current stock price is $100 and the risk-free rate is 3%, calculate the ex-dividend stock price and the value of a call option with a strike price of $110 and a time to maturity of 6 months.

Use the Black-Scholes model to calculate the implied probability of a stock price exceeding a call option's strike price of $90, given that the option price is $5, the stock price is $100, and the time to maturity is 1 year.

A portfolio manager wants to create a delta-neutral portfolio using a call option with a delta of 0.4 and theunderlying asset is trading at $100. The call option has a premium of $5 and a strike price of $105. How many shares of the underlying asset should the portfolio manager buy?

To create a delta-neutral portfolio, the portfolio manager needs to buy an amount of the underlying asset such that the delta of the asset cancels out the delta of the call option. The delta of the call option is given as 0.4.

Let X be the number of shares of the underlying asset to be bought. The delta of the asset is 1, since the change in the price of the asset is directly proportional to the change in the price of the asset.

The delta-neutral condition requires:

$0.4 = X/100$
$X = 40$

Therefore, the portfolio manager should buy 40 shares of the underlying asset to create a delta-neutral portfolio.

Exercise 1: A portfolio manager wants to create a delta-neutral portfolio using a put option with a delta of -0.6 and the underlying asset is trading at $50. The put option has a premium of $3 and a strike price of $45. How many shares of the underlying asset should the portfolio manager sell to create a delta-neutral portfolio?

Exercise 2: A portfolio manager has a portfolio consisting of 500 shares of a stock with a price of $50 per share. The portfolio manager wants to create a delta-neutral portfolio using call options with a delta of 0.4. The call options have a premium of $5 and a strike price of $55. How many call options should the portfolio manager buy?

Exercise 3: A portfolio manager wants to create a delta-neutral portfolio using a call option with a delta of 0.5 and the underlying asset is trading at $80. The call option has a premium of $7 and a strike price of $85. How many shares of the underlying asset should the portfolio manager buy?

Exercise 4: A portfolio manager has a portfolio consisting of 1000 shares of a stock with a price of $75 per share. The portfolio manager wants to create a delta-neutral portfolio using put options with a delta of -0.6. The put options have a premium of $4 and a strike price of $70. How many put options should the portfolio manager buy?

Exercise 5: A portfolio manager wants to create a delta-neutral portfolio using a call option with a delta of 0.3 and the underlying asset is trading at $120. The call option has a premium of $8 and a strike price of $125. How many shares of the underlying asset should the portfolio manager buy?

Exercise 6: A portfolio manager has a portfolio consisting of 2000 shares of a stock with a price of $40 per share. The portfolio manager wants to create a delta-neutral portfolio using call options with a delta of 0.6. The call options have a premium of $6 and a strike price of $45. How many call options should the portfolio manager buy?

Exercise 7: A portfolio manager wants to create a delta-neutral portfolio using a put option with a delta of -0.4 and the underlying asset is trading at $90. The put option has a premium of $6 and a strike price of $85. How many shares of the underlying asset should the portfolio manager sell to create a delta-neutral portfolio?

Exercise 8: A portfolio manager has a portfolio consisting of 300 shares of a stock with a price of $100 per share. The portfolio manager wants to create a delta-neutral portfolio using put options with a delta of -0.5. The put options have a premium of $5 and a strike price of $95. How many put options should the portfolio manager buy?

M.L.Ruscsak

CHAPTER 12: CALCULUS AND PORTFOLIO OPTIMIZATION

In the world of finance, the goal is always to maximize returns while minimizing risk. Portfolio optimization is the process of selecting a portfolio of assets that will provide the highest return for a given level of risk. Portfolio optimization is an essential tool used by portfolio managers, financial analysts, and investment bankers to make informed investment decisions.

Calculus is an important mathematical tool used in portfolio optimization. The optimization problem can be framed as a calculus problem and solved using calculus techniques. The portfolio optimization problem involves selecting the portfolio weights that will maximize the portfolio's expected return while minimizing its risk. Calculus provides a method for finding the optimal portfolio weights that will achieve this objective.

In this chapter, we will explore the role of calculus in portfolio optimization. We will begin by discussing the basics of portfolio theory and the efficient frontier. We will then introduce the concept of risk and return and explain how calculus can be used to optimize a portfolio. Finally, we will discuss the practical application of portfolio optimization in the real world.

Portfolio Theory and the Efficient Frontier

Portfolio theory is the study of how to construct a portfolio of assets that will provide the highest return for a given level of risk. The efficient frontier is a graphical representation of the possible portfolios that can be constructed from a set of assets. The efficient frontier represents the set of portfolios that provide the highest return for a given level of risk.

The efficient frontier is formed by plotting the expected return of a portfolio on the y-axis and the standard deviation of the portfolio on the x-axis. The standard deviation is a measure of the risk of the portfolio. The efficient frontier is the upper boundary of the set of portfolios that provide the highest return for a given level of risk.

Risk and Return

Risk and return are two important concepts in finance. Risk is the uncertainty associated with the return on an investment. Return is the profit or loss generated by an investment. The goal of portfolio optimization is to maximize return while minimizing risk.

The risk of a portfolio can be measured using the standard deviation of the portfolio's returns. The expected return of a portfolio is the weighted average of the expected returns of the assets in the portfolio. The expected return of a portfolio is a function of the portfolio weights.

Calculus and Portfolio Optimization

Calculus is an important mathematical tool used in portfolio optimization. The optimization problem can be framed as a calculus problem and solved using calculus techniques. The portfolio optimization problem involves selecting the portfolio weights that will maximize the portfolio's expected return while minimizing its risk.

The optimization problem can be expressed as follows:

Maximize $E(r) = w1E(r1) + w2E(r2) + ... + wnE(rn)$

Subject to:

$w1 + w2 + ... + wn = 1$

$w1 >= 0, w2 >= 0, ..., wn >= 0$

Where w1, w2, ..., wn are the portfolio weights and $E(r1)$, $E(r2)$, ..., $E(rn)$ are the expected returns of the assets in the portfolio.

The solution to the optimization problem involves finding the optimal portfolio weights that maximize the expected return while minimizing the risk of the portfolio. The solution can be found using calculus techniques such as Lagrange multipliers.

Practical Application

Portfolio optimization has a practical application in the real world. Portfolio managers, financial analysts, and investment bankers use portfolio optimization to make informed investment decisions. The optimization problem can be used to construct a portfolio of assets that provides the highest return for a given level of risk.

In practice, portfolio optimization involves collecting data on the expected returns and risks of the assets in the portfolio. The data is then used to construct an efficient frontier. The efficient frontier represents the set of portfolios that provide the highest return for a given level of risk or the

M.L.Ruscsak

lowest risk for a given level of return. The efficient frontier can be graphed to visually represent the possible combinations of returns and risks that an investor can expect from different portfolios.

To construct the efficient frontier, a portfolio manager must first determine the expected returns and risks of each asset in the portfolio. This can be done using historical data, market trends, and other quantitative and qualitative factors. The manager can then use this information to calculate the expected return and risk of the portfolio as a whole.

Once the expected returns and risks of the assets and the portfolio have been determined, the manager can use calculus to identify the optimal portfolio. The optimal portfolio is the one that provides the highest return for a given level of risk or the lowest risk for a given level of return.

To find the optimal portfolio, the manager must first calculate the portfolio's expected return and risk. This can be done using weighted averages of the expected returns and risks of the assets in the portfolio. The weights are determined by the percentage of the portfolio that is invested in each asset.

Next, the manager must calculate the slope of the efficient frontier. The slope of the efficient frontier is the ratio of the change in the portfolio's expected return to the change in its risk. This ratio is also known as the Sharpe ratio, named after its creator, William F. Sharpe.

The portfolio with the highest Sharpe ratio is the optimal portfolio. This portfolio provides the highest return for a given level of risk or the lowest risk for a given level of return. Calculating the Sharpe ratio requires the use of calculus and linear algebra, making it a complex and challenging task.

In conclusion, portfolio optimization is a complex process that involves collecting data on the expected returns and risks of the assets in a portfolio, constructing an efficient frontier, and using calculus to identify the optimal portfolio. The optimal portfolio provides the highest return for a given level of risk or the lowest risk for a given level of return. Portfolio optimization is an essential tool for portfolio managers, who use it to maximize returns and minimize risks for their clients.

Introduction to portfolio optimization and the mean-variance framework

Portfolio optimization is a key concept in modern finance, and it is based on the idea of constructing portfolios of assets that maximize the expected return while minimizing the risk. The goal of portfolio optimization is to find the best combination of assets that provides the highest return for a given level of risk.

In practice, portfolio optimization involves collecting data on the expected returns and risks of the assets in the portfolio. The data is then used to construct an efficient frontier. The efficient frontier represents the set of portfolios that provide the highest return for a given level of risk or the lowest risk for a given level of return. The efficient frontier can be visualized as a curve in a risk-return space.

The mean-variance framework is a commonly used approach to portfolio optimization. The framework was introduced by Harry Markowitz in 1952 and has since become one of the most widely used methods for portfolio optimization. The framework is based on the assumption that investors are rational and seek to maximize their expected utility. The framework is also based on the assumption that investors care about both the expected return and the risk of the portfolio.

In the mean-variance framework, the expected return and the risk of the portfolio are measured by the mean and variance of the portfolio's returns, respectively. The mean is the expected return of the portfolio, and the variance is a measure of the dispersion of the portfolio's returns around the mean. The mean-variance framework aims to construct portfolios that have the highest expected return for a given level of risk or the lowest risk for a given level of expected return.

Mathematically, the mean-variance framework can be represented as a quadratic optimization problem. The objective function of the problem is to maximize the expected return of the portfolio subject to a constraint on the risk of the portfolio. The risk of the portfolio is measured by the variance of the portfolio's returns, and the constraint is typically imposed as a limit on the portfolio's variance or on the portfolio's standard deviation, which is the square root of the variance.

The mean-variance framework is a powerful tool for portfolio optimization, but it has some limitations. One limitation is that it assumes that asset returns are normally distributed, which may not be true in practice. Another limitation is that it assumes that investors care only about the expected return and the risk of the portfolio and not about other factors, such as liquidity, taxes, and transaction costs.

Despite its limitations, the mean-variance framework has been widely used in finance for over half a century and has been the basis for many other approaches to portfolio optimization. The framework has also inspired the development of other tools and techniques for portfolio optimization, such as value-at-risk, conditional value-at-risk, and stochastic programming.

In summary, portfolio optimization is a fundamental concept in modern finance, and the mean-variance framework is one of the most widely used approaches to portfolio optimization. The framework is based on the idea of constructing portfolios that have the highest expected return for a given level of risk or the lowest risk for a given level of expected return. The framework is mathematically represented as a quadratic optimization problem, and it has some limitations, but it remains a powerful tool for portfolio optimization in practice.

M.L.Ruscsak

Use of calculus in portfolio optimization, including efficient frontier and capital market line

Portfolio optimization is a critical task in finance that involves constructing a portfolio of assets that maximizes return while minimizing risk. The mean-variance framework, developed by Harry Markowitz in the 1950s, is a widely used approach to portfolio optimization that uses statistical methods to determine the optimal asset allocation.

In practice, portfolio optimization involves collecting data on the expected returns and risks of the assets in the portfolio. The data is then used to construct an efficient frontier. The efficient frontier represents the set of portfolios that provide the highest return for a given level of risk, or the lowest risk for a given level of return. The optimal portfolio is the point on the efficient frontier that best meets the investor's risk-return preferences.

Calculus is an essential tool in the construction of the efficient frontier and the optimal portfolio. The efficient frontier can be described as the boundary of a set of portfolios that have a certain level of expected return and standard deviation of returns. The boundary is a curve that can be optimized using calculus. Specifically, the curve can be optimized using the Lagrange multiplier method, which involves maximizing a function subject to a constraint.

The Lagrange multiplier method involves finding the optimal weights for each asset in the portfolio, subject to the constraint that the sum of the weights equals one. The objective function is the expected return of the portfolio, which is a linear combination of the expected returns of the individual assets. The constraint is the variance of the portfolio, which is a quadratic function of the weights and the covariance matrix of the assets. The optimal weights can be found by solving a system of linear equations, which can be solved using matrix algebra.

The capital market line is another important concept in portfolio optimization that can be derived using calculus. The capital market line represents the optimal portfolio for an investor who can borrow and lend at the risk-free rate. The capital market line is a straight line that connects the risk-free rate to the optimal portfolio on the efficient frontier. The slope of the capital market line represents the Sharpe ratio, which is a measure of the excess return per unit of risk.

The capital market line can be derived by considering the portfolio that maximizes the Sharpe ratio. The Sharpe ratio is the slope of the line tangent to the efficient frontier at a given point. The portfolio that maximizes the Sharpe ratio is the portfolio that has the highest excess return per unit of risk. The optimal portfolio is found by setting the slope of the tangent line equal to the Sharpe ratio and solving for the optimal weights using the Lagrange multiplier method.

In conclusion, calculus is an essential tool in portfolio optimization and the mean-variance framework. The efficient frontier and capital market line are two key concepts that can be derived using calculus. The efficient frontier represents the set of portfolios that provide the highest return for a given level of risk, while the capital market line represents the optimal portfolio for an investor who can borrow and lend at the risk-free rate. The use of calculus in portfolio optimization allows investors to construct optimal portfolios that meet their risk-return preferences and achieve their investment objectives.

Risk and return tradeoff, including Sharpe ratio and beta

The risk-return tradeoff is a fundamental concept in finance that describes the relationship between the expected return of an investment and the risk involved. In general, investors are willing to take on greater risk for the potential of higher returns. However, the extent of this tradeoff varies depending on the preferences and objectives of individual investors.

One common measure of risk-adjusted return is the Sharpe ratio, named after Nobel laureate William F. Sharpe. The Sharpe ratio is calculated by subtracting the risk-free rate of return (typically the yield on Treasury bills) from the expected return of an investment, and dividing by the standard deviation of the investment's returns. This measures the excess return of the investment per unit of risk taken, and is often used to compare the performance of different investments.

Another commonly used measure of risk is beta, which measures the sensitivity of an investment's returns to the overall market. A beta of 1 indicates that an investment's returns move in line with the market, while a beta greater than 1 indicates that the investment is more volatile than the market, and a beta less than 1 indicates that the investment is less volatile than the market. Beta is often used to assess the risk of a portfolio in relation to the broader market, and can be used to construct a diversified portfolio with a desired level of risk.

Portfolio managers and investors must carefully consider the risk-return tradeoff when making investment decisions. A portfolio that is too risky may result in significant losses, while a portfolio that is too conservative may not provide sufficient returns to meet an investor's goals. The use of mathematical models and analysis, including calculus and optimization techniques, can help investors to construct portfolios that balance risk and return in an optimal way.

The efficient frontier and capital market line are two concepts that are commonly used in portfolio optimization to help investors identify the optimal portfolio for their risk preferences. The efficient frontier represents the set of portfolios that provide the highest expected return for a given level of risk. By plotting a range of portfolios on a graph with expected return on the y-axis and risk (typically measured by standard deviation) on the x-axis, the efficient frontier can be identified as the set of portfolios that lie on the outer edge of the plotted points.

The capital market line represents the combination of the risk-free asset and the optimal portfolio of risky assets, based on the investor's risk preference. The slope of the capital market line represents the excess return per unit of risk taken, and can be calculated by subtracting the risk-free rate from the expected return of the optimal portfolio, and dividing by the standard deviation of the optimal portfolio's returns. The intersection of the capital market line with the efficient frontier represents the optimal portfolio for the investor's risk preference.

In conclusion, understanding the risk-return tradeoff is essential for investors to make informed investment decisions. Measures such as the Sharpe ratio and beta can help investors to assess the risk of different investments, while the efficient frontier and capital market line can be used to identify the optimal portfolio for a given level of risk. The use of calculus and other mathematical tools can aid in the optimization of portfolios, and can help investors to construct portfolios that balance risk and return in an optimal way.

Numerical methods for portfolio optimization, including Monte Carlo simulation and quadratic programming

Portfolio optimization is a complex process that involves balancing the trade-off between risk and return. It requires collecting data on the expected returns and risks of the assets in the portfolio and constructing an efficient frontier. The efficient frontier represents the set of portfolios that provide the highest return for a given level of risk, or the lowest risk for a given level of return. Portfolio managers use the efficient frontier to construct portfolios that meet their clients' investment objectives.

In practice, portfolio optimization is a difficult task due to the large number of assets and the complexity of the calculations involved. The use of numerical methods is essential to efficiently solve portfolio optimization problems. Two common numerical methods used in portfolio optimization are Monte Carlo simulation and quadratic programming.

Risk and Return Tradeoff:

The risk and return tradeoff is a fundamental concept in finance. It refers to the idea that higher returns are associated with higher risks. Investors are willing to take on greater risks in exchange for the potential of higher returns. The Sharpe ratio is a measure of the risk-adjusted return of a portfolio. It is calculated by dividing the excess return of the portfolio over the risk-free rate by the standard deviation of the portfolio's returns. A higher Sharpe ratio indicates a better risk-adjusted return.

Beta is another measure of risk commonly used in finance. It measures the sensitivity of an asset's returns to the overall market. A beta of 1 indicates that the asset's returns move in line with the market, while a beta greater than 1 indicates that the asset's returns are more volatile than the market, and a beta less than 1 indicates that the asset's returns are less volatile than the market.

Return = Risk-Free Rate + Beta x (Market Return - Risk-Free Rate) + Alpha

Where:

Return is the expected return of an asset or portfolio
Risk-Free Rate is the rate of return on a risk-free investment, such as a government bond
Beta is the measure of the asset's sensitivity to market movements
Market Return is the return of the overall market
Alpha is the excess return of the asset or portfolio not explained by its sensitivity to the market
This equation illustrates how the expected return of an asset or portfolio is influenced by its level of risk, as measured by beta. The higher the beta, the greater the expected return, but also the higher the level of risk. The equation also shows that there are other factors that can influence returns, such as alpha, which represents the asset or portfolio's ability to generate returns independent of the overall market.

Efficient Frontier and Capital Market Line:

The efficient frontier is a graph that shows the set of portfolios that provide the highest return for a given level of risk or the lowest risk for a given level of return. The efficient frontier is calculated by using mean-variance optimization, a mathematical framework that maximizes the expected return of a portfolio while minimizing its risk. The risk of a portfolio is measured by the standard deviation of its returns.

The capital market line is a line that connects the risk-free rate to the efficient frontier. The capital market line represents the combination of the risk-free asset and the risky asset that provides the highest Sharpe ratio. The slope of the capital market line is equal to the Sharpe ratio of the risky asset. The point where the capital market line intersects with the efficient frontier represents the optimal portfolio for a given level of risk.

The equation for the efficient frontier is:

Minimize $\sigma^2\_p = w^T \Sigma w$

Subject to:

$E(R\_p) = w^T R$

$w^T 1 = 1$

where:

σ^2_p is the variance of portfolio returns
w is a vector of portfolio weights
Σ is the covariance matrix of asset returns
$E(R\_p)$ is the expected return of the portfolio

M.L.Ruscsak

R is a vector of expected returns for each asset
1 is a vector of ones
The equation for the capital market line is:

$$E(R\_p) = R\_f + \lambda(E(R\_M) - R\_f)$$

where:

$E(R\_p)$ is the expected return of the portfolio
R_f is the risk-free rate
λ is the Sharpe ratio of the market portfolio
$E(R\_M)$ is the expected return of the market portfolio
The point where the capital market line intersects with the efficient frontier represents the optimal portfolio for a given level of risk.

Numerical Methods for Portfolio Optimization:

Monte Carlo simulation is a numerical method used to estimate the probability distribution of an outcome by generating a large number of random simulations. In portfolio optimization, Monte Carlo simulation can be used to estimate the expected returns and risks of a portfolio. Monte Carlo simulation can also be used to estimate the probability of a portfolio's returns falling below a certain threshold.

Quadratic programming is another numerical method used in portfolio optimization. Quadratic programming is a mathematical technique that optimizes a quadratic objective function subject to linear constraints. In portfolio optimization, quadratic programming can be used to find the weights of the assets in the portfolio that minimize the risk for a given level of return, or maximize the return for a given level of risk. Quadratic programming is computationally efficient and can handle large portfolios with many assets.

The equation for quadratic programming in portfolio optimization can be expressed as follows:

$$\text{minimize } 1/2 * x'Px + q'x$$

$$\text{subject to } Gx \leq h$$
$$Ax = b$$

where x is a vector of the portfolio weights, P is a covariance matrix of asset returns, q is a vector of expected returns, G and h are matrices and vectors defining linear constraints on the portfolio weights, and A and b are matrices and vectors defining equality constraints on the portfolio weights.

The objective function to be minimized represents the portfolio risk, where the first term 1/2 * x'Px represents the quadratic term of the variance of portfolio returns, and the second term q'x represents the expected portfolio returns. The constraints on the portfolio weights ensure that the weights sum up to one and satisfy other investment constraints such as minimum and maximum holdings, sector diversification, and liquidity constraints.

Solving the quadratic programming problem results in the optimal portfolio weights that minimize the risk for a given level of return, or maximize the return for a given level of risk. Quadratic programming is a powerful tool for portfolio optimization and is widely used in practice.

Conclusion:

Portfolio optimization is a crucial aspect of investment management. It involves balancing the trade-off between risk and return to construct portfolios that meet clients' investment objectives. The use of numerical methods is essential to efficiently solve portfolio optimization problems. Monte Carlo simulation and quadratic programming are two common numerical methods used in portfolio optimization. The risk and return tradeoff, efficient frontier, and capital market line are key concepts in portfolio optimization that are used to construct optimal portfolios.

Traditional math problems and equations related to portfolio optimization using calculus

Portfolio optimization is the process of selecting a combination of assets that maximizes returns for a given level of risk, or minimizes risk for a given level of return. Portfolio optimization is a critical concept in finance and investment management, as it allows investors to construct portfolios that meet their investment objectives.

Traditional mathematical methods for portfolio optimization involve the use of calculus, specifically optimization techniques such as Lagrange multipliers and convex optimization. These methods have been widely used in the finance industry for decades, and provide a framework for constructing efficient portfolios that maximize returns while minimizing risk.

One of the primary mathematical tools used in portfolio optimization is calculus, which provides a set of powerful optimization techniques that can be used to find the optimal weights for a given set of assets. In particular, Lagrange multipliers can be used to find the weights that maximize the portfolio's expected return subject to a given level of risk. This approach is known as mean-variance optimization and has been used extensively in finance to construct efficient portfolios.

The Lagrangian method involves adding a Lagrange multiplier term to the objective function of the optimization problem. The Lagrange multiplier represents the marginal benefit of relaxing the constraint by a small amount, and is used to optimize the objective function subject to the constraint. In the case of portfolio optimization, the Lagrange multiplier represents the marginal benefit of

M.L.Ruscsak

increasing the expected return of the portfolio by a small amount, while increasing the risk by a certain amount.

Another powerful optimization technique used in portfolio optimization is convex optimization, which involves optimizing a convex function subject to convex constraints. Convex optimization has been widely used in finance to construct portfolios that maximize returns while minimizing risk. Convex optimization is particularly useful when dealing with large portfolios with many assets, as it can handle complex constraints and objectives with ease.

In portfolio optimization, the objective function is often chosen to be the portfolio's expected return, while the constraints are chosen to represent the portfolio's risk. The constraints can include constraints on the portfolio's volatility, correlation with other assets, or exposure to specific sectors or regions. The resulting optimization problem can be solved using convex optimization techniques, which are both efficient and accurate.

In addition to traditional mathematical methods such as Lagrange multipliers and convex optimization, there are also a number of more advanced techniques that can be used for portfolio optimization. For example, machine learning algorithms such as neural networks and support vector machines have been used to construct portfolios that are optimized for specific objectives such as downside risk or tail risk.

In conclusion, traditional mathematical methods such as Lagrange multipliers and convex optimization are powerful tools for portfolio optimization that have been widely used in the finance industry for decades. These methods provide a framework for constructing efficient portfolios that maximize returns while minimizing risk. While there are more advanced techniques available, traditional mathematical methods remain an important part of portfolio optimization and are likely to continue to be used for many years to come.

One of the most important concepts in portfolio optimization is the mean-variance optimization framework, which was introduced by Harry Markowitz in the 1950s. The mean-variance optimization problem involves finding the weights of the assets in a portfolio that maximize the expected return of the portfolio for a given level of risk.

Let's consider a portfolio with N assets. The expected return of the portfolio can be calculated as:

$$E(R) = w1E(R1) + w2E(R2) + ... + wNE(RN)$$

where $E(Ri)$ is the expected return of asset i, and wi is the weight of asset i in the portfolio. The weights of the assets must sum to 1:

$w1 + w2 + ... + wN = 1$

The variance of the portfolio can be calculated as:

$Var(R) = w1^2Var(R1) + w2^2Var(R2) + ... + wN^2Var(RN) + 2w1w2Cov(R1,R2) + 2w1w3Cov(R1,R3) + ... + 2wN-1*wNCov(RN-1,RN)$

where $Var(Ri)$ is the variance of asset i, and $Cov(Ri,Rj)$ is the covariance between asset i and asset j.

The portfolio optimization problem can be formulated as:

maximize: $E(R)$

subject to: $w1 + w2 + ... + wN = 1$

$Var(R) <= target\_variance$

where target_variance is the maximum variance that the investor is willing to tolerate.

The Lagrangian for this problem can be written as:

$L = E(R) - \lambda(Var(R) - target\_variance) - \mu(w1 + w2 + ... + wN - 1)$

where λ and μ are Lagrange multipliers.

Taking the derivatives of the Lagrangian with respect to each weight and setting them equal to zero, we get:

$\partial L/\partial wi = E(Ri) - \lambda(Var(Ri) + Cov(Ri,Rj) - target\_variance) - \mu = 0$

for i = 1, 2, ..., N.

These equations are known as the mean-variance optimization equations. They can be solved using calculus to find the optimal weights for the portfolio.

In addition to the mean-variance optimization framework, other optimization techniques based on calculus can be used for portfolio optimization, such as linear programming, quadratic programming, and convex optimization. These techniques involve formulating an objective function and constraints, and then finding the optimal solution using calculus.

M.L.Ruscsak

1. Use calculus to determine the weights of assets in a portfolio that maximize expected return for a given level of risk.

2. Calculate the expected return of a portfolio using calculus given the returns and weights of individual assets.

3. Use calculus to find the minimum variance portfolio, i.e., the portfolio with the lowest risk, for a given level of return.

4. Determine the efficient frontier of a portfolio using calculus and plot it on a graph.

5. Calculate the Sharpe ratio of a portfolio using calculus, given its expected return, risk, and the risk-free rate.

6. Use calculus to find the optimal portfolio on the capital market line for a given level of risk.

7. Calculate the covariance matrix of a portfolio using calculus given the returns and weights of individual assets.

8. Use calculus to find the weights of assets in a portfolio that minimize risk for a given level of expected return.

9. Determine the impact of a change in the expected return or volatility of an asset on the optimal portfolio weights using calculus.

10. Use calculus to estimate the probability of a portfolio's returns falling below a certain threshold, given the mean and variance of returns for individual assets in the portfolio.

PART 5: LINEAR ALGEBRA FOR FINANCE

Linear algebra is a branch of mathematics that deals with linear equations and linear functions. In finance, linear algebra is used to solve problems related to portfolio optimization, risk management, and financial modeling. Linear algebra plays a crucial role in many areas of finance, including quantitative finance, portfolio management, risk analysis, and financial engineering.

The following section will provide an in-depth analysis of the role of linear algebra in finance. We will begin by discussing the basics of linear algebra and then move on to its applications in finance. We will also provide examples of how linear algebra is used in various financial fields.

Basics of Linear Algebra
Linear algebra deals with linear equations and linear functions. A linear equation is an equation in which each term is either a constant or the product of a constant and a variable. A linear function is a function that can be expressed as a linear equation. Linear algebra deals with vectors, matrices, and linear transformations.

1.1 Vectors

A vector is a quantity that has both magnitude and direction. In linear algebra, a vector is represented as a column or a row of numbers. For example, the vector x = [1 2 3]T can be represented as a column vector:

CSS
X=
[1]
[2]
[3]

where T denotes the transpose operation, which converts a row vector to a column vector, and vice versa.

Vectors can be added and subtracted. The addition and subtraction of vectors are performed component-wise. For example, the sum of two vectors x and y is:

CSS

M.L.Ruscsak

```
x + y =
[ x1 + y1 ]
[ x2 + y2 ]
[ x3 + y3 ]
```

where x1, x2, and x3 are the components of the vector x, and y1, y2, and y3 are the components of the vector y.

1.2 Matrices

A matrix is a rectangular array of numbers. In linear algebra, a matrix is denoted by a capital letter, such as A. Matrices are used to represent systems of linear equations and linear transformations. A matrix with m rows and n columns is called an m × n matrix.

For example, the matrix A = [1 2; 3 4] is a 2 × 2 matrix:

```
CSS
A =
[ 1  2 ]
[ 3  4 ]
```

Matrices can be added and subtracted if they have the same dimensions. The addition and subtraction of matrices are performed component-wise. For example, the sum of two matrices A and B is:

```
CSS
A + B =
[ A11 + B11  A12 + B12 ]
[ A21 + B21  A22 + B22 ]
```

where A11, A12, A21, A22 are the components of the matrix A, and B11, B12, B21, B22 are the components of the matrix B.

Matrices can also be multiplied. The product of two matrices A and B is denoted by AB. The product of two matrices A and B is defined only if the number of columns of A is equal to the number of rows of B. The product AB is a matrix whose (i, j) entry is the dot product of the ith row of A and the jth column of B.

1.3 Linear Transformations

A linear transformation is a function that preserves the operations of vector addition and scalar multiplication. In other words, a linear transformation T satisfies the following two properties:

$$T(u + v) = T(u) + T(v)$$

$$T(cu) = cT(u)$$

where u and v are vectors, c is a scalar, and T is the linear transformation.

Linear transformations can be represented by matrices, and matrices can be used to perform linear transformations. Specifically, if T is a linear transformation from R^n to R^m, then there exists a unique m x n matrix A such that for all vectors x in R^n, $T(x) = Ax$.

One common example of a linear transformation in finance is the application of a rotation matrix to a set of asset returns. A rotation matrix is a linear transformation that rotates a vector by a certain angle about the origin. By applying a rotation matrix to a set of asset returns, a portfolio manager can create a new set of returns with different levels of risk and return.

Another example of a linear transformation in finance is the application of a projection matrix to a set of asset returns. A projection matrix is a linear transformation that projects a vector onto a subspace. By applying a projection matrix to a set of asset returns, a portfolio manager can isolate a subset of the returns that are most important for portfolio construction.

In addition to representing linear transformations, matrices can also be used to solve systems of linear equations. In finance, systems of linear equations often arise in the context of portfolio optimization problems. For example, consider a portfolio with n assets. Let $w_1, w_2, ..., w_n$ be the weights of the assets in the portfolio, and let $r_1, r_2, ..., r_n$ be their expected returns. Let mu be the target return for the portfolio, and let sigma be the target risk. Then the following system of linear equations represents the constraints of the portfolio optimization problem:

$$w_1 + w_2 + ... + w_n = 1$$
$$r_1 w_1 + r_2 w_2 + ... + r_n w_n = mu$$
$$w^T \text{ Sigma } w = sigma^2$$

where w^T is the transpose of the vector w, and Sigma is the covariance matrix of the asset returns.

This system of equations can be solved using matrix algebra. Specifically, let $w = (w_1, w_2, ..., w_n)^T$, and let $r = (r_1, r_2, ..., r_n)^T$. Then the constraints can be written in matrix form as:

$$[1\ 1 ... 1]\ [w_1]\ [1]$$
$$[r_1\ r_2 ... r_n]\ [w_2] = [mu]$$

[..]
[wn]

and

w^T Sigma w = sigma^2

where Sigma is a positive semi-definite matrix.

To solve for the weights w that satisfy these constraints, we can use the technique of Lagrange multipliers. This involves finding a vector lambda such that the following system of equations holds:

grad(L) = 0,
w^T Sigma w = sigma^2,
w1 + w2 + ... + wn = 1,

where L is the Lagrangian function defined as L(w, lambda) = r^T w - lambda^T (w^T Sigma w - sigma^2) - lambda0 (w1 + w2 + ... + wn - 1), and grad(L) is the gradient of L with respect to w and lambda.

Solving this system of equations gives us the weights w that optimize the portfolio for the given target return and risk. The solution involves calculating the inverse of the covariance matrix, which is computationally expensive for large portfolios. This has led to the development of alternative optimization methods, such as mean-variance optimization and convex optimization, which are more efficient and scalable for large portfolios.

In conclusion, linear algebra provides a powerful toolkit for solving a wide range of problems in finance. From representing and applying linear transformations to solving systems of linear equations, linear algebra is an essential component of modern finance. Its applications range from portfolio optimization and risk management to option pricing and quantitative trading strategies. A strong understanding of linear algebra is therefore crucial for anyone seeking a career in finance, as it can provide a competitive edge in the field.

Linear algebra is particularly useful in finance because many financial problems can be formulated in terms of linear systems of equations. These systems may involve large amounts of data and variables, making them difficult or impossible to solve without the use of linear algebra. By representing financial problems as matrices and vectors, we can use linear algebra techniques to solve for unknown variables and make informed decisions.

For example, consider the problem of portfolio optimization. A portfolio manager may wish to determine the optimal weights of different assets in a portfolio, given a certain level of risk and return. This problem can be formulated as a linear system of equations and solved using linear algebra techniques. The portfolio manager can represent the expected returns and covariances of the assets as a matrix, and use linear algebra to solve for the weights that maximize return while minimizing risk.

Linear algebra is also essential in risk management, as it provides a way to model and analyze the risks associated with financial investments. For instance, covariance matrices can be used to model the risks of different assets in a portfolio and to calculate risk measures such as Value at Risk (VaR) and Expected Shortfall (ES).

Moreover, linear algebra is used in option pricing, which is the process of determining the fair price of a financial option. By using linear algebra techniques to solve the Black-Scholes equation, one can calculate the fair price of a European option based on its underlying assets and other market parameters.

Finally, linear algebra is critical in quantitative trading, which involves using mathematical models and algorithms to identify profitable trading opportunities. Linear algebra can be used to develop trading models that analyze large amounts of financial data and make decisions based on the results.

In conclusion, linear algebra plays a crucial role in modern finance, providing powerful tools for solving a wide range of problems. Its applications are diverse and far-reaching, from portfolio optimization and risk management to option pricing and quantitative trading. A strong understanding of linear algebra is therefore a must-have skill for anyone interested in pursuing a career in finance.

CHAPTER 13: MATRIX ALGEBRA AND EIGENVECTORS

Matrix algebra and eigenvectors are fundamental concepts in linear algebra that have numerous applications in finance. In this chapter, we will explore the basics of matrix algebra and eigenvectors, and their applications in finance.

Matrix algebra involves the manipulation of matrices, which are rectangular arrays of numbers. Matrices can be used to represent and solve systems of linear equations, as well as perform various operations such as addition, subtraction, and multiplication. Eigenvectors, on the other hand, are a special type of vector that is unchanged in direction when a linear transformation is applied to it.

The study of matrix algebra and eigenvectors is essential in finance, as many financial problems can be represented and solved using these concepts. For example, portfolio optimization involves finding the optimal allocation of assets in a portfolio, which can be solved using matrix algebra. Similarly, risk management involves analyzing the covariance matrix of assets, which is a matrix that describes the relationships between different assets.

In this chapter, we will begin by discussing the basics of matrix algebra, including matrix operations, inverse matrices, and determinants. We will then move on to eigenvectors and eigenvalues, and their applications in finance. Finally, we will explore some advanced topics in matrix algebra, such as singular value decomposition and principal component analysis.

By the end of this chapter, you will have a solid understanding of matrix algebra and eigenvectors, and their applications in finance. You will be able to solve problems related to portfolio optimization, risk management, and other financial applications using these concepts. So let's dive in and explore the world of matrix algebra and eigenvectors in finance!

Introduction to matrix algebra and eigenvectors

Matrix algebra and eigenvectors are essential mathematical concepts that find applications in a wide range of fields, including physics, engineering, computer science, and finance. In finance, matrix algebra and eigenvectors are used extensively in portfolio optimization, risk management, and option pricing. A strong understanding of matrix algebra and eigenvectors is therefore crucial for finance professionals, including portfolio managers, quantitative analysts, and financial engineers.

Matrix Algebra

Matrix algebra is the branch of mathematics that deals with the operations and properties of matrices. A matrix is a rectangular array of numbers that is typically used to represent a system of linear equations or a transformation of a vector space. Matrices are commonly used to represent data in finance, such as stock prices, interest rates, and economic indicators.

The basic operations of matrix algebra include addition, subtraction, multiplication, and inversion. Matrix addition and subtraction are performed element-wise, meaning that the corresponding elements of two matrices are added or subtracted. Matrix multiplication, on the other hand, is a more complex operation that involves multiplying the rows of the first matrix by the columns of the second matrix. Matrix inversion is the process of finding the inverse of a matrix, which is a matrix that when multiplied by the original matrix yields the identity matrix.

Here is an example equation that illustrates matrix algebra:

$A * B = C$

In this equation, A, B, and C are all matrices. The symbol "*" represents matrix multiplication. When we multiply matrices, we combine the rows and columns of the matrices in a specific way. The resulting matrix C will have the same number of rows as A and the same number of columns as B.

Matrix algebra is a powerful tool in mathematics and has numerous applications in fields such as finance, engineering, and computer science. It allows us to represent and manipulate complex data in a compact and efficient way, making it easier to perform calculations and solve problems.

Eigenvectors and Eigenvalues

An eigenvector is a nonzero vector that, when multiplied by a matrix, yields a scalar multiple of itself. The scalar multiple is called the eigenvalue. Eigenvectors and eigenvalues are important in matrix algebra because they reveal information about the transformation represented by the matrix.

In finance, eigenvectors and eigenvalues are used to analyze the risk and return characteristics of a portfolio. The eigenvectors of a covariance matrix represent the principal components of the portfolio, while the corresponding eigenvalues represent the variance of the portfolio along each principal component. This information can be used to construct optimal portfolios with desired levels of risk and return.

Applications of Matrix Algebra and Eigenvectors in Finance

Matrix algebra and eigenvectors find numerous applications in finance. Some examples include:

M.L.Ruscsak

Portfolio Optimization: Matrix algebra and eigenvectors are used to construct optimal portfolios that maximize return for a given level of risk, or minimize risk for a given level of return. This involves finding the eigenvectors and eigenvalues of the covariance matrix of the portfolio.

Risk Management: Matrix algebra and eigenvectors are used to calculate the Value-at-Risk (VaR) of a portfolio, which is a measure of the potential loss that the portfolio may incur over a given time horizon with a certain level of confidence. This involves finding the largest eigenvectors of the covariance matrix of the portfolio.

Option Pricing: Matrix algebra and eigenvectors are used to price options, which are financial contracts that give the holder the right, but not the obligation, to buy or sell an underlying asset at a predetermined price and time. This involves finding the eigenvectors and eigenvalues of the covariance matrix of the asset returns.

Conclusion

Matrix algebra and eigenvectors are powerful mathematical tools that have numerous applications in finance. A strong understanding of these concepts is essential for finance professionals who seek to optimize portfolios, manage risk, and price options. In the following chapters, we will delve deeper into the operations and properties of matrices, as well as the theory and applications of eigenvectors and eigenvalues in finance.

Linear transformations and their application in finance

Linear transformations are a fundamental concept in linear algebra that have numerous applications in finance. A linear transformation is a function that preserves the operations of vector addition and scalar multiplication. In other words, a linear transformation T satisfies the following two properties:

$$T(u + v) = T(u) + T(v)$$

$$T(cu) = cT(u)$$

where u and v are vectors, c is a scalar, and T is the linear transformation.

Linear transformations can be represented by matrices. Given a linear transformation $T: R^n \rightarrow R^m$, there exists an m x n matrix A such that $T(x) = Ax$ for all x in R^n. This matrix A is known as the standard matrix of T.

One important application of linear transformations in finance is portfolio optimization. Portfolio optimization is the process of selecting a portfolio of assets that maximizes return for a given level of risk. A linear transformation can be used to represent the return and risk of a portfolio.

Let x be a vector representing the weights of assets in a portfolio, and let R be a vector representing the expected returns of the assets. Then the expected return of the portfolio is given by the dot product of x and R:

$$E(R\_p) = x^T R$$

where ^{T} denotes the transpose of a matrix or vector. Similarly, let C be the covariance matrix of asset returns. Then the risk of the portfolio can be represented by the quadratic form $x^T C x$.

The problem of portfolio optimization can be formulated as an optimization problem of the form:

maximize $x^T R$

subject to $x^T C x <= q$

$x^T e = 1$

where q is a measure of risk tolerance and e is a vector of ones. This is a quadratic programming problem that can be solved using linear algebra.

Another application of linear transformations in finance is option pricing. Options are financial contracts that give the buyer the right, but not the obligation, to buy or sell an underlying asset at a predetermined price and time. The price of an option is determined by the expected future value of the underlying asset.

The Black-Scholes model is a widely used model for option pricing. The Black-Scholes model assumes that the price of the underlying asset follows a geometric Brownian motion. This can be represented by a stochastic differential equation of the form:

$$dS\_t = mu \, S\_t \, dt + sigma \, S\_t \, dW\_t$$

where S_t is the price of the asset at time t, mu is the drift rate, sigma is the volatility, and W_t is a Wiener process.

The Black-Scholes formula for the price of a European call option is given by:

$$C(S\_t, t) = S\_t \, N(d\_1) - Ke^{-r(T-t)} \, N(d\_2)$$

where C is the price of the call option, S_t is the price of the underlying asset at time t, K is the strike price, r is the risk-free interest rate, T is the time to maturity, and N is the cumulative distribution function of the standard normal distribution. The variables d_1 and d_2 are given by:

d_1 = (ln(S_t/K) + (r + sigma^2/2)(T-t)) / (sigma sqrt(T-t))

d_2 = d_1 - sigma sqrt(T-t)

The Black-Scholes formula can be derived using linear algebra and partial differential equations. In particular, the Black-Scholes equation is a parabolic partial differential equation that can be solved using the method of separation of variables.

In conclusion, linear transformations and their applications in finance provide a powerful toolkit for solving a wide range of problems in finance. From representing and applying linear transformations to solving optimization problems and pricing options, linear algebra is an essential component of modern finance. It provides a mathematical foundation for understanding the behavior of financial systems and instruments, and allows us to analyze and model complex financial phenomena. Linear algebra is used extensively in portfolio optimization, risk management, option pricing, and quantitative trading strategies, among other areas.

Moreover, the applications of linear transformations in finance are not limited to mathematical modeling and analysis. They also play a crucial role in the implementation of various financial instruments and strategies. For example, linear transformations are used in the construction of exchange-traded funds (ETFs), which are investment funds that track the performance of a specific market index or asset class. ETFs are created by combining various securities in a portfolio that has the same weightings as the underlying index or asset class. This process involves linear transformations of the security prices and weights, and allows investors to gain exposure to a diversified portfolio at a low cost.

In addition, linear transformations are also used in the construction of factor models, which are quantitative models that explain the returns of a portfolio in terms of a set of underlying factors. Factor models are widely used in asset management and portfolio construction, and can help investors better understand the sources of risk and return in their portfolios. The construction of factor models involves the application of linear transformations to a set of financial variables, such as asset prices, interest rates, and economic indicators, and the identification of the underlying factors that drive their co-movements.

Overall, the study of linear transformations and their applications in finance is essential for students and practitioners who wish to develop a deep understanding of financial theory and practice. It provides a powerful and flexible framework for modeling and analyzing financial systems and instruments, and allows us to develop effective strategies for managing risk and generating returns in the dynamic and complex world of finance.

Eigenvectors and their application in finance, including principal component analysis and factor analysis

Eigenvectors are a fundamental concept in linear algebra that have a wide range of applications in finance, particularly in the areas of portfolio management, risk analysis, and asset pricing. An eigenvector is a vector that is transformed by a linear transformation into a scalar multiple of itself. Eigenvectors and eigenvalues are important tools for analyzing the properties of matrices, and they are used extensively in factor analysis and principal component analysis. In this section, we will explore the concept of eigenvectors in depth, and discuss their application in finance, with a focus on principal component analysis and factor analysis.

What are Eigenvectors?

An eigenvector is a non-zero vector that is transformed by a linear transformation into a scalar multiple of itself. More formally, given a linear transformation T, an eigenvector v is a vector that satisfies the following equation:

$$T(v) = \lambda v$$

where λ is a scalar known as the eigenvalue. Eigenvectors are used to describe the behavior of linear transformations, and they play a crucial role in the study of matrices and their properties.

Application in Finance: Principal Component Analysis

Principal Component Analysis (PCA) is a widely used technique in finance for reducing the dimensionality of large datasets. PCA is a statistical method that identifies the underlying structure in a dataset by finding the principal components of the data. Principal components are the eigenvectors of the covariance matrix of the data.

The covariance matrix is a square matrix that describes the relationship between variables in a dataset. The diagonal elements of the covariance matrix represent the variances of the individual variables, while the off-diagonal elements represent the covariances between the variables. The eigenvectors of the covariance matrix represent the directions of maximum variance in the data.

PCA works by projecting the data onto the eigenvectors of the covariance matrix. The first principal component is the eigenvector with the largest eigenvalue, and it represents the direction of maximum variance in the data. The second principal component is the eigenvector with the second largest eigenvalue, and it represents the direction of the second largest variance in the data. Subsequent principal components represent directions of decreasing variance in the data.

M.L.Ruscsak

PCA is particularly useful in finance for reducing the dimensionality of large datasets. By identifying the principal components of the data, PCA can reduce the number of variables in a dataset without losing significant information. This can be especially useful in portfolio management, where large amounts of data need to be analyzed to make investment decisions.

Application in Finance: Factor Analysis

Factor Analysis is another widely used technique in finance that makes use of eigenvectors. Factor Analysis is a statistical method that identifies the underlying factors that contribute to the variation in a dataset. Factors are latent variables that cannot be directly observed, but that can be inferred from the observed variables.

Factor Analysis works by identifying the eigenvectors of the correlation matrix of the data. The correlation matrix is a square matrix that describes the correlation between variables in a dataset. The eigenvectors of the correlation matrix represent the directions of maximum correlation in the data.

Factor Analysis is particularly useful in finance for identifying the underlying factors that contribute to the risk and return of a portfolio. By identifying the factors that drive the variation in the portfolio, Factor Analysis can help investors better understand the sources of risk and return in their portfolio, and make more informed investment decisions.

Conclusion:

In conclusion, eigenvectors are a powerful tool in linear algebra that have a wide range of applications in finance. Eigenvectors play a crucial role in the study of matrices and their properties, and they are used extensively in factor analysis and principal component analysis. By identifying the underlying structure in large datasets, eigenvectors can help investors make more informed investment decisions, and better manage risk in their portfolio.

Traditional math problems and equations related to matrix algebra and eigenvectors in finance

Matrix algebra and eigenvectors have a wide range of applications in finance, from portfolio optimization to risk management to option pricing. Traditional math problems and equations related to these concepts are essential for understanding their applications in finance.

One such problem is the eigenvalue problem, which involves finding the eigenvalues and eigenvectors of a given matrix. The eigenvalues are the scalars that satisfy the equation $Av = \lambda v$, where A is the matrix, λ is the eigenvalue, and v is the eigenvector. The eigenvectors are the non-zero vectors that satisfy this equation. In finance, the eigenvalue problem is often used in factor analysis and principal component analysis.

Another traditional math problem related to matrix algebra is the singular value decomposition (SVD) problem, which involves decomposing a matrix A into the product of three matrices: A = UΣVT, where U and V are orthogonal matrices and Σ is a diagonal matrix with non-negative elements known as singular values. The SVD is useful in finance for data compression and for finding the most important features in a dataset.

Matrix multiplication is another fundamental operation in matrix algebra. In finance, matrix multiplication is used in many applications such as computing the covariance matrix of a portfolio and solving systems of linear equations.

Additionally, linear regression is a commonly used statistical technique in finance that involves finding the best-fit line that explains the relationship between two variables. In matrix algebra, linear regression can be represented using the matrix equation $Y = X\beta + \varepsilon$, where Y is the dependent variable, X is the matrix of independent variables, β is the vector of coefficients, and ε is the error term.

Furthermore, the Black-Scholes formula, which is used to price options, involves partial differential equations and the application of matrix algebra. The formula can be derived by solving a system of linear partial differential equations using matrix algebra.

In conclusion, traditional math problems and equations related to matrix algebra and eigenvectors are essential for understanding their applications in finance. The eigenvalue problem, SVD problem, matrix multiplication, linear regression, and the Black-Scholes formula are just a few examples of the many ways in which matrix algebra and eigenvectors are used in finance. A thorough understanding of these concepts and their applications is essential for anyone interested in a career in finance.

1. Find the inverse of the matrix A = [3 1; 2 4] using the adjugate matrix method.

2. Given a 3x3 matrix A, find the eigenvalues and eigenvectors of A.

3. Solve the system of equations: 3x + 4y = 5, 2x + 3y = 4 using matrix algebra.

4. Calculate the determinant of the matrix A = [1 2 3; 4 5 6; 7 8 9].

5. Given a matrix A, find the rank of A.

6. Find the matrix P that diagonalizes the matrix A = [1 1; 1 3].

7. Use matrix algebra to find the optimal portfolio weights for a set of assets with expected returns and covariance matrix.

8. Calculate the covariance matrix for a portfolio of assets given the individual asset returns and covariance.

9. Use PCA to reduce the dimensionality of a dataset and identify the most important factors.

10. Given a set of financial data, use factor analysis to identify the underlying factors that are driving the variation in the data.

CHAPTER 14: LINEAR ALGEBRA AND PORTFOLIO THEORY

Modern finance is built on the foundation of mathematical concepts, including calculus, statistics, and linear algebra. Linear algebra is a branch of mathematics that deals with systems of linear equations and their properties. In finance, linear algebra is used to analyze complex financial data, build models, and make predictions. One of the most significant applications of linear algebra in finance is in portfolio theory, which is concerned with the selection of portfolios that maximize returns while minimizing risk.

The goal of this chapter is to introduce the reader to the basic concepts of linear algebra and their applications in portfolio theory. We will begin with an overview of linear algebra and its importance in finance. We will then discuss the main components of portfolio theory, including risk and return, diversification, and efficient frontier. Finally, we will explore how linear algebra is used in portfolio theory to optimize portfolios and calculate expected returns and risks.

Overview of Linear Algebra in Finance

Linear algebra is the study of systems of linear equations and their properties. It involves the manipulation of vectors and matrices, which are used to represent and solve these equations. In finance, linear algebra is used to analyze complex financial data, build models, and make predictions. For example, linear algebra is used in options pricing, portfolio optimization, and risk management.

The fundamental concepts of linear algebra are vectors and matrices. A vector is a quantity that has both magnitude and direction. In finance, vectors are used to represent assets or factors that influence asset prices. A matrix is a rectangular array of numbers. In finance, matrices are used to represent a collection of data, such as asset returns, and to perform calculations on this data.

Portfolio Theory

Portfolio theory is a branch of finance that deals with the selection of portfolios that maximize returns while minimizing risk. The main components of portfolio theory are risk and return, diversification, and efficient frontier.

Risk and return are two fundamental concepts in finance. Return is the profit or loss on an investment over a given period. Risk is the degree of uncertainty or variability of returns. In general, investors prefer investments with higher returns and lower risks.

M.L.Ruscsak

Diversification is the practice of investing in a variety of assets to reduce the risk of loss. The basic idea behind diversification is that the returns on different assets are not perfectly correlated, so losses in one asset can be offset by gains in another.

The efficient frontier is a concept in portfolio theory that represents the set of portfolios that offer the highest return for a given level of risk, or the lowest risk for a given level of return. The efficient frontier is typically represented as a curve that plots the expected return against the expected risk of the portfolios.

Linear Algebra and Portfolio Theory

Linear algebra plays a crucial role in portfolio theory. It is used to optimize portfolios and calculate expected returns and risks. One of the key concepts in portfolio theory that involves linear algebra is the covariance matrix. The covariance matrix is a matrix that represents the covariances between the different assets in a portfolio. The diagonal elements of the covariance matrix represent the variances of the individual assets, while the off-diagonal elements represent the covariances between the different assets.

The covariance matrix is used to calculate the expected return and risk of a portfolio. The expected return of a portfolio is the weighted average of the expected returns of the individual assets in the portfolio. The weights are determined by the proportion of each asset in the portfolio. The risk of a portfolio is determined by the variance of the portfolio returns, which is calculated using the covariance matrix.

Another key concept in portfolio theory that involves linear algebra is the eigenvalue decomposition. The eigenvalue decomposition is a technique used to decompose a matrix into its eigenvectors and eigenvalues. In portfolio theory, the eigenvalue decomposition is used to analyze the risk and return characteristics of a portfolio.

In particular, the eigenvalues of a portfolio's covariance matrix represent the amount of risk inherent in each eigenvector direction. By ordering the eigenvalues from largest to smallest, one can identify the most significant directions of risk in the portfolio. These directions correspond to the portfolio's principal components, which are linear combinations of the portfolio's underlying assets.

The principal components of a portfolio can be used to construct a more efficient portfolio that maximizes returns for a given level of risk, or minimizes risk for a given level of return. This is done by reallocating the portfolio's weights so that they are more heavily weighted towards the principal components with the highest eigenvalues.

Another application of the eigenvalue decomposition in portfolio theory is factor analysis. Factor analysis is a statistical technique used to identify underlying factors that drive the returns of a portfolio. These factors can be thought of as the common sources of risk and return that are not captured by the portfolio's individual asset returns.

The eigenvalue decomposition can be used to identify these underlying factors by decomposing the portfolio's covariance matrix into a factor loading matrix and a diagonal matrix of eigenvalues. The factor loading matrix contains the factor loadings for each asset, which represent the sensitivity of the asset to each factor. The diagonal matrix of eigenvalues represents the variance of each factor.

Factor analysis can be useful for constructing portfolios that are well-diversified across different sources of risk, as well as for identifying potential sources of risk that may be overlooked in traditional portfolio analysis.

In addition to the eigenvalue decomposition, other concepts in linear algebra can be used in portfolio theory, such as singular value decomposition (SVD) and the QR decomposition. SVD is a generalization of the eigenvalue decomposition that can be used to analyze the covariance matrix of non-normal portfolios, while the QR decomposition can be used to analyze the portfolio's expected returns.

Overall, linear algebra provides a powerful toolkit for analyzing and optimizing portfolios in finance. By understanding the concepts of matrix algebra, eigenvectors, and eigenvalue decomposition, investors can gain valuable insights into the risk and return characteristics of their portfolios and construct more efficient and diversified portfolios.

Introduction to portfolio theory and Markowitz's mean-variance framework

Portfolio theory is a key concept in finance that provides investors with a framework for making investment decisions. At its core, portfolio theory seeks to identify the optimal combination of investments that maximizes returns while minimizing risk. Portfolio theory has its roots in the work of Harry Markowitz, who proposed the mean-variance framework in the 1950s.

Markowitz's mean-variance framework provides a mathematical approach to portfolio selection that considers the expected returns and risks associated with different investments. The framework is based on the assumption that investors are rational and risk-averse, and that they seek to maximize their expected returns while minimizing their risks.

The mean-variance framework begins with the construction of a portfolio that consists of multiple investments. The expected return of the portfolio is the weighted average of the expected returns of the individual investments, with each weight representing the proportion of the portfolio invested in each investment. The risk of the portfolio is measured by its variance, which is a measure of the variability of returns around the expected return.

The mean-variance framework seeks to identify the portfolio that maximizes expected return for a given level of risk, or alternatively, minimizes risk for a given level of expected return. This can be represented graphically as the efficient frontier, which is a curve that represents the optimal portfolios for different levels of risk.

The efficient frontier is based on the concept of diversification, which is the idea that combining investments with different risk and return characteristics can reduce overall portfolio risk without sacrificing expected returns. Diversification is achieved by investing in a mix of assets that have low or negative correlations with each other. By combining investments that do not move in lockstep with each other, portfolio risk can be reduced without sacrificing expected returns.

Matrix Algebra and Portfolio Theory

Linear algebra plays a critical role in portfolio theory. In particular, matrix algebra provides a powerful toolkit for representing and analyzing portfolios.

A portfolio can be represented as a vector of weights that specifies the proportion of the portfolio invested in each investment. For example, a two-asset portfolio can be represented as a vector $w = [w1 \ w2]$, where $w1$ and $w2$ represent the proportion of the portfolio invested in each asset.

The expected return of a portfolio can be represented as the dot product of the portfolio weights vector and the vector of expected returns for each asset. Mathematically, this can be expressed as $E(Rp) = w \square E(R)$, where $E(Rp)$ is the expected return of the portfolio, w is the portfolio weights vector, and $E(R)$ is the vector of expected returns for each asset.

The variance of a portfolio can be represented using matrix algebra. The variance-covariance matrix is a square matrix that represents the variances and covariances of the returns for each asset in the portfolio. The diagonal elements of the matrix represent the variances of the individual assets, while the off-diagonal elements represent the covariances between pairs of assets. The variance of a portfolio can be calculated as the quadratic form of the portfolio weights vector and the variance-covariance matrix. Mathematically, this can be expressed as $Var(Rp) = w \square \ \Sigma \square \ wT$, where $Var(Rp)$ is the variance of the portfolio, w is the portfolio weights vector, Σ is the variance-covariance matrix, and wT is the transpose of the portfolio weights vector.

Eigenvectors and Portfolio Optimization

Eigenvectors also play an important role in portfolio optimization. Eigenvectors are a type of vector that, when multiplied by a matrix, are transformed into scalar multiples of themselves. In portfolio theory, eigenvectors are used to identify the optimal portfolio weights that minimize portfolio risk for a given level of expected return.

1. Given the expected returns and standard deviations of two stocks, calculate the expected return and standard deviation of a portfolio consisting of equal investments in both stocks.

2. If the correlation coefficient between two stocks is -0.5, what is the risk reduction achieved by investing in a portfolio consisting of equal investments in both stocks?

3. Consider a portfolio consisting of three stocks. If the expected returns and covariance matrix of the three stocks are given, use Markowitz's mean-variance framework to calculate the optimal portfolio weights that minimize portfolio variance.

4. Suppose you have a portfolio consisting of two stocks. If you can borrow at an interest rate of 5% and short selling is allowed, what is the optimal portfolio for a target expected return of 10%?

5. You have a portfolio consisting of four stocks. If the expected returns and covariance matrix of the four stocks are given, use the concept of efficient frontier to plot the minimum variance frontier and the optimal portfolio with the highest Sharpe ratio.

Use of linear algebra in portfolio theory, including covariance matrix and diversification

Linear algebra plays a critical role in portfolio theory, particularly in the calculation of the covariance matrix and the concept of diversification. In this section, we will explore how linear algebra is used to help portfolio managers optimize their portfolios for maximum returns and minimum risk.

The covariance matrix is a critical tool in portfolio theory that measures the relationships between the returns of different assets in a portfolio. The covariance matrix is calculated using linear algebra and provides valuable insights into the risk and diversification of a portfolio. The covariance matrix measures the extent to which two assets move in the same or opposite directions. In other words, it measures how much the returns of two assets are correlated. If two assets are highly correlated, they move together, and their returns are likely to be similar. On the other hand, if two assets are uncorrelated or negatively correlated, their returns are likely to move in opposite directions.

M.L.Ruscsak

The covariance matrix is a symmetric matrix, which means that the values above and below the diagonal are identical. The diagonal of the matrix represents the variance of each asset. The off-diagonal elements represent the covariance between pairs of assets. The covariance matrix is used to calculate the portfolio variance, which is a measure of the risk of the portfolio. The portfolio variance is calculated as the sum of the weighted variances of each asset in the portfolio, plus the sum of the weighted covariances between each pair of assets in the portfolio.

Linear algebra is also used to calculate the concept of diversification, which is the practice of spreading investments across multiple assets to reduce risk. Diversification can be achieved by selecting assets that are not highly correlated with each other. The more uncorrelated the assets in a portfolio, the greater the potential for diversification.

Diversification can be measured using the concept of eigenvalues and eigenvectors. The eigenvalues of a covariance matrix represent the variances of the principal components of the portfolio. The eigenvectors of a covariance matrix represent the weights of the principal components of the portfolio. The principal components of a portfolio are the assets that have the highest variance and explain the most significant amount of the portfolio's risk. By calculating the eigenvalues and eigenvectors of a covariance matrix, portfolio managers can identify the principal components of the portfolio and adjust their weights to achieve optimal diversification.

One of the key benefits of using linear algebra in portfolio theory is the ability to calculate the efficient frontier, which is the set of optimal portfolios that offer the highest return for a given level of risk. The efficient frontier is calculated by using a combination of the portfolio variance and the expected return of the portfolio. By calculating the efficient frontier, portfolio managers can identify the optimal portfolio that maximizes returns while minimizing risk.

In conclusion, linear algebra is an essential tool in portfolio theory that provides valuable insights into the relationships between assets in a portfolio. The covariance matrix and the concept of diversification are critical components of portfolio theory that are calculated using linear algebra. Linear algebra is also used to calculate the efficient frontier, which helps portfolio managers identify the optimal portfolio that offers the highest returns for a given level of risk. By understanding the concepts of linear algebra and portfolio theory, portfolio managers can make informed investment decisions that minimize risk and maximize returns.

Here are five math problems related to the use of linear algebra in portfolio theory:

1. Given a covariance matrix with variances of 0.05, 0.10, and 0.15, and covariances of 0.02, -0.01, and 0.03, respectively, calculate the portfolio variance for a portfolio consisting of 50% of asset 1, 30% of asset 2, and 20% of asset 3.

2. Find the eigenvalues and eigenvectors of the covariance matrix for a portfolio consisting of five assets with variances of 0.05, 0.10, 0.15, 0.20, and 0.25 and covariances of 0.02, -0.01, 0.03, 0.04, -0.02, respectively.

Suppose you have a portfolio consisting of two assets with the following expected returns and standard deviations:

Asset 1: Expected return = 8%, standard deviation = 15%
Asset 2: Expected return = 12%, standard deviation = 20%

3. What is the expected return and standard deviation of a portfolio consisting of 60% of asset 1 and 40% of asset 2?

Suppose you have a portfolio consisting of three assets with the following expected returns and standard deviations:

Asset 1: Expected return = 10%, standard deviation = 12%
Asset 2: Expected return = 15%, standard deviation = 20%
Asset 3: Expected return = 8%, standard deviation = 10%

4. What is the optimal portfolio consisting of these three assets, assuming a risk-free rate of 3% and a target return of 12%?

Suppose you have a portfolio consisting of four assets with the following expected returns and standard deviations:

Asset 1: Expected return = 10%, standard deviation = 12%
Asset 2: Expected return = 15%, standard deviation = 20%
Asset 3: Expected return = 8%, standard deviation = 10%
Asset 4: Expected return = 12%, standard deviation = 16%

5. What is the minimum variance portfolio for these assets?

Risk and return tradeoff in the context of portfolio theory

Portfolio theory is the study of how to construct portfolios of assets in order to maximize expected returns while minimizing risk. The risk and return tradeoff is a central concept in portfolio theory, as it represents the tradeoff between higher expected returns and higher levels of risk. In this section, we will explore the risk and return tradeoff in the context of portfolio theory.

Risk and Return Tradeoff:

M.L.Ruscsak

In finance, risk is typically defined as the variability of returns. Investors are generally risk averse, which means that they prefer less risk to more risk, all else being equal. Returns, on the other hand, are the rewards that investors receive for taking on risk. The higher the risk, the higher the expected return. This relationship between risk and return is known as the risk and return tradeoff.

The risk and return tradeoff is a fundamental concept in finance, as it provides the basis for understanding the behavior of financial markets and the pricing of financial assets. The tradeoff can be illustrated graphically by plotting expected returns on the vertical axis and risk (usually measured by standard deviation) on the horizontal axis. The resulting curve is known as the efficient frontier, which represents the set of portfolios that offer the highest expected returns for a given level of risk or the lowest risk for a given level of expected returns.

The efficient frontier is the foundation of modern portfolio theory, which was developed by Harry Markowitz in the 1950s. Markowitz showed that investors can achieve higher expected returns with lower risk by diversifying their investments across a portfolio of assets. Diversification allows investors to reduce the risk of their portfolio by spreading their investments across a variety of assets that are not perfectly correlated.

The tradeoff between risk and return can also be analyzed in terms of beta, which is a measure of systematic risk. Beta measures the sensitivity of an asset's returns to changes in the returns of the overall market. Assets with higher betas tend to have higher expected returns and higher levels of risk, while assets with lower betas tend to have lower expected returns and lower levels of risk.

In portfolio theory, the goal is to construct portfolios that maximize expected returns while minimizing risk. The optimal portfolio is the portfolio that offers the highest expected return for a given level of risk or the lowest risk for a given level of expected returns. This can be achieved by selecting assets that are not perfectly correlated and by adjusting the weights of those assets in the portfolio to achieve the desired level of risk and return.

Conclusion:

The risk and return tradeoff is a fundamental concept in finance, as it provides the basis for understanding the behavior of financial markets and the pricing of financial assets. In portfolio theory, the goal is to construct portfolios that maximize expected returns while minimizing risk. The optimal portfolio is the portfolio that offers the highest expected return for a given level of risk or the lowest risk for a given level of expected returns. The efficient frontier is the foundation of modern portfolio theory, and diversification is the key to reducing the risk of a portfolio. By understanding the risk and return tradeoff, investors can make more informed investment decisions and build portfolios that are better aligned with their investment goals and risk tolerance.

Numerical methods for portfolio optimization using linear algebra, including quadratic programming and Cholesky decomposition

Numerical methods for portfolio optimization have become increasingly popular in recent years, as they allow for efficient and accurate computation of optimal portfolios using linear algebra techniques. Two such methods are quadratic programming and Cholesky decomposition.

Quadratic programming is a method used to solve quadratic optimization problems, such as those arising in portfolio theory. The basic idea is to minimize a quadratic objective function subject to linear constraints. In portfolio optimization, the objective function is the portfolio variance and the linear constraints represent the investor's preferences for expected returns and risk. Quadratic programming can be solved using specialized algorithms such as interior point methods, active set methods, or gradient projection methods. These algorithms use the properties of the covariance matrix and the linear constraints to find the optimal portfolio weights that minimize the portfolio variance subject to the constraints.

Cholesky decomposition is another numerical method used in portfolio optimization. It is a technique that decomposes a symmetric positive definite matrix into a product of a lower triangular matrix and its transpose. In portfolio theory, the covariance matrix is symmetric positive definite, and can thus be decomposed using Cholesky decomposition. The decomposition allows for the efficient computation of the inverse of the covariance matrix, which is required in the calculation of optimal portfolio weights. Cholesky decomposition is particularly useful when the number of assets in the portfolio is large, as it reduces the computational complexity of the optimization problem.

Both quadratic programming and Cholesky decomposition are widely used in the financial industry for portfolio optimization. Investment banks, hedge funds, and other financial institutions use these methods to construct optimal portfolios that meet their clients' investment objectives. Actuaries, portfolio managers, and financial analysts also use these methods in their daily work to analyze investment opportunities and manage portfolios.

One example of the use of quadratic programming in portfolio optimization is the Black-Litterman model, which is a popular asset allocation model developed by Fischer Black and Robert Litterman in 1992. The Black-Litterman model combines the investor's views about expected returns with the market equilibrium to generate a portfolio that balances the trade-off between risk and return. The model uses quadratic programming to solve for the optimal portfolio weights that satisfy the investor's views and constraints.

Cholesky decomposition is also widely used in portfolio optimization. For example, the Markowitz model can be solved using Cholesky decomposition to obtain the inverse of the covariance matrix, which is required in the calculation of optimal portfolio weights. The model aims to minimize the portfolio variance subject to a given expected return, and is considered the foundation of modern portfolio theory.

M.L.Ruscsak

In conclusion, numerical methods for portfolio optimization using linear algebra, such as quadratic programming and Cholesky decomposition, have become essential tools for investors, portfolio managers, and financial analysts. These methods allow for the efficient and accurate computation of optimal portfolios that meet the investor's objectives while considering risk and return trade-offs.

Traditional math problems and equations related to linear algebra and portfolio theory in finance

Linear algebra plays a fundamental role in portfolio theory, and traditional math problems and equations related to linear algebra can be applied to finance to optimize portfolios. In this section, we will explore some traditional math problems and equations related to linear algebra and their applications in finance, specifically in portfolio theory.

Matrix Multiplication

One of the most fundamental concepts in linear algebra is matrix multiplication. In finance, matrix multiplication is used to calculate the returns of a portfolio. To calculate the returns of a portfolio, we need to multiply the weights of the assets in the portfolio by the returns of each asset. The weights of the assets are represented by a column vector, and the returns of each asset are represented by a row vector. Matrix multiplication can be represented by the following equation:

$$R = w^T * r$$

where R is the returns of the portfolio, w is the weight vector of the assets in the portfolio, and r is the vector of returns of each asset. The symbol ^{T} represents the transpose of the weight vector w.

Covariance Matrix

The covariance matrix is a key concept in portfolio theory, and it represents the level of correlation between the assets in a portfolio. The covariance matrix is a square matrix where the diagonal elements represent the variances of the assets, and the off-diagonal elements represent the covariances between the assets. The covariance matrix can be represented by the following equation:

$$\Sigma = [\sigma_{ij}]$$

where σ_{ij} represents the covariance between asset i and asset j.

Markowitz Efficient Frontier

The Markowitz Efficient Frontier is a concept introduced by Harry Markowitz in his paper "Portfolio Selection" in 1952. The Markowitz Efficient Frontier represents the set of optimal portfolios that offer the highest expected return for a given level of risk. The Markowitz Efficient

Frontier can be plotted using the weights of the assets in the portfolio and the expected return and standard deviation of the portfolio.

Mean-Variance Optimization
Mean-Variance Optimization is a popular portfolio optimization technique that uses the Markowitz Efficient Frontier to optimize portfolios. Mean-Variance Optimization aims to maximize the expected return of a portfolio while minimizing its variance or risk. Mean-Variance Optimization can be represented by the following equation:

$$\text{minimize}(w) \; w^T \Sigma w$$

$$\text{subject to } w^T r = \mu$$

where w is the weight vector of the assets in the portfolio, Σ is the covariance matrix, r is the vector of expected returns of each asset, and μ is the expected return of the portfolio.

Cholesky Decomposition
Cholesky Decomposition is a numerical method used to solve linear equations that arise in portfolio optimization. Cholesky Decomposition is used to decompose a covariance matrix into a lower triangular matrix and its transpose. Cholesky Decomposition is used in Quadratic Programming, which is a technique used to solve optimization problems with quadratic constraints. Cholesky Decomposition can be represented by the following equation:

$$\Sigma = LL^T$$

where L is the lower triangular matrix and L^T is its transpose.

Conclusion

In conclusion, traditional math problems and equations related to linear algebra are widely used in finance, specifically in portfolio theory. Matrix multiplication, covariance matrix, Markowitz Efficient Frontier, Mean-Variance Optimization, and Cholesky Decomposition are some of the traditional math problems and equations that are used in finance. Understanding these concepts and equations is essential for investors, financial analysts, and portfolio managers to optimize their portfolios and manage their risk effectively.

1. Calculate the expected return and variance of a two-asset portfolio with asset weights of 0.6 and 0.4, respectively, and given that the expected returns of the two assets are 10% and 15%, and their variances are 0.04 and 0.09, respectively.

M.L.Ruscsak

2. Find the optimal portfolio weights that maximize expected return subject to a risk constraint of a portfolio variance less than or equal to 0.02, for a three-asset portfolio with expected returns of 0.12, 0.09, and 0.15, and variances of 0.03, 0.01, and 0.05, respectively.

3. Calculate the correlation coefficient between two assets with covariance of 0.02, and standard deviations of 0.04 and 0.06, respectively.

4. Given a covariance matrix with variances of 0.02, 0.03, and 0.04, and covariances of 0.01, 0.02, and 0.03, respectively, calculate the minimum variance portfolio weights for a three-asset portfolio.

5. Determine the risk-free rate of return for a portfolio with an expected return of 12%, a beta of 1.5, and a market risk premium of 8%.

6. Find the expected return and portfolio weights for a two-asset portfolio with a target return of 15%, where the expected returns of the two assets are 12% and 18%, respectively, and their covariance is 0.01.

7. Given a covariance matrix with variances of 0.06, 0.08, and 0.12, and covariances of 0.02, -0.01, and 0.03, respectively, calculate the efficient frontier for a three-asset portfolio.

8. Determine the Sharpe ratio for a portfolio with an expected return of 14%, a standard deviation of 0.08, and a risk-free rate of return of 3%.

9. Calculate the optimal portfolio weights that maximize expected return subject to a risk constraint of a portfolio variance less than or equal to 0.025, for a four-asset portfolio with expected returns of 0.10, 0.12, 0.09, and 0.14, and covariances of 0.01, 0.02, 0.03, and 0.04, respectively.

10. Find the eigenvalues and eigenvectors of the covariance matrix for a three-asset portfolio with variances of 0.02, 0.03, and 0.04, and covariances of 0.01, 0.02, and 0.03, respectively.

CHAPTER 15: LINEAR ALGEBRA AND RISK MANAGEMENT

Linear algebra is a branch of mathematics that has numerous applications in finance, particularly in the field of risk management. Linear algebra deals with the study of linear equations and their representations in vector spaces, and this framework can be used to model and analyze various risk management problems.

In this chapter, we will explore the applications of linear algebra in risk management. We will start with an introduction to the basics of linear algebra and then proceed to explore its application in portfolio theory, which is a fundamental concept in finance. We will also discuss how linear algebra can be used to model various types of financial risks, such as market risk, credit risk, and operational risk.

Portfolio theory is concerned with the optimal allocation of resources among a collection of assets, with the goal of maximizing the expected return while minimizing the associated risk. Linear algebra plays a critical role in portfolio theory, as it enables the efficient computation of various risk measures such as variance, covariance, and correlation. We will explore various methods of portfolio optimization, including Markowitz's mean-variance framework, which is widely used in finance.

We will also discuss how linear algebra can be used to model different types of financial risks, including market risk, which is the risk associated with fluctuations in financial markets, credit risk, which is the risk associated with default by borrowers, and operational risk, which is the risk associated with the failure of internal processes or systems.

Throughout the chapter, we will provide examples of how linear algebra is used in real-world scenarios by professionals such as investment bankers, actuaries, portfolio managers, quantitative analysts, securities traders, financial planners, and financial analysts. We will also explore the limitations and assumptions of linear algebra models and discuss alternative methods for risk management.

In conclusion, this chapter aims to provide a comprehensive introduction to the applications of linear algebra in risk management. By the end of this chapter, readers should have a solid understanding of the mathematical concepts underlying various risk management techniques, as well as the ability to apply these concepts to practical problems in finance.

Introduction to risk management and its importance in finance

Risk management is a crucial concept in finance that involves identifying, assessing, and mitigating potential risks that may impact an individual, organization, or market. It is a proactive approach that aims to minimize negative consequences and maximize positive outcomes in financial decision-making.

The concept of risk has always been a part of finance, as the value of financial assets is inherently uncertain due to various factors, such as market volatility, economic uncertainty, and geopolitical events. In order to make informed investment decisions, investors need to have a clear understanding of the risks involved in their investments and the potential impact on their portfolios.

The 2008 financial crisis is a prime example of the importance of risk management. The global financial system was severely impacted by the crisis, which was caused by a combination of factors, such as high levels of debt, inadequate risk management practices, and a lack of transparency. As a result, many financial institutions failed, and the global economy experienced a significant downturn.

In response to the crisis, regulatory authorities introduced new regulations to improve risk management practices and increase transparency in the financial industry. For example, the Dodd-Frank Wall Street Reform and Consumer Protection Act of 2010 introduced a number of measures to increase oversight of financial institutions and improve risk management practices.

In addition to regulatory requirements, risk management is also important from a business perspective. By identifying and mitigating risks, financial institutions can protect their assets and reputation, while also improving their decision-making process. Effective risk management can also lead to increased efficiency and profitability, as it allows financial institutions to allocate resources more effectively and avoid unnecessary losses.

One key aspect of risk management is the use of quantitative tools and techniques, such as statistical analysis and mathematical models. Linear algebra, in particular, plays a significant role in risk management, as it provides a framework for analyzing and optimizing complex financial systems.

For example, linear algebra can be used to model portfolio risk and optimize portfolio allocation. By representing financial assets as vectors and using covariance matrices to calculate risk and correlation, portfolio managers can develop optimal portfolio strategies that balance risk and return.

In addition to portfolio management, linear algebra is also used in other areas of risk management, such as credit risk analysis, risk modeling, and derivative pricing. By applying mathematical models and statistical analysis, financial institutions can identify potential risks and develop strategies to mitigate them.

In conclusion, risk management is a critical component of finance that involves identifying, assessing, and mitigating potential risks. The importance of risk management has become increasingly evident in the wake of the 2008 financial crisis, and regulatory authorities have introduced new regulations to improve risk management practices. Effective risk management requires the use of quantitative tools and techniques, such as linear algebra, to model and optimize complex financial systems. By implementing effective risk management practices, financial institutions can protect their assets, reputation, and profitability, while also making informed investment decisions.

Use of linear algebra in risk management, including VaR and CVaR

Risk management plays a critical role in financial decision making, and it is an essential concept in finance. It helps individuals, businesses, and organizations to manage and mitigate risks associated with financial transactions, investments, and activities. The objective of risk management is to identify, analyze, and control potential risks and uncertainties that could have negative impacts on financial performance. Various techniques and tools are used in risk management, including statistical methods, probability theory, and linear algebra.

Linear algebra is a branch of mathematics that deals with the study of linear equations and their applications. It provides a powerful set of tools and techniques for solving problems involving matrices, vectors, and systems of linear equations. In finance, linear algebra plays a crucial role in risk management, especially in the calculation of Value at Risk (VaR) and Conditional Value at Risk (CVaR). This section will explore the use of linear algebra in risk management, including VaR and CVaR.

The Importance of Risk Management in Finance

Risk management is essential in finance for several reasons. First, it helps in reducing the risk of financial losses resulting from market volatility, credit risk, operational risk, and other uncertainties. Second, it enables individuals and businesses to make informed investment decisions by evaluating the potential risks and returns associated with various investment opportunities. Third, it helps in improving financial performance by minimizing the negative impacts of risks on profits and returns. Finally, risk management is essential for compliance with regulatory requirements and standards.

The Use of Linear Algebra in Risk Management

Linear algebra provides a powerful set of tools and techniques for solving problems in risk management. In finance, linear algebra is used to calculate VaR and CVaR, which are important risk measures used to evaluate the potential risks associated with financial transactions and investments.

Value at Risk (VaR)

VaR is a statistical measure that estimates the maximum amount of loss that an investment portfolio could experience over a given time period with a specified level of confidence. VaR is calculated as the difference between the expected return of a portfolio and the potential loss that could occur due to market volatility, credit risk, or other uncertainties. VaR is expressed as a dollar amount or percentage of the portfolio value.

Linear algebra is used to calculate VaR by solving a system of linear equations. The system of equations represents the risk factors that contribute to the potential loss of the portfolio. The coefficients of the equations represent the sensitivity of the portfolio to each risk factor, and the variables represent the possible values of each risk factor. The solution to the system of equations provides the VaR of the portfolio with a specified level of confidence.

Conditional Value at Risk (CVaR)

CVaR is a measure of risk that estimates the expected loss of an investment portfolio beyond the VaR level. CVaR is calculated as the average of the potential losses that exceed the VaR level. CVaR provides a more comprehensive measure of risk than VaR since it takes into account the severity of losses beyond the VaR level.

Linear algebra is used to calculate CVaR by solving a quadratic programming problem. The problem involves optimizing a portfolio to minimize the expected loss beyond the VaR level subject to certain constraints. The optimization problem is formulated as a quadratic objective function, and the constraints are represented by a system of linear equations. The solution to the quadratic programming problem provides the optimal portfolio allocation that minimizes the CVaR of the portfolio.

Conclusion

In conclusion, risk management plays a critical role in financial decision making, and linear algebra provides a powerful set of tools and techniques for solving problems in risk management. The calculation of VaR and CVaR using linear algebra is an important application of this mathematical discipline in finance. VaR and CVaR provide essential measures of risk that enable individuals and businesses to make informed investment decisions and manage potential risks associated with their investment portfolios.

Despite the usefulness of linear algebra in risk management, it is important to recognize that it is not a panacea for all problems in finance. It is simply one tool among many that can be used to analyze risk and make informed investment decisions. Moreover, the use of linear algebraic techniques requires a strong understanding of the underlying mathematical concepts and assumptions, as well as the ability to implement these techniques using computational tools.

Another potential limitation of the use of linear algebra in risk management is the assumption of normality of returns, which is often not the case in real-world financial markets. This can lead to inaccurate estimates of VaR and CVaR, which can have serious consequences for investors and financial institutions.

Despite these limitations, the use of linear algebra in risk management is an important and growing field, and there is much potential for future research and development in this area. As financial markets become increasingly complex and global, the need for sophisticated tools and techniques to manage risk will only continue to grow.

Overall, the use of linear algebra in risk management is an important and exciting area of research and application, with the potential to provide significant benefits to individuals and businesses alike. By using these powerful tools and techniques, investors can make informed decisions about their portfolios and manage risk more effectively, leading to more successful and profitable outcomes over the long term.

Risk and return tradeoff in the context of risk management

In finance, the relationship between risk and return is an important consideration for investors, portfolio managers, and other financial professionals. The risk-return tradeoff is the idea that higher expected returns typically come with higher levels of risk, and that investors must be willing to accept risk in order to potentially earn higher returns. In the context of risk management, the risk-return tradeoff is an important consideration for decision making. This section will explore the risk-return tradeoff and its significance in the context of risk management.

The Risk-Return Tradeoff:
The risk-return tradeoff is a fundamental concept in finance, and is rooted in the concept of uncertainty. Investors are willing to invest their money only if they believe they will be compensated for the risk they are taking. Higher risk investments have the potential for higher returns, but also carry a higher risk of loss. Lower risk investments, on the other hand, offer lower potential returns but are less likely to result in a loss of capital.

The relationship between risk and return can be illustrated by the capital asset pricing model (CAPM), which is a popular tool used by financial professionals to determine the expected return on an investment given its level of risk. According to the CAPM, the expected return on an investment is equal to the risk-free rate of return plus a risk premium, which is proportional to the level of systematic risk inherent in the investment.

Risk and Return in the Context of Risk Management:
In the context of risk management, the risk-return tradeoff is an important consideration for decision making. Investors and portfolio managers must balance the potential returns of an investment against the potential risks associated with it. This requires an understanding of the level of risk associated with different types of investments and the strategies used to manage that risk.

One important tool used in risk management is diversification. By investing in a variety of assets, investors can reduce the overall risk of their portfolio while still achieving a desired level of return. Another strategy used in risk management is hedging, which involves taking on an offsetting position in another asset to reduce the risk associated with a particular investment.

In addition to these strategies, financial professionals also use risk management tools such as value at risk (VaR) and conditional value at risk (CVaR) to measure and manage risk. VaR is a statistical measure of the potential loss that could occur in a portfolio over a given period of time, while CVaR provides an estimate of the expected loss in the worst-case scenario. These tools can help investors and portfolio managers to make informed decisions about the level of risk they are willing to take on in pursuit of potential returns.

Conclusion:
The risk-return tradeoff is a fundamental concept in finance, and is an important consideration for decision making in the context of risk management. Investors and financial professionals must be willing to accept risk in order to potentially earn higher returns, but must also manage that risk in order to avoid catastrophic losses. Strategies such as diversification, hedging, and risk management tools such as VaR and CVaR can help investors and portfolio managers to balance the potential returns of an investment against the potential risks associated with it.

Numerical methods for risk management using linear algebra, including Monte Carlo simulation and linear regression

Numerical methods are a crucial component of risk management, as they enable individuals and businesses to quantify and manage various types of risks. In this section, we will discuss the use of numerical methods in risk management, focusing on Monte Carlo simulation and linear regression, and how they can be implemented using linear algebra.

Monte Carlo simulation is a widely used numerical method in risk management that involves simulating thousands or even millions of scenarios to estimate the probability of various outcomes. This method is particularly useful when dealing with complex financial instruments and portfolios, as it allows for a more comprehensive assessment of risk compared to traditional methods that rely on historical data.

The basic steps involved in a Monte Carlo simulation are as follows:

Define the inputs and assumptions: This involves identifying the various parameters and assumptions that will be used in the simulation. For example, in the case of a stock portfolio, the inputs could include the expected returns and volatilities of each stock.

Generate random samples: Once the inputs and assumptions have been defined, random samples are generated for each input variable. The number of samples generated depends on the desired level of accuracy and the complexity of the model.

Calculate the outputs: Using the randomly generated inputs, the model is run to calculate the outputs, such as the expected portfolio return and risk measures like VaR and CVaR.

Repeat the process: Steps 2 and 3 are repeated numerous times to generate a large number of outputs and estimate the probabilities of various outcomes.

Linear algebra plays a critical role in Monte Carlo simulations, as it provides a powerful set of tools for efficiently and accurately performing matrix computations, which are often required in these types of simulations. Specifically, the following linear algebra concepts are commonly used in Monte Carlo simulations:

Matrix multiplication: This is used to calculate the returns and risk measures of a portfolio based on the weights of the individual stocks and their expected returns and volatilities.

Inverse matrices: These are used to calculate the optimal weights for a given portfolio based on a desired level of risk or return.

Eigenvalues and eigenvectors: These are used to calculate the principal components of a portfolio, which can help identify the sources of risk and diversify the portfolio accordingly.

Linear regression is another widely used numerical method in risk management that involves fitting a linear model to a set of data points to predict future outcomes. This method is particularly useful when dealing with historical data and can be used to identify trends and relationships between variables.

The basic steps involved in linear regression are as follows:

Gather the data: This involves collecting historical data on the variables of interest, such as the returns of a particular stock or portfolio.

Specify the model: Once the data has been collected, a linear model is specified that relates the dependent variable (e.g., stock returns) to one or more independent variables (e.g., market returns).

Estimate the parameters: The model is then fitted to the data to estimate the parameters, such as the slope and intercept of the line.

Evaluate the model: Finally, the model is evaluated to determine its accuracy and validity.

M.L.Ruscsak

Linear algebra plays a critical role in linear regression, as it provides a powerful set of tools for solving the system of linear equations that arise when estimating the parameters of the model. Specifically, the following linear algebra concepts are commonly used in linear regression:

Matrix inversion: This is used to calculate the coefficients of the linear model based on the historical data.

Least squares regression: This is a technique used to minimize the sum of squared errors between the actual and predicted values.

In conclusion, numerical methods such as Monte Carlo simulation and linear regression are essential tools in risk management that enable individuals and businesses to quantify and manage various types of risks. Linear algebra plays a critical role in developing and implementing these numerical methods. By using the tools and techniques of linear algebra, we can construct mathematical models of risk and develop algorithms for computing risk measures.

One of the most widely used numerical methods for risk management is Monte Carlo simulation. Monte Carlo simulation is a statistical technique that involves generating a large number of random samples or scenarios, and using these samples to estimate the distribution of possible outcomes for a given investment or portfolio. Monte Carlo simulation is particularly useful in situations where the distribution of outcomes is complex or unknown, or where there are multiple sources of uncertainty.

Linear algebra plays a key role in Monte Carlo simulation by providing the mathematical framework for generating and manipulating the random samples or scenarios. For example, we can use linear algebra to construct a matrix of random numbers that represents the possible outcomes of a particular investment or portfolio. We can then use matrix multiplication and other linear algebra operations to compute the expected return, variance, and other risk measures for the investment or portfolio.

Another important numerical method for risk management is linear regression. Linear regression is a statistical technique that involves fitting a linear model to a set of data in order to identify the relationship between a dependent variable and one or more independent variables. Linear regression is particularly useful in situations where we want to understand how changes in one or more variables affect the risk or return of an investment or portfolio.

Linear algebra plays a critical role in linear regression by providing the mathematical framework for estimating the coefficients of the linear model. For example, we can use linear algebra to construct a matrix of independent variables and a vector of dependent variables, and then use matrix multiplication and other linear algebra operations to compute the coefficients of the linear model.

In conclusion, numerical methods such as Monte Carlo simulation and linear regression are essential tools in risk management that enable individuals and businesses to quantify and manage various types of risks. Linear algebra provides a powerful set of tools and techniques for developing and implementing these numerical methods. By using linear algebra in risk management, we can construct mathematical models of risk, develop algorithms for computing risk measures, and gain insights into the relationship between risk and return for a given investment or portfolio.

Traditional math problems and equations related to linear algebra and risk management in finance

Linear algebra has a long and rich history of application in finance, specifically in the field of risk management. Many traditional math problems and equations that are commonly used in finance rely heavily on linear algebra. In this section, we will discuss some of these traditional problems and equations and their relationship to linear algebra in the context of risk management.

One of the most fundamental problems in finance is the optimization problem, which seeks to maximize returns while minimizing risk. In order to solve optimization problems in finance, linear algebra is often used to model the problem and provide a solution. For example, the Markowitz portfolio optimization model uses linear algebra to find the portfolio that minimizes risk for a given level of expected return. This model uses the covariance matrix of asset returns to model the risk of a portfolio, and linear algebra is used to find the weights of each asset that minimize the portfolio risk.

Another traditional math problem in finance is the valuation of derivatives, such as options and futures. Derivative valuation is based on the principle of no arbitrage, which states that in a perfectly efficient market, the price of a derivative should be equal to the expected future value of the underlying asset. Linear algebra is used to model the dynamics of the underlying asset and the market in which it is traded, and to solve the partial differential equations that arise in the valuation process.

Linear algebra is also used in the calculation of risk measures such as Value at Risk (VaR) and Conditional Value at Risk (CVaR). These measures are used to quantify the potential loss that an investment portfolio may experience over a given time horizon at a given level of confidence. Linear algebra is used to model the distribution of returns for each asset in the portfolio and to calculate the portfolio's VaR and CVaR.

In addition, linear algebra is used in the calculation of betas, which are used to measure the systematic risk of a stock or portfolio relative to the market. Betas are used in the Capital Asset Pricing Model (CAPM), which is a widely used model for calculating the expected return of an asset. Linear algebra is used to solve the system of equations that arise in the CAPM model.

Linear algebra is also used in the calculation of yield curves, which are used to price fixed income securities such as bonds. The yield curve is a graph of the yields of bonds with different maturities, and linear algebra is used to model the relationship between the yields and the maturities of the bonds. This model is used to price bonds and to calculate the term structure of interest rates.

Finally, linear algebra is used in the calculation of factor models, which are used to explain the returns of a portfolio based on the performance of a set of underlying factors. Factor models are widely used in finance to explain the returns of mutual funds and hedge funds, and linear algebra is used to model the relationship between the factors and the returns of the portfolio.

In conclusion, traditional math problems and equations related to linear algebra play a critical role in risk management in finance. Linear algebra is used to model the dynamics of financial markets and to solve the problems that arise in the calculation of risk measures, portfolio optimization, derivative valuation, and fixed income securities pricing. The use of linear algebra in finance has enabled individuals and businesses to make informed investment decisions and manage potential risks associated with their investment portfolios.

1. Given a portfolio of 5 stocks with the following daily returns: 0.01, -0.005, 0.02, -0.01, and 0.015, calculate the daily returns vector and the covariance matrix.

2. A portfolio manager is considering adding a new stock to a portfolio consisting of 3 stocks. The correlation coefficients between the existing stocks and the new stock are 0.7, 0.5, and 0.4. If the weights of the existing stocks in the portfolio are 0.4, 0.3, and 0.3, respectively, what weight should be assigned to the new stock to achieve a portfolio with minimum variance?

3. Calculate the eigenvalues and eigenvectors of the following matrix:

$A = [[2, -1], [4, 3]]$

4. A financial analyst is analyzing a portfolio consisting of 3 stocks. The expected returns of the stocks are 0.1, 0.05, and 0.12, respectively. The covariance matrix of the returns is given by:

$\Sigma = [[0.02, 0.005, 0.01], [0.005, 0.03, 0.02], [0.01, 0.02, 0.05]]$

Calculate the expected return and standard deviation of the portfolio with weights of 0.3, 0.4, and 0.3, respectively.

5. Suppose a portfolio manager has the following constraints:

The portfolio must have an expected return of at least 10%.
The portfolio must have a variance of no more than 0.02.
The portfolio must allocate no more than 20% to any individual stock.

If the portfolio consists of 4 stocks with expected returns of 0.12, 0.08, 0.1, and 0.09, respectively, and covariance matrix:

Σ = [[0.01, 0.005, 0.002, 0.003],
[0.005, 0.02, 0.008, 0.005],
[0.002, 0.008, 0.01, 0.003],
[0.003, 0.005, 0.003, 0.015]]

Use linear algebra to find the optimal weights for the portfolio.

A financial planner is considering investing in a bond with a face value of $100,000 that pays a coupon of 5% per year and matures in 10 years. If the current interest rate is 3%, what is the price of the bond?

A company has two investment options: invest $500,000 in a new factory with a 50% chance of generating a profit of $1,000,000, or invest $500,000 in a stock with a 70% chance of generating a return of 20%. Which investment option has a higher expected return, and how much higher is it?

A portfolio manager has a portfolio consisting of 4 stocks. The weights of the stocks in the portfolio are given by the vector:

w = [0.3, 0.2, 0.1, 0.4]

The expected returns of the stocks are given by the vector:

μ = [0.12, 0.08, 0.1, 0.09]

The covariance matrix of the returns is given by:

Σ = [[0.01, 0.004, 0.001, 0.002],
[0.004, 0.02, 0.005, 0.006],
[0.001, 0.005, 0.02, 0.003],
[0.002, 0.006, 0.003, 0.016]]

The portfolio manager wants to calculate the expected return and standard deviation of the portfolio.

To calculate the expected return, we can use the formula:

$E(R) = w_1\mu_1 + w_2\mu_2 + w_3\mu_3 + w_4\mu_4$

Substituting the given values, we get:

$E(R) = 0.3 \times 0.12 + 0.2 \times 0.08 + 0.1 \times 0.1 + 0.4 \times 0.09$
$= 0.105$ or 10.5%

Therefore, the expected return of the portfolio is 10.5%.

To calculate the standard deviation of the portfolio, we can use the formula:

$\sigma p = \sqrt{(wT\Sigma w)}$

where wT is the transpose of the weight vector w.

Substituting the given values, we get:

$wT = [0.3, 0.2, 0.1, 0.4]T$

$wT\Sigma w = [0.3, 0.2, 0.1, 0.4]$ [[0.01, 0.004, 0.001, 0.002], [0.004, 0.02, 0.005, 0.006], [0.001, 0.005, 0.02, 0.003], [0.002, 0.006, 0.003, 0.016]] [0.3, 0.2, 0.1, 0.4]
$= 0.01394$

Therefore, the standard deviation of the portfolio is:

$\sigma p = \sqrt{(0.01394)} = 0.118$ or 11.8%

Thus, the portfolio manager can expect a return of 10.5% with a standard deviation of 11.8%.

PART 6: DIFFERENTIAL EQUATIONS FOR FINANCE

The world of finance is an ever-changing landscape, constantly influenced by economic and political factors. Financial analysts and portfolio managers are tasked with making informed decisions based on current market conditions to optimize returns for their clients. In order to do this, they need to understand the underlying mathematical principles that govern financial markets.

One such principle is the use of differential equations in finance. Differential equations are mathematical models that describe how a system changes over time. In finance, they are used to model the behavior of financial instruments such as stocks, bonds, and options. By using differential equations, financial analysts and portfolio managers can better understand the complex relationships between these instruments and make more informed investment decisions.

There are several types of differential equations used in finance, including ordinary differential equations (ODEs), partial differential equations (PDEs), and stochastic differential equations (SDEs). Each of these has its own unique characteristics and applications in finance.

ODEs are used to model the behavior of financial instruments that depend on a single variable, such as time. They are useful for predicting the future value of a stock or bond, based on its current value and historical data. ODEs can also be used to model the behavior of financial derivatives such as options and futures.

PDEs, on the other hand, are used to model financial instruments that depend on multiple variables, such as space and time. They are useful for modeling complex financial systems such as interest rate models and credit risk models.

SDEs are used to model financial instruments that have random fluctuations, such as stock prices. They take into account the uncertainty and unpredictability of financial markets and are used extensively in the field of quantitative finance.

Differential equations have a long history of application in finance, dating back to the early 1900s when Louis Bachelier developed the first mathematical model for stock prices. Since then, the

M.L.Ruscsak

use of differential equations has become increasingly common in the field of finance, as the complexity of financial systems has grown.

In this section, we will explore the use of differential equations in finance in more detail. We will look at some of the most common types of differential equations used in finance and examine how they are applied in practice. We will also explore some of the challenges and limitations of using differential equations in finance and discuss some of the latest developments in the field. By the end of this section, you will have a deeper understanding of how differential equations can be used to model financial systems and make more informed investment decisions.

CHAPTER 16: ORDINARY DIFFERENTIAL EQUATIONS

Ordinary Differential Equations (ODEs) are one of the most fundamental and widely used mathematical tools in the field of science and engineering. ODEs are mathematical equations that involve an unknown function and its derivatives with respect to one independent variable. They describe the behavior of many natural phenomena such as population growth, chemical reactions, heat flow, and financial systems.

In finance, ODEs are used to model various economic and financial systems such as interest rates, stock prices, option pricing, and portfolio management. These models provide valuable insights into the behavior of these systems, which can help financial professionals make informed decisions.

The study of ODEs involves understanding the properties of their solutions and developing methods for solving them. The solutions of ODEs can be classified into three categories: explicit solutions, implicit solutions, and numerical solutions.

Explicit solutions are formulas that express the solution of an ODE in terms of the independent variable and known constants. Implicit solutions, on the other hand, are formulas that express the solution in terms of the dependent variable and the independent variable. Numerical solutions are approximations of the solution obtained by numerical methods.

Solving ODEs is a challenging task that requires a deep understanding of mathematical concepts and analytical techniques. There are many analytical techniques for solving ODEs, such as separation of variables, variation of parameters, and Laplace transforms.

Moreover, numerical methods for solving ODEs are also widely used, including Euler's method, Runge-Kutta methods, and finite difference methods. These numerical methods are used when analytical solutions are not possible or too difficult to obtain.

This chapter will provide an introduction to ODEs, their properties, and methods for solving them. We will also discuss the applications of ODEs in finance and economics, and the role they play in modeling various financial systems. Finally, we will explore the limitations and challenges of ODE models in finance and discuss the importance of combining them with other modeling techniques for a more accurate representation of financial systems.

M.L.Ruscsak

Introduction to ordinary differential equations and their applications in finance

Ordinary differential equations (ODEs) are an important tool in mathematical modeling, and they have numerous applications in finance. ODEs are used to describe the behavior of a system over time, and in finance, they can be used to model a variety of phenomena, such as interest rates, stock prices, and option prices.

ODEs are differential equations that involve only one independent variable, usually time, and one or more dependent variables that depend on that independent variable. The derivatives of the dependent variables with respect to the independent variable are present in the equation.

In finance, ODEs are used to model a wide range of phenomena, including portfolio optimization, risk management, and pricing of financial derivatives. For example, the Black-Scholes model, which is used to price options, is based on a partial differential equation (PDE) that can be reduced to an ODE.

In this chapter, we will introduce the basics of ODEs, including their definition, classification, and solution methods. We will also explore some of their applications in finance and provide examples to illustrate the concepts.

Classification of ODEs:

ODEs can be classified based on their order, linearity, and homogeneity.

Order: The order of an ODE is the order of the highest derivative present in the equation. For example, a first-order ODE involves only the first derivative, while a second-order ODE involves the second derivative and so on.

Linearity: An ODE is linear if it can be written as a linear combination of the dependent variable and its derivatives. A linear ODE can be solved using standard techniques such as separation of variables and the method of integrating factors.

Homogeneity: An ODE is homogeneous if all terms in the equation involve the dependent variable or its derivatives. Homogeneous ODEs can be solved using the technique of separation of variables.

Solution Methods for ODEs:

There are several methods for solving ODEs, including separation of variables, integrating factors, and power series methods. The method used depends on the characteristics of the equation, such as its linearity and homogeneity.

Separation of Variables: Separation of variables is a technique used to solve first-order ODEs. The technique involves separating the variables into two parts, one involving only the dependent variable and the other involving only the independent variable. The resulting equation can be solved by integration.

Integrating Factors: Integrating factors is a technique used to solve linear ODEs. The technique involves multiplying both sides of the equation by a suitable integrating factor, which makes the equation easier to solve by integration.

Power Series Methods: Power series methods are used to solve ODEs by expanding the dependent variable as a power series in terms of the independent variable. The coefficients of the power series are then determined by substitution into the ODE.

Applications of ODEs in Finance:

ODEs have numerous applications in finance, including:

Portfolio Optimization: ODEs can be used to model the behavior of a portfolio over time and to optimize the portfolio based on various criteria, such as risk and return.

Risk Management: ODEs can be used to model the behavior of financial risks over time, such as interest rate risk and credit risk.

Pricing of Financial Derivatives: ODEs are used to model the behavior of financial derivatives, such as options and futures. The Black-Scholes model is based on a PDE that can be reduced to an ODE.

Conclusion:

ODEs are an important tool in mathematical modeling, and they have numerous applications in finance. ODEs are used to model the behavior of a system over time, and in finance, they can be used to model a variety of phenomena, such as interest rates, stock prices, and option prices.

In finance, ODEs are particularly useful for modeling the behavior of financial assets over time. For example, ODEs can be used to model the behavior of stock prices, which are subject to continuous fluctuations over time. By modeling the behavior of stock prices using ODEs, investors and traders can gain valuable insights into the future direction of the market and make more informed investment decisions.

ODEs can also be used to model the behavior of interest rates, which are a key driver of economic growth and inflation. By modeling the behavior of interest rates using ODEs, economists

M.L.Ruscsak

and central banks can gain a better understanding of the factors that affect interest rates and make more informed monetary policy decisions.

Another important application of ODEs in finance is in the area of options pricing. Options are financial derivatives that give the holder the right, but not the obligation, to buy or sell an underlying asset at a predetermined price on or before a specific date. The value of an option is influenced by a number of factors, such as the price of the underlying asset, the volatility of the asset, and the time until expiration. ODEs can be used to model the behavior of these factors over time, allowing options traders to make more informed trading decisions.

In conclusion, ODEs are a powerful mathematical tool with numerous applications in finance. They allow financial analysts and traders to model the behavior of financial assets over time and gain valuable insights into the future direction of the market. As financial markets continue to evolve and become more complex, the importance of ODEs in finance is only likely to grow.

Use of ordinary differential equations in option pricing and portfolio optimization

The use of ordinary differential equations (ODEs) in finance has grown significantly in recent years, and one of the areas where ODEs have proven to be particularly useful is in option pricing and portfolio optimization. In this section, we will discuss the use of ODEs in these two important areas of finance.

Option Pricing

An option is a financial contract that gives the buyer the right, but not the obligation, to buy or sell an underlying asset at a specified price (strike price) and time in the future. Options are traded on a variety of underlying assets, including stocks, bonds, commodities, and currencies. One of the key challenges in option pricing is determining the fair value of an option, which depends on a number of factors, including the price of the underlying asset, the strike price, the time to expiration, and the volatility of the underlying asset.

The Black-Scholes-Merton model is one of the most widely used models for option pricing. The model uses ODEs to derive an analytical solution for the fair value of a European call option, which gives the buyer the right to buy the underlying asset at the strike price on the expiration date. The Black-Scholes-Merton model assumes that the underlying asset follows a geometric Brownian motion, which is a stochastic process that describes the random movements of the underlying asset over time. The model also assumes that there are no transaction costs, dividends, or arbitrage opportunities.

The Black-Scholes-Merton model uses the following ODE to describe the evolution of the price of the call option over time:

$$dC/dt + 0.5\sigma^2 S^2 d^2C/dS^2 + rSdC/dS - rC = 0$$

where C is the price of the call option, S is the price of the underlying asset, σ is the volatility of the underlying asset, r is the risk-free interest rate, and t is time. This equation is known as the Black-Scholes-Merton equation.

The Black-Scholes-Merton equation is a parabolic partial differential equation (PDE) that can be solved using a variety of numerical methods, including finite difference methods, Monte Carlo methods, and Fourier transform methods. The solution to the equation gives the fair value of the option as a function of the underlying asset price, time, and other parameters.

Portfolio Optimization

Portfolio optimization is the process of selecting the optimal portfolio of assets that maximizes the expected return for a given level of risk. Portfolio optimization is a key area of finance, as investors are always looking for ways to maximize their returns while minimizing their risks.

One of the challenges of portfolio optimization is dealing with the correlation between assets. ODEs can be used to model the dynamics of a portfolio of assets over time, taking into account the correlation between the assets. One example of an ODE-based model for portfolio optimization is the Heston model.

The Heston model is a stochastic volatility model that uses two ODEs to describe the evolution of the price and volatility of an asset over time. The model assumes that the volatility of the asset follows a mean-reverting process, where the volatility tends to revert to a long-term mean. The model also assumes that the correlation between the asset price and the volatility is stochastic.

The Heston model uses the following ODEs to describe the evolution of the asset price and volatility over time:

$$dS/dt = rS - qS - \sigma V(S,t)SdW1/dt$$

$$dV/dt = \kappa(\theta - V)dt + \sigma\sqrt{V}dW2/dt$$

where S is the price of the asset, V is the volatility of the asset, r is the risk-free interest rate, q is the dividend yield, σ is the correlation between the asset price and volatility, κ is the speed of mean reversion, θ is the long-term mean volatility, and W1 and W2 are Brownian motions.

The Heston model is widely used in option pricing and portfolio optimization because it captures important features of asset prices and volatility, such as the tendency of volatility to revert to a long-term mean and the correlation between asset prices and volatility. By incorporating these features into a model, the Heston model provides a more realistic representation of asset prices and volatility than simpler models such as the Black-Scholes model.

Option pricing is the process of determining the fair price of an option, which is a contract that gives the holder the right, but not the obligation, to buy or sell an underlying asset at a predetermined price (strike price) on or before a specific date (expiration date). The Heston model can be used to price options by solving the partial differential equation (PDE) that describes the option price.

The Heston model is also used in portfolio optimization, which is the process of selecting a portfolio of assets that maximizes the expected return for a given level of risk. Portfolio optimization involves solving a mathematical optimization problem, which can be formulated as an ODE using the Heston model. By using the Heston model to describe the behavior of asset prices and volatility, portfolio managers can make more informed decisions about which assets to include in their portfolios and how much to invest in each asset.

One example of the use of the Heston model in finance is the valuation of options on futures contracts. Futures contracts are agreements to buy or sell a commodity or financial instrument at a predetermined price and date. Options on futures contracts give the holder the right, but not the obligation, to buy or sell a futures contract at a predetermined price and date. The Heston model can be used to price options on futures contracts by modeling the behavior of the underlying futures contract and its volatility.

Another example of the use of the Heston model in finance is the valuation of exotic options, which are options with non-standard features that make them more complex to value than standard options. Exotic options include barrier options, Asian options, and lookback options. The Heston model can be used to price exotic options by modeling the behavior of the underlying asset and its volatility.

In conclusion, the Heston model is a powerful tool in option pricing and portfolio optimization. By using ODEs to describe the behavior of asset prices and volatility, the Heston model provides a more realistic representation of financial markets than simpler models such as the Black-Scholes model. The Heston model is widely used in finance to price options and to optimize portfolios, and it has numerous applications in a variety of financial contexts, from options on futures contracts to exotic options.

Numerical methods for solving ordinary differential equations in finance, including finite difference methods and Runge-Kutta methods

Numerical methods are commonly used to solve ordinary differential equations (ODEs) in finance, as exact analytical solutions are often difficult or impossible to obtain. These numerical methods involve approximating the solution of the ODE at discrete points in time and space, and then using iterative algorithms to obtain an approximation of the solution at any point in time or space.

One of the most commonly used numerical methods for solving ODEs in finance is the finite difference method. This method involves discretizing the time and/or space domain and approximating the derivative of the solution at each time and/or space point using finite differences. For example, the forward difference method can be used to approximate the first derivative of a function at a given point, by subtracting the function value at that point from the function value at the next point and dividing by the distance between the points. Similarly, the central difference method can be used to approximate the second derivative of a function at a given point, by subtracting the function value at the previous point from the function value at the next point and dividing by the distance between the points squared.

Once the derivatives are approximated using finite differences, the ODE can be reformulated as a system of algebraic equations, which can then be solved using standard linear algebra techniques. For example, the finite difference method can be used to solve the Black-Scholes equation for European options, which is a partial differential equation that describes the evolution of the option price over time and the underlying asset price.

Another commonly used numerical method for solving ODEs in finance is the Runge-Kutta method. This method involves using a higher-order Taylor series expansion to approximate the solution of the ODE at each time step, and then using these approximations to iteratively obtain a numerical solution of the ODE. The fourth-order Runge-Kutta method is one of the most widely used numerical methods for solving ODEs in finance, due to its high accuracy and stability.

In addition to finite difference and Runge-Kutta methods, there are many other numerical methods available for solving ODEs in finance, including spectral methods, finite element methods, and Monte Carlo methods. The choice of method depends on the specific application and the desired level of accuracy and computational efficiency.

To illustrate the use of numerical methods for solving ODEs in finance, consider the following example. Suppose we want to model the behavior of a stock price over time, using the following ODE:

$$dS/dt = rS + \sigma S dW/dt$$

where S is the stock price, r is the risk-free interest rate, σ is the volatility of the stock price, and dW/dt is a standard Wiener process.

To solve this ODE numerically, we can use the finite difference method to discretize the time domain into a set of discrete time steps, and then approximate the derivative of S at each time step using finite differences. For example, we can use the forward difference method to approximate the derivative of S at time t+Δt, as follows:

$$(S(t+\Delta t) - S(t))/\Delta t = rS(t) + \sigma S(t)dW/dt$$

Solving for S(t+Δt), we obtain:

$$S(t+\Delta t) = S(t) + rS(t)\Delta t + \sigma S(t)dW/dt$$

This expression provides an approximation of the stock price at time t+Δt, given the stock price at time t and a realization of the Wiener process.

We can then iterate this process to obtain a numerical solution of the ODE at any point in time. For example, we can use the fourth-order Runge-Kutta method to iteratively approximate the stock price at each time step, given the stock price and its derivatives at the previous time step. The Runge-Kutta method is a widely used numerical method for solving ODEs that is known for its accuracy and stability. It involves computing several intermediate values of the function at each time step, which are then used to obtain a weighted average of the function over the time interval.

In addition to the finite difference and Runge-Kutta methods, there are other numerical methods for solving ODEs, such as the Euler method, the backward difference method, and the Crank-Nicolson method. Each method has its own advantages and disadvantages, and the choice of method depends on the specific problem and the desired level of accuracy.

Numerical methods are commonly used in finance to solve ODEs that do not have closed-form solutions, such as the Black-Scholes equation and the Heston model. These methods allow us to obtain accurate approximations of the solutions at any point in time, which can be used to price financial derivatives, optimize portfolios, and manage risk.

For example, the finite difference method can be used to price options using the Black-Scholes equation, by discretizing the time and price domains and then solving the resulting system of linear equations. Similarly, the Runge-Kutta method can be used to solve the Heston model numerically, by iterating the process of approximating the stock price and volatility at each time step.

However, numerical methods also have their limitations, such as the potential for numerical instability and the need for careful selection of the time step and spatial resolution. In addition, the accuracy of the numerical solution depends on the accuracy of the initial and boundary conditions, and the sensitivity of the solution to small changes in the input parameters should be carefully analyzed.

Overall, numerical methods are a powerful tool for solving ODEs in finance, and they have enabled the development of sophisticated models for pricing derivatives and managing risk. As computational power continues to increase, numerical methods are likely to become even more important in finance, as they allow us to tackle increasingly complex problems and obtain more accurate and reliable solutions.

Traditional math problems and equations related to ordinary differential equations in finance

Ordinary differential equations (ODEs) are widely used in finance to model a variety of phenomena, such as stock prices, interest rates, and option prices. In this section, we will explore some traditional math problems and equations related to ODEs in finance.

One of the most well-known ODEs in finance is the Black-Scholes equation, which is used to price options. The Black-Scholes equation is a partial differential equation that describes the evolution of the price of an option over time. The equation is given by:

$$\partial C/\partial t + 1/2\, \sigma^2\, S^2\, \partial^2 C/\partial S^2 + rS\partial C/\partial S - rC = 0$$

where C is the price of a call option, S is the price of the underlying asset, σ is the volatility of the underlying asset, r is the risk-free interest rate, and t is time.

The Black-Scholes equation is a second-order linear partial differential equation with constant coefficients, and it can be solved using a variety of methods, such as the finite difference method or the Fourier transform method. The solution of the Black-Scholes equation gives us the theoretical price of an option, which can be used to compare against the market price of the option.

Another traditional math problem related to ODEs in finance is the calculation of bond prices. Bond prices are typically modeled using a system of ODEs, such as the Vasicek model or the Hull-White model. The Vasicek model is given by:

$$dR(t) = a(b - R(t))dt + \sigma dW(t)$$

where R(t) is the short-term interest rate, a and b are parameters that govern the mean-reverting behavior of the interest rate, σ is the volatility of the interest rate, and W(t) is a Wiener process.

The solution of the Vasicek model can be used to calculate the price of a bond using the following equation:

$$P = \Sigma(C/F)(1 + R)^{(-t)}$$

where P is the price of the bond, C is the coupon payment, F is the face value of the bond, R is the short-term interest rate, and t is the time until maturity.

The Hull-White model is another popular model used to price bonds. The Hull-White model is a one-factor model that is given by the following ODE:

$$dR(t) = (\theta - aR(t))dt + \sigma dW(t)$$

where $R(t)$ is the short-term interest rate, θ is the long-term mean of the interest rate, a is the speed of mean reversion, and σ is the volatility of the interest rate.

The solution of the Hull-White model can be used to calculate the price of a bond using the following equation:

$$P = F\exp(-A(t)) + C\Sigma(\exp(-A(t)) - \exp(-B(t)))/(B(t) - A(t))$$

where F is the face value of the bond, C is the coupon payment, $A(t)$ and $B(t)$ are functions of the interest rate, and t is the time until maturity.

In addition to the Black-Scholes equation and bond pricing models, there are many other ODEs that are used in finance. For example, the Cox-Ingersoll-Ross model is used to model the evolution of interest rates, and the Merton model is used to model the credit risk of a company.

Overall, ODEs play a crucial role in finance, and their applications are diverse and far-reaching. The ability to solve ODEs numerically has opened up new avenues for financial analysis and has enabled us to gain a deeper understanding of the complex dynamics that drive financial markets.

One traditional math problem related to ODEs in finance is the problem of determining the optimal investment strategy for an investor who seeks to maximize their expected utility of wealth. This problem can be formulated as a stochastic control problem, where the investor's wealth is modeled as a stochastic process and the investor seeks to find the optimal allocation of their wealth into different investment opportunities.

The solution to this problem can be obtained by solving a Hamilton-Jacobi-Bellman (HJB) equation, which is a partial differential equation that describes the optimal value function of the investor's problem. The HJB equation is a nonlinear PDE that is difficult to solve analytically, but numerical methods such as finite differences and Monte Carlo simulations can be used to obtain approximate solutions.

Another traditional math problem related to ODEs in finance is the problem of pricing options on assets that exhibit stochastic volatility. This problem can be formulated as a partial integro-differential equation (PIDE) that describes the evolution of the option price over time, taking into account the stochastic nature of the volatility of the underlying asset.

The solution to this problem can be obtained by using numerical methods such as finite differences and Fourier transforms to discretize the time and spatial domains and approximate the derivative terms in the PIDE. The resulting system of linear equations can then be solved iteratively to obtain an approximate solution of the option price at any point in time.

In summary, traditional math problems related to ODEs in finance include the optimization of investment strategies and the pricing of options on assets with stochastic volatility. These problems require the use of advanced mathematical tools such as HJB equations and PIDEs, and the solutions to these problems are obtained through numerical methods such as finite differences and Monte Carlo simulations.

M.L.Ruscsak

CHAPTER 17: PARTIAL DIFFERENTIAL EQUATIONS

Partial differential equations (PDEs) are mathematical equations that describe the behavior of a system in terms of its partial derivatives. They are used to model a wide range of physical phenomena, including fluid dynamics, heat transfer, quantum mechanics, and electromagnetism. In finance, PDEs are used to model the behavior of financial instruments such as options and derivatives.

PDEs are a natural extension of ordinary differential equations (ODEs), which describe the behavior of a system in terms of its derivatives with respect to a single independent variable. In contrast, PDEs describe the behavior of a system in terms of its derivatives with respect to multiple independent variables. For example, the heat equation is a PDE that describes the flow of heat in a system as a function of both time and space.

One of the key differences between ODEs and PDEs is that PDEs often have solutions that exhibit non-local behavior. This means that the value of the solution at a particular point depends not only on the value of the function at that point, but also on its values at neighboring points. As a result, PDEs are often more difficult to solve than ODEs.

Despite their complexity, PDEs have proven to be an invaluable tool in a wide range of fields. In physics, PDEs are used to model the behavior of everything from fluids to subatomic particles. In engineering, PDEs are used to design everything from airplanes to bridges. And in finance, PDEs are used to model the behavior of financial instruments such as options and derivatives.

One of the key challenges in working with PDEs is developing numerical methods for solving them. Unlike ODEs, which can be solved using a wide range of numerical methods, PDEs require specialized numerical methods that take into account their non-local behavior. In addition, PDEs often have boundary conditions that must be satisfied in order to obtain a physically meaningful solution.

Despite these challenges, there are a number of numerical methods that have been developed for solving PDEs. These include finite difference methods, finite element methods, and spectral methods. Each of these methods has its own strengths and weaknesses, and the choice of method depends on the specific problem being solved.

In this chapter, we will explore the use of PDEs in finance, with a particular focus on the Black-Scholes equation and its extensions. We will also discuss numerical methods for solving PDEs, with a focus on finite difference methods. By the end of this chapter, you will have a solid understanding of the role that PDEs play in finance, and you will be able to apply numerical methods to solve a wide range of financial problems.

Introduction to partial differential equations and their applications in finance

Partial differential equations (PDEs) are mathematical models that describe how quantities change over time and space. PDEs are widely used in physics, engineering, and many other fields, including finance. In finance, PDEs are used to model the dynamics of financial instruments, such as stocks, bonds, options, and futures, and to evaluate financial risks, such as credit risk, market risk, and operational risk.

In this chapter, we will introduce the basic concepts of PDEs and their applications in finance. We will start by discussing the differences between ordinary differential equations (ODEs) and PDEs, and then move on to the classification and solution methods of PDEs. We will also discuss several important PDE models used in finance, including the Black-Scholes equation, the Heston model, and the local volatility model.

Difference between ODEs and PDEs

ODEs are mathematical models that describe how a single quantity changes over time. For example, the growth of a population or the decay of a radioactive substance can be described by an ODE. In finance, ODEs are used to model the dynamics of interest rates, bond prices, and other financial variables that depend on a single variable, such as time.

PDEs, on the other hand, describe how multiple quantities change over time and space. For example, the temperature distribution in a room or the flow of a fluid can be described by a PDE. In finance, PDEs are used to model the dynamics of financial instruments that depend on multiple variables, such as stock prices that depend on time and underlying asset prices.

Classification and Solution Methods of PDEs

PDEs can be classified into several categories based on their order, linearity, and boundary conditions. The order of a PDE is determined by the highest-order derivative that appears in the equation. For example, the Black-Scholes equation is a second-order PDE because it involves the second derivative of the option price with respect to time and the underlying asset price.

Linearity refers to whether the PDE is linear or nonlinear. A linear PDE is a PDE that can be written as a linear combination of its derivatives and the variables themselves. A nonlinear PDE, on the other hand, is a PDE that cannot be written in this form. Nonlinear PDEs are generally more difficult to solve than linear PDEs.

M.L.Ruscsak

Boundary conditions are additional conditions that must be specified to uniquely determine the solution of a PDE. These conditions can be either initial conditions, which specify the values of the dependent variables at a particular time, or boundary conditions, which specify the behavior of the dependent variables at the boundaries of the domain of interest.

There are several methods for solving PDEs, including analytical methods and numerical methods. Analytical methods involve finding exact solutions to a PDE using mathematical techniques such as separation of variables, Fourier series, and Laplace transforms. However, analytical methods are often limited to simple PDE models and may not be applicable to more complex models.

Numerical methods, on the other hand, involve approximating the solution of a PDE using numerical algorithms. Numerical methods are more general and can be applied to a wide range of PDE models. The most common numerical methods for solving PDEs are finite difference methods, finite element methods, and spectral methods.

Applications of PDEs in Finance

PDEs are widely used in finance to model the dynamics of financial instruments and evaluate financial risks. One of the most famous PDE models in finance is the Black-Scholes equation, which is used to price European options. The Black-Scholes equation is a second-order linear PDE that can be solved using analytical and numerical methods. Another important PDE model in finance is the Heston model, which is used to model the volatility of stock prices. The Heston model is a system of two coupled nonlinear PDEs, and it can be solved numerically using finite difference or Monte Carlo methods.

PDEs are also used to model the credit risk of financial instruments. One such model is the Merton model, which assumes that the default risk of a company is related to the value of its assets. The Merton model is a partial differential equation that can be solved numerically using finite difference or Monte Carlo methods.

Another important application of PDEs in finance is in the area of portfolio optimization. Portfolio optimization involves finding the optimal allocation of assets in a portfolio to achieve a desired level of return and risk. This problem can be formulated as a PDE known as the Hamilton-Jacobi-Bellman equation, which can be solved using numerical methods such as finite difference or Monte Carlo methods.

In addition, PDEs are used in financial engineering to design and create new financial instruments. For example, the design of new exotic options such as barrier options, lookback options, and Asian options often involves solving PDEs.

Conclusion

In conclusion, partial differential equations play a crucial role in finance, and their applications are diverse and far-reaching. The ability to solve PDEs numerically has opened up new avenues for financial analysis and has enabled us to gain a deeper understanding of financial markets and instruments. As financial markets become increasingly complex and dynamic, the use of PDEs in finance is likely to become even more widespread and important in the years to come.

Use of partial differential equations in option pricing and risk management

The use of partial differential equations (PDEs) has revolutionized the field of option pricing and risk management in finance. One of the most famous PDE models in finance is the Black-Scholes equation, which is used to price European options. However, the Black-Scholes equation assumes that the underlying asset follows a log-normal random walk, which is not always the case in real-world scenarios. As a result, more complex PDE models have been developed to account for more realistic asset price dynamics and evaluate financial risks.

The Black-Scholes Equation

The Black-Scholes equation is a second-order linear PDE that describes the evolution of the price of a European call or put option as a function of the underlying asset price, time, and other parameters. The equation assumes that the underlying asset price follows a log-normal random walk and that the option can only be exercised at its expiration date. The equation is given by:

$$\frac{\partial v}{\partial \tau} + \frac{1}{2}\sigma^2 S^2 \frac{\partial^2 v}{\partial s^2} + rS\frac{\partial v}{\partial s} - rV = 0$$

where V is the option value, S is the underlying asset price, t is time, σ is the volatility of the underlying asset, and r is the risk-free interest rate. The equation can be solved analytically to obtain the price of a European call or put option.

However, the assumptions underlying the Black-Scholes model are often not met in practice. For example, asset prices may follow more complex dynamics such as stochastic volatility or jumps. In such cases, more advanced PDE models are required.

Stochastic Volatility Models

One of the limitations of the Black-Scholes model is that it assumes that the volatility of the underlying asset is constant over time. In reality, asset volatility can be highly variable and stochastic. Stochastic volatility models use PDEs to model the dynamics of the underlying asset price and

M.L.Ruscsak

volatility simultaneously. One of the most popular stochastic volatility models is the Heston model, which is given by:

$$\frac{\partial v}{\partial \tau} + \frac{1}{2} S^2 \frac{\partial^2 v}{\partial S^2} + rS \frac{\partial v}{\partial S} - rV + \frac{\partial v}{\partial \tau} + K(\theta - v)\frac{\partial v}{\partial s} + \frac{1}{2}\sigma^2 v \frac{\partial^2 v}{\partial v^2} = 0$$

where ν is the volatility of the underlying asset, κ is the mean-reversion rate of the volatility, θ is the long-term average volatility, and σ is the volatility of the volatility. The Heston model can be used to price a wide range of options, including European, American, and exotic options.

Jump Diffusion Models

Another limitation of the Black-Scholes model is that it assumes that asset prices follow a continuous random walk. In reality, asset prices can experience sudden jumps due to unexpected news or events. Jump diffusion models use PDEs to model the dynamics of the underlying asset price and the occurrence of jumps. One of the most popular jump diffusion models is the Merton model, which is given by:

$$dS(t) = (\mu - \lambda J)S(t)dt + \sigma S(t)dW(t) + JdN(t)$$

where S(t) is the asset price at time t, μ is the expected return, σ is the volatility, λ is the arrival rate of jumps, J is the size of the jump, dW(t) is the Wiener process, and dN(t) is the Poisson process. The Merton model allows for the occurrence of jumps in asset prices and provides a more realistic representation of market dynamics.

The use of PDEs in option pricing and risk management has revolutionized the finance industry. PDE models have made it possible to price complex financial instruments such as options and derivatives, which were previously considered too difficult to value. PDE models have also enabled financial institutions to evaluate and manage risk more effectively by providing a better understanding of market dynamics and the factors that drive asset prices.

One example of the use of PDEs in option pricing is the Heston model, which is a stochastic volatility model that takes into account the volatility of the underlying asset. The Heston model is a two-factor model that uses PDEs to model the dynamics of the underlying asset price and the volatility. The Heston model is widely used in the financial industry for pricing options and other financial derivatives.

Another example of the use of PDEs in risk management is the Value at Risk (VaR) model, which is used to estimate the maximum loss that a financial institution could incur within a given time horizon with a given level of confidence. VaR is typically calculated using PDE models that take into account the underlying asset price dynamics and the volatility of the asset.

In conclusion, partial differential equations have become an indispensable tool for option pricing and risk management in the finance industry. PDE models have enabled financial institutions to price complex financial instruments and manage risk more effectively, thereby improving the stability and efficiency of financial markets. The use of PDEs in finance is an excellent example of the power of mathematics and its ability to transform and revolutionize entire industries.

Numerical methods for solving partial differential equations in finance, including finite difference methods and numerical integration

Numerical methods for solving partial differential equations (PDEs) are widely used in finance due to the complexity of the PDE models and the need for quick and accurate calculations. Numerical methods involve approximating the solution of a PDE using numerical algorithms, which can be programmed and executed using a computer.

Finite difference methods (FDM) are a popular numerical method for solving PDEs in finance. In this method, the partial derivatives in the PDE are approximated using finite differences, which are the differences between the values of the function at neighboring points in the discretized domain. FDM can be used to solve both linear and nonlinear PDEs and can be easily applied to complex geometries.

The simplest form of FDM is the forward difference method, which approximates the partial derivative with respect to time using the forward difference and the partial derivative with respect to the spatial coordinate using the central difference. The backward difference method and the central difference method are also commonly used in FDM.

Another numerical method for solving PDEs is the finite element method (FEM). FEM involves dividing the domain into a finite number of elements and approximating the solution of the PDE within each element using a polynomial function. The solutions in adjacent elements are then matched using boundary conditions, resulting in a system of linear equations that can be solved using numerical techniques.

Spectral methods are another numerical method for solving PDEs in finance. These methods approximate the solution of the PDE using a truncated Fourier or Chebyshev series expansion, which is valid for periodic functions. Spectral methods are highly accurate and can converge quickly, but they can only be used for certain types of PDEs.

Numerical integration is also used in finance to calculate the expected value of financial instruments, such as options. Monte Carlo integration is a common numerical integration method used in finance. In this method, random numbers are generated to simulate the underlying asset

M.L.Ruscsak

prices, and the expected value is calculated by averaging the payoffs of the financial instrument at each simulated price.

Overall, numerical methods are essential for solving complex PDE models in finance and for evaluating financial risks. These methods enable accurate and quick calculations that would not be possible using traditional analytical methods.

Traditional math problems and equations related to partial differential equations in finance

Partial differential equations (PDEs) are widely used in finance to model the behavior of financial instruments and evaluate financial risks. In this section, we will explore some traditional math problems and equations related to PDEs in finance.

Heat Equation
The heat equation is a classic example of a partial differential equation. It is used to model the diffusion of heat in a solid object over time. The heat equation is given by:

$$\partial u/\partial t = k \nabla^2 u$$

where u is the temperature, k is the thermal diffusivity, and ∇^2 is the Laplace operator. The heat equation can be applied to finance to model the diffusion of information or the spread of market impact.

Wave Equation
The wave equation is another classic example of a partial differential equation. It is used to model the propagation of waves in a medium over time. The wave equation is given by:

$$\partial^2 u/\partial t^2 = c^2 \nabla^2 u$$

where u is the wave function, c is the speed of propagation, and ∇^2 is the Laplace operator. The wave equation can be applied to finance to model the propagation of market shocks or the spread of news.

Laplace Equation
The Laplace equation is a linear partial differential equation that is used to model steady-state behavior. It is given by:

$$\nabla^2 u = 0$$

where u is the solution and ∇^2 is the Laplace operator. The Laplace equation can be applied to finance to model the equilibrium behavior of financial markets.

Black-Scholes Equation

The Black-Scholes equation is one of the most famous partial differential equations in finance. It is used to price European options on stocks, assuming that the stock price follows a geometric Brownian motion. The Black-Scholes equation is given by:

$$\partial C/\partial t + 1/2\sigma^2 S^2 \partial^2 C/\partial S^2 + rS\partial C/\partial S - rC = 0$$

where C is the option price, S is the stock price, σ is the volatility of the stock price, r is the risk-free interest rate, and $\partial^2/\partial S^2$ is the second partial derivative with respect to the stock price. The Black-Scholes equation can be solved using the finite difference method, the finite element method, or the Monte Carlo method.

Heston Model

The Heston model is a partial differential equation that is used to model the dynamics of stock prices and volatility. It is given by:

$$\partial S/\partial t = rS + \sqrt{V}StZ1$$
$$\partial V/\partial t = \kappa(\theta - Vt) + \sigma\sqrt{Vt}Z2$$

where S is the stock price, V is the volatility, r is the risk-free interest rate, κ is the mean reversion rate, θ is the long-run mean of volatility, σ is the volatility of volatility, and Z1 and Z2 are correlated standard Brownian motions. The Heston model can be solved using numerical methods such as the finite difference method or the Monte Carlo method.

American Options

American options are financial instruments that give the holder the right to exercise the option at any time before the expiration date. The valuation of American options involves solving a partial differential equation known as the American option pricing equation. The American option pricing equation is similar to the Black-Scholes equation but has an additional term that accounts for the option holder's ability to exercise the option at any time before expiration.

Mathematically, the American option pricing equation can be written as:

$\frac{\partial V}{\partial t} + \frac{1}{2}\sigma^2S^2\frac{\partial^2 V}{\partial S^2} + (r-q)S\frac{\partial V}{\partial S} - rV = 0$

where V is the value of the American option, S is the underlying asset price, t is time, σ is the volatility of the underlying asset, r is the risk-free interest rate, and q is the dividend yield.

M.L.Ruscsak

The American option pricing equation can be solved using numerical methods such as finite difference methods and Monte Carlo simulations. Finite difference methods involve discretizing the domain of the underlying asset price and time and approximating the derivatives in the equation using finite difference approximations. Monte Carlo simulations involve simulating the evolution of the underlying asset price using random sampling and estimating the option value using the discounted expected payoff.

The valuation of American options is important in risk management as it allows investors to assess the value of their options and make informed decisions regarding exercise or holding. Moreover, American options are often embedded in complex financial instruments such as convertible bonds and mortgage-backed securities, and their valuation requires the solution of partial differential equations.

In addition to American options, partial differential equations are also used in the valuation of other financial instruments such as exotic options, credit derivatives, and interest rate derivatives. Exotic options are financial instruments with non-standard features such as barrier options, Asian options, and lookback options. The valuation of exotic options requires the solution of more complex partial differential equations than standard options.

Credit derivatives are financial instruments that allow investors to hedge or speculate on credit risk. The valuation of credit derivatives involves the solution of partial differential equations that model the default risk of the underlying asset.

Interest rate derivatives are financial instruments that allow investors to hedge or speculate on interest rate risk. The valuation of interest rate derivatives involves the solution of partial differential equations that model the dynamics of interest rates.

In conclusion, partial differential equations are powerful mathematical tools for modeling the dynamics of financial instruments and evaluating financial risks. The use of partial differential equations in finance has revolutionized the field of quantitative finance and enabled the development of sophisticated financial instruments and risk management strategies.

1. Solve the Black-Scholes equation for a European call option with a strike price of $50, a time to maturity of 3 months, a risk-free interest rate of 2%, a dividend yield of 1%, and a volatility of 20%.

2. Use the heat equation to model the temperature distribution in a thin rod of length 1 that is initially at a temperature of 0 and has boundary conditions of 0 at both ends. Solve for the temperature distribution at time $t = 0.1$.

3. Apply the wave equation to model the motion of a guitar string of length 1 that is initially at rest and is plucked at the midpoint. Solve for the displacement of the string at time t = 0.01.

4. Use the Black-Scholes equation to price a European put option with a strike price of $100, a time to maturity of 6 months, a risk-free interest rate of 1.5%, a dividend yield of 2%, and a volatility of 25%.

5. Apply the diffusion equation to model the spread of a disease in a population of 10,000 individuals. Assume an initial infected population of 100 individuals and a diffusion coefficient of 0.1. Solve for the infection rate at time t = 30.

6. Use the heat equation to model the temperature distribution in a circular plate of radius 1 that is initially at a temperature of 0 and has a boundary condition of 0 at the edge. Solve for the temperature distribution at time t = 0.05.

7. Apply the wave equation to model the motion of a piano wire of length 2 that is initially at rest and is struck at one end. Solve for the displacement of the wire at time t = 0.02.

8. Use the Black-Scholes equation to price a European call option with a strike price of $75, a time to maturity of 9 months, a risk-free interest rate of 2.5%, a dividend yield of 1.5%, and a volatility of 30%.

9. Apply the diffusion equation to model the diffusion of a chemical in a container of volume 10. Assume an initial concentration of 5 units and a diffusion coefficient of 0.05. Solve for the concentration at time t = 20.

10. Use the heat equation to model the temperature distribution in a rectangular plate of length 2 and width 1 that is initially at a temperature of 0 and has a boundary condition of 0 on all sides. Solve for the temperature distribution at time t = 0.1.

M.L.Ruscsak

CHAPTER 18: ADVANCED TOPICS IN DIFFERENTIAL EQUATIONS FOR FINANCE

Differential equations play a vital role in finance, especially in the area of quantitative finance. The field of quantitative finance deals with the application of mathematical and statistical methods to financial problems. This involves developing models that can be used to value financial instruments, manage risk, and make investment decisions. Differential equations provide a powerful tool for developing such models, as they allow us to describe the behavior of financial variables over time.

This chapter will cover advanced topics in differential equations for finance. We will discuss some of the more sophisticated techniques used in the valuation of financial instruments, including stochastic calculus, partial differential equations, and Monte Carlo simulation. These techniques are essential for dealing with complex financial instruments that cannot be valued using traditional techniques.

We will begin by discussing stochastic calculus, which is the study of calculus applied to stochastic processes. Stochastic processes are random variables that evolve over time, and they are used to model the behavior of financial variables, such as stock prices or interest rates. Stochastic calculus provides a powerful framework for analyzing such processes, and it is a key tool in the valuation of financial derivatives.

Next, we will discuss partial differential equations (PDEs), which are used to model complex financial instruments, such as options with early exercise features. PDEs provide a powerful tool for valuing such instruments, as they allow us to describe the evolution of the underlying asset price over time. We will discuss some of the most common PDE models used in finance, including the Black-Scholes equation and the Heston model.

Finally, we will discuss Monte Carlo simulation, which is a technique used to value financial instruments by generating random scenarios for the future evolution of financial variables. Monte Carlo simulation provides a powerful tool for modeling complex financial instruments, as it allows us to consider a wide range of possible scenarios and generate probability distributions for the value of the instrument.

Overall, this chapter will provide an overview of some of the more advanced techniques used in differential equations for finance. These techniques are essential for dealing with the complex financial instruments that are becoming increasingly common in today's financial markets. By understanding these techniques, students will be better equipped to analyze financial markets and make informed investment decisions.

Introduction to advanced topics in differential equations for finance

Differential equations play a critical role in the analysis and modeling of financial phenomena. They provide a powerful mathematical tool for describing the complex and dynamic behavior of financial markets, and for developing quantitative models that can be used to make informed investment decisions. In this section, we will introduce advanced topics in differential equations for finance, building on the fundamental concepts and techniques discussed in earlier chapters.

We will begin by reviewing some of the basic concepts in differential equations, including classification, solution methods, and boundary conditions. We will then explore more advanced topics, such as nonlinear and stochastic differential equations, partial differential equations, and numerical methods for solving differential equations.

Nonlinear differential equations arise frequently in financial modeling, where they are used to describe phenomena such as option pricing and asset pricing. We will discuss the characteristics of nonlinear differential equations, including stability and chaos, and examine various methods for analyzing and solving these equations.

Stochastic differential equations are another important class of differential equations that are widely used in finance. These equations incorporate random fluctuations into the dynamics of financial models, which is essential for capturing the inherent uncertainty and volatility of financial markets. We will discuss the properties of stochastic differential equations, such as mean reversion and diffusion, and explore techniques for analyzing and solving these equations.

Partial differential equations are used extensively in finance, particularly for option pricing and risk management. We will provide an introduction to partial differential equations, including classification, solution methods, and boundary conditions. We will then examine specific examples of partial differential equations that are commonly used in finance, such as the Black-Scholes equation and the heat equation.

Numerical methods are essential for solving differential equations in finance, as most real-world problems cannot be solved analytically. We will discuss the basic principles of numerical methods, such as finite difference and finite element methods, and explore their applications in finance. We will also examine advanced numerical methods, such as Monte Carlo simulations and numerical optimization, that are used for solving complex financial models.

In conclusion, the study of advanced topics in differential equations is essential for understanding and modeling the complex behavior of financial markets. By building on the fundamental concepts and techniques discussed in earlier chapters, we can develop sophisticated quantitative models that can be used to make informed investment decisions.

Use of stochastic calculus and partial differential equations in option pricing and risk management

Stochastic calculus and partial differential equations (PDEs) are essential tools in the pricing of options and the management of financial risk. In this section, we will explore the use of stochastic calculus and PDEs in option pricing and risk management.

Stochastic calculus is a branch of mathematics that deals with processes that evolve randomly over time. In finance, stochastic calculus is used to model the behavior of asset prices and other financial variables, such as interest rates and volatilities. One of the most widely used stochastic calculus models is the Black-Scholes-Merton model, which is based on the assumption that asset prices follow a geometric Brownian motion.

However, in reality, asset prices can experience sudden jumps due to unexpected news or events, and the geometric Brownian motion model may not be adequate to capture these sudden jumps. In such cases, jump diffusion models, which combine stochastic calculus and PDEs, can be used to model the dynamics of the underlying asset price and the occurrence of jumps.

The pricing of options involves solving a PDE known as the Black-Scholes equation, which is derived using the Black-Scholes-Merton model. However, the Black-Scholes equation assumes that the option can only be exercised at the expiration date. In reality, some options, such as American options, can be exercised at any time before the expiration date. The valuation of American options involves solving a PDE known as the American option pricing equation, which is more complex than the Black-Scholes equation.

Risk management is an important aspect of financial management, and stochastic calculus and PDEs play a crucial role in managing financial risk. Value at Risk (VaR) is a widely used measure of financial risk, which measures the maximum potential loss that a portfolio may incur over a specified time horizon at a given level of confidence. The calculation of VaR involves solving a PDE known as the VaR equation, which is based on stochastic calculus.

In conclusion, the use of stochastic calculus and PDEs in option pricing and risk management has become increasingly important in the field of finance. Understanding the mathematical concepts and techniques behind these models is crucial for professionals in fields such as investment banking, actuarial science, portfolio management, quantitative analysis, securities trading, financial planning, and financial analysis.

Numerical methods for solving advanced differential equations in finance, including Monte Carlo simulation and finite difference methods

Numerical methods have become an integral part of solving advanced differential equations in finance. They allow practitioners to obtain approximate solutions to complex problems that do not have a closed-form analytical solution. Two of the most commonly used numerical methods in finance are Monte Carlo simulation and finite difference methods. These methods are particularly useful in pricing complex financial derivatives, managing risk, and optimizing portfolios.

Monte Carlo Simulation:

Monte Carlo simulation is a powerful numerical method for pricing financial derivatives and estimating risk. It involves simulating the possible future paths of an underlying asset or portfolio using random numbers. This method is particularly useful when the underlying asset follows a stochastic process that cannot be solved analytically.

The basic steps in a Monte Carlo simulation are as follows:

✧ Specify the stochastic process governing the evolution of the underlying asset(s).

✧ Simulate many possible future paths of the asset(s) using random numbers.

✧ Calculate the payoff of the derivative at each time step for each path.

✧ Average the payoffs across all paths to obtain an estimate of the derivative's price.

✧ Monte Carlo simulation can be used to price a wide variety of derivatives, including options, exotic options, and credit derivatives. It is also useful for estimating Value-at-Risk (VaR), which is a measure of the potential loss of a portfolio over a given time horizon.

Finite Difference Methods:

Finite difference methods are numerical techniques used to solve differential equations by discretizing them into a set of algebraic equations. This method involves approximating the derivatives of the underlying asset using a set of difference equations. These difference equations can then be solved numerically to obtain an approximate solution to the differential equation.

The basic steps in a finite difference method are as follows:

✧ Discretize the domain into a grid.

✧ Approximate the derivatives using finite differences.

M.L.Ruscsak

✧ Write down the difference equations for the discretized problem.

✧ Solve the difference equations numerically to obtain an approximate solution to the differential equation.

✧ Finite difference methods are commonly used in option pricing, risk management, and portfolio optimization. They are particularly useful when the underlying asset follows a diffusion process and the option pricing problem is formulated as a partial differential equation.

Conclusion:

Numerical methods such as Monte Carlo simulation and finite difference methods are essential tools for solving advanced differential equations in finance. They provide practitioners with a flexible and powerful way to approximate complex problems that do not have an analytical solution. These methods have wide-ranging applications in option pricing, risk management, and portfolio optimization. Students seeking a career in finance should have a strong understanding of these numerical methods and their applications.

Math Exercises:

1. Use Monte Carlo simulation to price a European call option on a stock that follows a geometric Brownian motion process.

2. Use Monte Carlo simulation to estimate the VaR of a portfolio consisting of stocks and bonds.

3. Use finite difference methods to price a European put option on a stock that follows a diffusion process.

4. Use finite difference methods to price an American call option on a stock that follows a diffusion process.

5. Use Monte Carlo simulation to price a lookback option on a stock that follows a stochastic volatility model.

6. Use finite difference methods to solve the Black-Scholes partial differential equation for a European call option.

7. Use Monte Carlo simulation to estimate the expected shortfall of a portfolio consisting of options.

8. Use finite difference methods to price a barrier option on a stock that follows a diffusion process.

9. Use Monte Carlo simulation to price a credit default swap on a bond.

10. Use finite difference methods to solve the Heston partial differential equation for a European call option.

Traditional math problems and equations related to advanced differential equations in finance

In finance, advanced differential equations are used to model various financial instruments and their prices. These equations often involve complex mathematical concepts, such as stochastic calculus and partial differential equations, making them difficult to solve analytically. As a result, numerical methods are often used to solve these equations.

However, it's important to have a good understanding of traditional math problems and equations related to advanced differential equations in finance. These problems form the building blocks of advanced differential equations and are essential for understanding the underlying concepts. In this section, we will explore some of these traditional math problems and equations.

Stochastic Differential Equations:

Stochastic differential equations (SDEs) are used to model financial processes that involve randomness or uncertainty. These equations are similar to ordinary differential equations, but with an additional stochastic term.

M.L.Ruscsak

One example of an SDE is the geometric Brownian motion, which is used in the Black-Scholes model. This equation is given by:

$$dS_t = \mu S_t dt + \sigma S_t dW_t$$

where S is the price of the asset, μ is the expected return, σ is the volatility, and dW is a Wiener process (a type of random walk).

Solving SDEs is difficult, but there are several numerical methods available, including the Euler-Maruyama method and the Milstein method. These methods involve discretizing the equation in time and then using approximations to solve the equation at each time step.

Numerical Integration:

Numerical integration is a numerical method used to approximate the value of a definite integral. In finance, numerical integration is often used to calculate the value of option prices.

For example, to price a European call option using numerical integration, we can use the followingsteps:

Define the function that represents the payoff of the option at expiration, which depends on the stock price at expiration.

Calculate the expected payoff of the option at expiration by integrating the function over all possible stock prices at expiration, weighted by the probability density function of the stock price at expiration.

Discount the expected payoff back to the present value using the risk-free interest rate.

The resulting value is the price of the option.

One method for numerical integration is the trapezoidal rule, which approximates the area under a curve by approximating the curve with a series of trapezoids. The more trapezoids used, the more accurate the approximation.

Another method for numerical integration is Simpson's rule, which approximates the area under a curve by approximating the curve with a series of parabolic curves. Simpson's rule can be more accurate than the trapezoidal rule with fewer intervals, but requires the function to be twice-differentiable.

In addition to numerical integration, other numerical methods used in finance include Monte Carlo simulation and finite difference methods. Monte Carlo simulation is a method for solving complex mathematical problems using random numbers, and can be used to price options by simulating the future prices of the underlying asset. Finite difference methods approximate the solutions of partial differential equations using a discretization of the domain and finite difference approximations of the derivatives.

Overall, numerical methods play an important role in the field of finance by allowing complex mathematical models to be solved efficiently and accurately.

1. Evaluate the integral of e^x from 0 to 1 using the trapezoidal rule with n = 4.

2. Use Simpson's rule to approximate the integral of cos(x) from 0 to pi/2 with n = 6.

3. Calculate the value of the integral of ln(x) from 1 to 2 using the midpoint rule with n = 8.

4. Use the trapezoidal rule with n = 10 to approximate the integral of sin(x) from 0 to pi.

5. Estimate the value of the integral of x^2 + 1 from 0 to 2 using Simpson's rule with n = 5.

6. Evaluate the integral of 1/x from 1 to 3 using the trapezoidal rule with n = 6.

7. Use the midpoint rule with n = 4 to approximate the integral of e^(-x^2) from 0 to 1.

8. Calculate the value of the integral of x*sin(x) from 0 to pi/2 using Simpson's rule with n = 6.

9. Estimate the integral of (1+x^2)^(-1) from 0 to 1 using the trapezoidal rule with n = 8.

10. Use Simpson's rule with n = 10 to approximate the integral of e^(2x) from 0 to 1.

11. Evaluate the integral of (1+x)^(-2) from 0 to 1 using the midpoint rule with n = 6.

12. Calculate the value of the integral of ln(1+x) from 0 to 1 using the trapezoidal rule with n = 10.

13. Estimate the integral of (2x+1)^(-1) from 0 to 2 using Simpson's rule with n = 5.

14. Use the midpoint rule with n = 8 to approximate the integral of x*cos(x) from 0 to pi.

15. Evaluate the integral of 1/(1+x^2) from 0 to 1 using the trapezoidal rule with n = 4.

16. Calculate the value of the integral of x*e^(2x) from 0 to 1 using Simpson's rule with n = 10.

17. Estimate the integral of (1-x)^(-1/2) from 0 to 0.5 using the trapezoidal rule with n = 8.

18. Use Simpson's rule with n = 6 to approximate the integral of e^(x^2) from 0 to 1.

19. Evaluate the integral of 1/(1+x) from 0 to 1 using the midpoint rule with n = 10.

20. Calculate the value of the integral of x^2*e^x from 0 to 1 using the trapezoidal rule with n = 6.

21. Estimate the integral of cos(x^2) from 0 to pi/4 using Simpson's rule with n = 4.

22. Use the midpoint rule with n = 5 to approximate the integral of ln(x) from 1 to 2.

23. Evaluate the integral of 1/(x+1) from 0 to 2 using the trapezoidal rule with n = 8.

24. Calculate the value of the integral of x^3*e^(x^2) from 0 to 1 using Simpson's rule with n = 10.

PART 7: FINANCIAL ENGINEERING

Financial engineering is a multidisciplinary field that involves the application of mathematical models, statistical techniques, and computer programming to solve complex financial problems. It emerged in the 1980s as a response to the growing demand for sophisticated financial products and services. Since then, financial engineering has become an essential part of the financial industry, helping companies manage risk, optimize investment strategies, and create innovative financial products.

The goal of financial engineering is to use mathematical and computational methods to design financial instruments that meet the needs of investors and issuers. These instruments can include stocks, bonds, options, futures, and derivatives. By analyzing market trends and using advanced mathematical models, financial engineers can create products that are tailored to specific market conditions and investor preferences.

The field of financial engineering is multidisciplinary, combining elements of finance, mathematics, economics, statistics, and computer science. Financial engineers must have a deep understanding of financial markets and products, as well as the mathematical and computational tools needed to model and analyze financial data.

One of the key areas of financial engineering is risk management. Financial engineers use sophisticated mathematical models to measure and manage risk in financial portfolios. These models can take into account a wide range of factors, such as market volatility, credit risk, and interest rate risk. By carefully managing risk, financial engineers can help investors maximize returns while minimizing the possibility of losses.

Another area of financial engineering is quantitative analysis. Financial engineers use advanced mathematical techniques to analyze financial data and develop investment strategies. These strategies can be based on factors such as historical market data, economic indicators, and investor sentiment. By using quantitative analysis, financial engineers can identify patterns and trends in financial data that may not be visible to the naked eye.

Financial engineering has become increasingly important in the wake of the global financial crisis of 2008. In the aftermath of the crisis, financial institutions faced new regulatory requirements and increased pressure to manage risk and improve transparency. Financial engineering has played a crucial role in helping these institutions navigate the complex regulatory landscape and develop innovative solutions to meet the needs of investors.

In this section, we will explore the key concepts and techniques used in financial engineering. We will examine the mathematical models and computational tools used to analyze financial data, manage risk, and develop investment strategies. We will also examine the role of financial engineering in the broader financial industry, and the challenges and opportunities that lie ahead for this rapidly evolving field.

CHAPTER 19: OVERVIEW OF FINANCIAL ENGINEERING

Financial engineering is a branch of finance that combines mathematical and engineering techniques to design financial products, models, and strategies. It involves the use of advanced mathematical models, statistical analysis, computer programming, and financial theory to create and manage complex financial instruments and products. Financial engineering is essential for modern financial markets, as it helps to manage risks, create investment opportunities, and design innovative financial products that meet the diverse needs of investors and businesses.

The origins of financial engineering can be traced back to the 1970s, when the Black-Scholes model was developed to price options. The model revolutionized the financial industry by providing a mathematical framework for valuing options and other derivatives. It also laid the foundation for further advances in financial engineering, such as the development of interest rate models, credit risk models, and portfolio optimization techniques.

Today, financial engineering is used in a wide range of financial applications, including asset management, risk management, trading, and investment banking. It has become an integral part of the financial industry, as it enables market participants to create and manage sophisticated financial products and strategies that were previously impossible or impractical.

One of the key strengths of financial engineering is its ability to combine different financial instruments to create new products that meet the specific needs of investors and businesses. For example, financial engineers can combine stocks, bonds, and options to create structured products that offer customized risk-return profiles. They can also design derivatives that provide insurance against specific risks, such as interest rate movements, currency fluctuations, or commodity price changes.

Financial engineering is also essential for managing risk in financial markets. It enables market participants to quantify and manage various types of risk, such as market risk, credit risk, and operational risk. By using advanced risk management techniques, financial engineers can help investors and businesses to minimize the impact of adverse events on their portfolios and operations.

In this chapter, we will provide an overview of financial engineering, including its history, key concepts, and applications. We will also discuss the different types of financial instruments and products that financial engineers can create, as well as the mathematical and engineering techniques used in financial engineering. Finally, we will examine the challenges and opportunities in financial engineering, and how it can contribute to the future development of financial markets.

M.L.Ruscsak

Introduction to financial engineering and its applications in finance

Financial engineering is a field that combines mathematics, computer science, finance, and economics to create financial instruments and products that meet the needs of investors, traders, and financial institutions. Financial engineers use mathematical models and algorithms to develop investment strategies, risk management techniques, and hedging instruments. The field has gained popularity in recent years due to its ability to create complex financial products that can be customized to meet the needs of individual investors or institutions.

Financial engineering has many applications in finance, including portfolio management, risk management, derivative pricing, and trading strategies. The use of financial engineering in these areas has allowed for more sophisticated investment strategies and better risk management techniques. In this section, we will provide an overview of financial engineering and its applications in finance.

Overview of Financial Engineering

Financial engineering is a broad field that encompasses many different areas of finance. At its core, financial engineering involves the use of mathematical models and computer algorithms to create financial products and strategies that meet the needs of investors and financial institutions. Financial engineering can be applied to many different areas of finance, including portfolio management, risk management, derivative pricing, and trading strategies.

Portfolio Management

Portfolio management is the process of selecting and managing a portfolio of investments in order to achieve a specific investment objective. Financial engineers use mathematical models to analyze and optimize portfolios to achieve the desired return for a given level of risk. This involves creating a diversified portfolio of assets that is tailored to the specific investment objectives of the investor.

Risk Management

Risk management is the process of identifying, assessing, and managing risks that could affect an investment portfolio. Financial engineers use mathematical models to analyze and quantify the risks associated with different investments and create risk management strategies that minimize the impact of these risks. This involves hedging against risks using financial instruments such as options, futures, and swaps.

Derivative Pricing

Derivative pricing is the process of determining the value of financial instruments such as options, futures, and swaps. Financial engineers use mathematical models to calculate the fair value of these instruments and to develop pricing strategies that take into account the risks associated with these instruments. This involves using mathematical models to simulate the behavior of financial instruments and to determine their value under different market conditions.

Trading Strategies

Trading strategies are the methods and techniques used by traders to make investment decisions. Financial engineers use mathematical models and algorithms to create trading strategies that take into account market conditions, historical data, and other factors that may affect the performance of investments. This involves creating algorithms that can analyze large amounts of data in real-time and make investment decisions based on this data.

Conclusion

Financial engineering is a rapidly evolving field that has many applications in finance. It involves the use of mathematical models and computer algorithms to create financial products and strategies that meet the needs of investors and financial institutions. Financial engineering has allowed for more sophisticated investment strategies and better risk management techniques, making it an important field in modern finance. In the following sections, we will explore some of the key concepts and tools used in financial engineering, including options pricing, stochastic calculus, and Monte Carlo simulation.

Historical overview of financial engineering and its development

Financial engineering is a field of study that emerged in the late 1970s and early 1980s, as financial markets began to rapidly evolve and increase in complexity. This field is the intersection of finance, mathematics, statistics, and computer science. It involves the development of financial models, investment strategies, and risk management techniques, with the aim of creating financial products that meet the specific needs of investors and businesses.

The development of financial engineering can be traced back to the early days of financial markets, when basic financial instruments such as stocks, bonds, and options were traded. However, it was not until the 1970s that the field began to emerge as a formal discipline. The growth of financial engineering was driven in part by the increasing use of computers and quantitative methods in finance.

One of the pioneers of financial engineering was Fischer Black, who along with Myron Scholes, developed the Black-Scholes model for option pricing in 1973. This model is still widely used today, and was a major breakthrough in the field of financial engineering. Black also played a key role in the development of the Capital Asset Pricing Model (CAPM), which is another widely used model in finance.

Another important figure in the history of financial engineering is Robert Merton, who worked with Black and Scholes to develop the Black-Scholes-Merton model, an extension of the Black-Scholes model that takes into account the possibility of default by the issuer of the option. Merton also made significant contributions to the development of other financial models and risk management techniques.

The field of financial engineering continued to evolve in the 1980s and 1990s, as financial markets became increasingly global and interconnected. This led to the development of new financial instruments such as swaps, futures, and derivatives, which required increasingly sophisticated models and techniques to accurately price and manage risk.

The financial crisis of 2008 highlighted the importance of risk management and the limitations of financial models. The crisis led to increased scrutiny of financial engineering and its role in the financial system. However, despite these challenges, the field of financial engineering continues to play an important role in the development of new financial products and investment strategies.

In summary, financial engineering has a relatively short but rich history. The field has been shaped by the rapid evolution of financial markets and the increasing use of quantitative methods and computer science in finance. Pioneers such as Fischer Black and Robert Merton played a critical role in the development of financial models and risk management techniques, and their contributions continue to be felt today. Despite challenges and criticisms, the field of financial engineering remains a dynamic and important area of study in finance.

CHAPTER 20: MATHEMATICAL MODELS IN FINANCIAL ENGINEERING

Financial engineering is an interdisciplinary field that combines financial theory, mathematics, statistics, and computer science to design and develop innovative financial products and solutions. One of the essential tools used in financial engineering is mathematical modeling, which allows the quantitative analysis of financial data and the evaluation of financial risks.

In this chapter, we will explore mathematical models in financial engineering, including their applications and limitations. We will begin by discussing the importance of mathematical models in finance and financial engineering, followed by an overview of the different types of models used in finance.

We will also delve into the assumptions and limitations of mathematical models and their potential impact on the accuracy of financial predictions. Additionally, we will discuss the role of computer simulations in financial modeling, including their advantages and disadvantages.

Overall, this chapter aims to provide students with a comprehensive understanding of mathematical models in financial engineering, their applications in the financial industry, and the challenges and limitations involved in their development and use.

Importance of Mathematical Models in Finance

Mathematical models are essential in finance and financial engineering, as they enable analysts and practitioners to understand complex financial data and make informed decisions. They help to quantify financial risks, forecast future trends, and develop investment strategies.

For example, mathematical models can be used to price financial derivatives, such as options, futures, and swaps, by estimating the probabilities of different market outcomes. These models provide a framework for evaluating the risk and return of financial instruments, which is crucial for investment management and portfolio optimization.

Furthermore, mathematical models are used in risk management, where they enable financial institutions to assess their exposure to various types of risk, such as credit risk, market risk, and operational risk. By developing mathematical models that account for different sources of risk, financial institutions can identify and mitigate potential losses, thereby safeguarding their financial stability.

Types of Mathematical Models in Finance

✧ There are different types of mathematical models used in finance, depending on the specific problem being addressed. Some of the most commonly used models include:

✧ Black-Scholes Model: This model is used to price European options and is based on the assumption that stock prices follow a log-normal distribution.

✧ Binomial Option Pricing Model: This model is used to price American options and assumes that the price of the underlying asset can take only two values in each time period.

✧ Monte Carlo Simulation: This model is used to simulate the behavior of financial instruments by generating a large number of random samples from the probability distribution of the underlying asset.

✧ Value at Risk (VaR) Model: This model is used to measure the maximum loss that a portfolio of financial assets could experience with a given probability over a specified period.

Assumptions and Limitations of Mathematical Models

While mathematical models are powerful tools for analyzing financial data, they are not perfect and are subject to certain assumptions and limitations. For example, models that assume a normal distribution of market returns may not be accurate in extreme market conditions, such as during a financial crisis.

Additionally, models may be based on incomplete or inaccurate data, which can lead to incorrect predictions. Moreover, the assumptions made in developing a model may not hold in real-world situations, making it difficult to apply the model to practical problems.

Therefore, it is essential to use mathematical models in conjunction with other analytical tools and to regularly review and update them to reflect changing market conditions and data.

Role of Computer Simulations in Financial Modeling

Computer simulations are an integral part of financial modeling, as they allow analysts to simulate the behavior of financial instruments under different scenarios. They are particularly useful for analyzing complex financial products, such as structured products and derivatives, which involve multiple underlying assets and cash flows.

However, computer simulations also have limitations. They require a large amount of computational power and can be time-consuming, particularly when simulating large portfolios of financial instruments. Additionally, they rely on assumptions and inputs that may not accurately reflect the behavior of financial markets, which can lead to inaccuracies in the results.

To mitigate these limitations, financial engineers use a variety of mathematical models to describe the behavior of financial instruments and markets. These models are based on mathematical concepts such as probability theory, stochastic calculus, and optimization theory, and allow analysts to make predictions about the behavior of financial instruments and markets under different scenarios.

One of the most widely used mathematical models in financial engineering is the Black-Scholes model, which is used to price options. The Black-Scholes model is based on the assumption that stock prices follow a geometric Brownian motion, and it allows analysts to calculate the theoretical value of an option based on inputs such as the stock price, strike price, time to expiration, risk-free interest rate, and volatility.

Other popular models used in financial engineering include the binomial option pricing model, the Monte Carlo simulation model, and the Vasicek model for interest rate modeling. Each of these models has its own strengths and weaknesses, and financial engineers must carefully consider which model is appropriate for a particular application.

In addition to mathematical modeling, financial engineering also involves the use of computational tools and programming languages such as MATLAB, Python, and R. These tools allow analysts to implement and test financial models, simulate the behavior of financial instruments and markets, and analyze large amounts of financial data.

Overall, financial engineering is an important field that plays a critical role in the development and implementation of financial products and strategies. By combining mathematical modeling, computer simulations, and computational tools, financial engineers are able to create innovative financial products that meet the needs of investors and businesses while managing risk and uncertainty.

Use of mathematical models in finance, including stochastic calculus and option pricing models

The use of mathematical models in finance has become increasingly popular over the past few decades. Mathematical models are used to understand and predict financial market behavior, and they are essential in making informed investment decisions. These models are based on mathematical equations and statistical analysis of historical data.

M.L.Ruscsak

One of the most widely used mathematical models in finance is stochastic calculus. Stochastic calculus is a branch of mathematics that deals with random variables and their evolution over time. It is used to model the behavior of financial instruments, such as stocks, bonds, and options, which are subject to random price movements. Stochastic calculus has been used to develop a variety of models, such as the Black-Scholes model, which is widely used for option pricing.

Option pricing models are used to determine the fair value of options contracts. Options contracts give the buyer the right, but not the obligation, to buy or sell an underlying asset at a predetermined price and time. The Black-Scholes model is a widely used option pricing model that uses stochastic calculus to determine the fair value of options contracts. It takes into account various factors such as the current price of the underlying asset, the strike price, the time to expiration, and the volatility of the underlying asset.

Another widely used model in finance is the binomial options pricing model. This model is used to price options contracts that have more complex payoff structures. It is based on the assumption that the underlying asset can move up or down by a certain percentage in each time period. The model then calculates the probability of the asset moving up or down, and the expected payoff at each node of the tree. This allows analysts to determine the fair value of options contracts that have more complex payoff structures, such as American options, which can be exercised at any time before expiration.

In addition to option pricing models, mathematical models are used in a variety of other applications in finance. For example, they are used in portfolio optimization, risk management, and asset pricing. Portfolio optimization models are used to determine the optimal mix of assets in a portfolio based on the investor's risk preferences and return expectations. Risk management models are used to identify and manage risks in a portfolio, such as credit risk and market risk. Asset pricing models are used to determine the fair value of various financial assets, such as stocks and bonds.

However, mathematical models in finance are not without their limitations. One of the major challenges is that financial markets are constantly evolving, and historical data may not always be a good indicator of future performance. In addition, models are often based on assumptions that may not hold true in all market conditions. For example, the Black-Scholes model assumes that the underlying asset follows a lognormal distribution, which may not always be the case.

Furthermore, the use of mathematical models in finance can be controversial. Some critics argue that models are often used to justify risky investment strategies and may give investors a false sense of security. They also argue that models can be manipulated to produce desired results, leading to unintended consequences.

In conclusion, mathematical models have become an essential tool in finance, allowing analysts to understand and predict financial market behavior. They have been used to develop a variety of models, such as option pricing models, portfolio optimization models, risk management models, and asset pricing models. While these models have limitations, they are an important tool in making informed investment decisions. It is important for investors to understand the assumptions and limitations of these models and to use them in conjunction with other analytical tools and expert judgment.

Exercise:

1. What is stochastic calculus and how is it used in finance?

2. What is the Black-Scholes model and what is it used for?

3. What is the binomial options pricing model and how is it different from the Black-Scholes model?

4. Explain the concept of implied volatility and its relationship with option pricing.

5. Describe the assumptions and limitations of the Black-Scholes model.

6. Discuss how the binomial options pricing model can be used to value American options.

7. Provide an example of how the Monte Carlo simulation can be used to value financial derivatives.

Implied volatility is a measure of the market's expectation for future volatility of an underlying asset. It is calculated by taking the market price of an option and solving for the volatility that would make the Black-Scholes model's theoretical value of the option equal to the market price. Implied volatility is important in option pricing because it can be used to infer the market's expectation for future price movements of the underlying asset. Higher implied volatility indicates that the market expects greater price movements, which leads to higher option prices.

The Black-Scholes model is a mathematical model used to value European-style options. It is based on several assumptions, including constant volatility, no dividends paid on the underlying asset, and efficient markets. The model assumes that the underlying asset follows a geometric Brownian motion and that the risk-free interest rate is constant over the life of the option. Some of the limitations of the Black-Scholes model include its assumptions, such as the assumption of constant volatility, which may not hold in real-world markets. Additionally, the model assumes that the underlying asset follows a continuous process, which may not be the case for certain types of assets.

The binomial options pricing model is a discrete-time model used to value American-style options. It assumes that the underlying asset can move up or down by a certain percentage in each period and that the risk-free interest rate is constant. The model works by constructing a binomial tree that represents the possible price movements of the underlying asset over time. At each node of the tree, the option is valued using the risk-neutral probabilities of the underlying asset moving up or down. The binomial options pricing model is different from the Black-Scholes model in that it can handle American-style options and does not require the assumption of constant volatility.

Monte Carlo simulation is a computational technique used to value financial derivatives by simulating the future price movements of the underlying asset. The method involves generating a large number of random price paths for the underlying asset based on its historical volatility and using these paths to calculate the expected payoff of the derivative. Monte Carlo simulation can be used to value a wide range of financial derivatives, including options, forwards, and swaps. For example, it can be used to value a European call option on a stock by simulating the future price movements of the stock and using these simulations to calculate the expected payoff of the option.

Overview of option pricing models, including the Black-Scholes model and its assumptions

Options are financial contracts that give the holder the right, but not the obligation, to buy or sell an underlying asset at a predetermined price and date. Options are used by investors and traders to hedge risks and speculate on future market movements. The price of an option is determined by a variety of factors, including the current price of the underlying asset, the option's strike price, the time to expiration, and the volatility of the underlying asset. Option pricing models use mathematical techniques to determine the fair value of an option based on these factors.

One of the most widely used option pricing models is the Black-Scholes model, developed by Fischer Black and Myron Scholes in 1973. The Black-Scholes model assumes that the underlying asset follows a random walk and that the option is European-style, meaning it can only be exercised on the expiration date. The model also assumes that there are no dividends paid on the underlying asset, and that the risk-free rate of return and volatility of the underlying asset are constant over the life of the option.

The Black-Scholes model uses the following formula to determine the fair value of a call option:

$$C = SN(d1) - Xe^{(-rT)} * N(d2)$$

where C is the fair value of the call option, S is the current price of the underlying asset, X is the option's strike price, r is the risk-free rate of return, T is the time to expiration, and d1 and d2 are calculated as follows:

$$d1 = [ln(S/X) + (r + (\sigma^2)/2)T] / (\sigma sqrt(T))$$
$$d2 = d1 - \sigma * sqrt(T)$$

In this formula, σ represents the volatility of the underlying asset.

The Black-Scholes model is a powerful tool for valuing options, but it has some limitations. One of the main criticisms of the Black-Scholes model is that it assumes that the volatility of the underlying asset is constant over the life of the option, which is often not the case in practice. Other criticisms include the assumption of no dividends and the assumption of a constant risk-free rate of return.

Another popular option pricing model is the binomial options pricing model, which was developed by Cox, Ross, and Rubinstein in 1979. The binomial model assumes that the underlying asset can either go up or down in value at each time step, and that the option can be exercised at any time prior to expiration. The model calculates the fair value of the option by working backwards from the expiration date, creating a binomial tree of possible future prices for the underlying asset.

The binomial model can be used to value both European and American-style options and can handle options with complex features, such as path-dependent options. However, it requires more computational power than the Black-Scholes model and can be more difficult to implement in practice.

In summary, option pricing models are essential tools for valuing options and managing risk in financial markets. The Black-Scholes model and the binomial options pricing model are two of the most widely used models, each with its own strengths and weaknesses. Investors and traders must carefully consider the assumptions and limitations of these models when using them to value options and make investment decisions.

Analysis of the strengths and weaknesses of various option pricing models

M.L.Ruscsak

Option pricing models are essential tools used by financial practitioners and researchers to determine the fair value of an option. These models come with their own set of strengths and weaknesses, which are important to consider when selecting a model for a particular application. In this section, we will analyze the strengths and weaknesses of various option pricing models, including the Black-Scholes model, the binomial options pricing model, and the Monte Carlo simulation method.

Black-Scholes Model:

The Black-Scholes model is a widely used option pricing model that was introduced in 1973 by Fischer Black and Myron Scholes. The model provides a closed-form solution for the price of a European call or put option, assuming that the underlying asset follows a lognormal distribution and that there are no dividends paid on the underlying asset. The model takes into account the risk-free rate of return, the volatility of the underlying asset, the time to expiration of the option, and the strike price of the option.

The strengths of the Black-Scholes model include its simplicity, its ability to provide a quick and accurate estimate of the fair value of an option, and its applicability to a wide range of underlying assets, including stocks, bonds, currencies, and commodities. Additionally, the Black-Scholes model provides insights into the relationships between the parameters that determine the price of an option, such as the relationship between the volatility of the underlying asset and the price of the option.

However, the Black-Scholes model has its weaknesses. Firstly, it assumes that the underlying asset follows a lognormal distribution, which may not always be the case in practice. Secondly, the model assumes that there are no dividends paid on the underlying asset, which may not be true for many stocks. Lastly, the Black-Scholes model assumes that the risk-free rate of return is constant over time, which may not hold true in reality.

Binomial Options Pricing Model:

The binomial options pricing model is a discrete-time option pricing model that was introduced by Cox, Ross, and Rubinstein in 1979. The model provides a tree-like representation of the possible prices that the underlying asset can take on at each time step, with the price of the option being determined by backward induction through the tree. The model takes into account the risk-free rate of return, the volatility of the underlying asset, the time to expiration of the option, and the strike price of the option.

The strengths of the binomial options pricing model include its ability to handle a wide range of underlying asset price distributions, including those that are not lognormal, and its ability to incorporate dividends paid on the underlying asset. Additionally, the binomial model can be easily adapted to handle American-style options, which can be exercised at any time prior to expiration.

However, the binomial options pricing model also has its weaknesses. Firstly, it can be computationally intensive and time-consuming to calculate, especially for options with a large number of time steps. Secondly, the model assumes that the volatility of the underlying asset remains constant over time, which may not be true in practice.

Monte Carlo Simulation Method:

The Monte Carlo simulation method is a stochastic simulation method that was introduced in the early 20th century by Enrico Fermi and Stanislaw Ulam. The method involves simulating the possible future paths of the underlying asset, using random numbers to generate a set of possible outcomes for the asset price at each time step. The price of the option is then determined by averaging the payoff of the option across the simulated paths. The Monte Carlo simulation method takes into account the risk-free rate of return, the volatility of the underlying asset, the time to expiration of the option, and the strike price of the option.

The strengths of the Monte Carlo simulation method include its ability to handle a wide range of complex financial instruments and to incorporate a large number of factors that can affect the price of an option. Additionally, Monte Carlo simulations can be used to generate a large number of potential outcomes, making it possible to get a more accurate estimate of the value of an option compared to other pricing models. Furthermore, the Monte Carlo simulation method is very flexible, allowing analysts to model a wide variety of option contracts, including American options, exotic options, and multi-asset options.

However, the Monte Carlo simulation method also has several weaknesses. One of the main weaknesses is its computational complexity. Monte Carlo simulations require a large number of iterations to achieve accurate results, which can be time-consuming and computationally expensive. Moreover, the Monte Carlo simulation method requires the input of a number of parameters, including the volatility of the underlying asset, which can be difficult to estimate accurately. Additionally, the Monte Carlo simulation method may not provide a closed-form solution, which can make it difficult to compare results with other models.

Despite its limitations, the Monte Carlo simulation method remains a popular choice for pricing complex financial instruments. In particular, it is widely used for valuing options on assets with complex price dynamics, such as commodities and energy products, as well as for credit risk modeling and economic scenario analysis.

Exercise:

M.L.Ruscsak

1. What is the Monte Carlo simulation method and how is it used in option pricing?

2. What are the strengths of the Monte Carlo simulation method in option pricing?

3. What are the weaknesses of the Monte Carlo simulation method in option pricing?

4. In what types of financial instruments is the Monte Carlo simulation method particularly useful?

CHAPTER 21: NUMERICAL METHODS IN FINANCIAL ENGINEERING

The field of financial engineering involves the use of mathematical and computational techniques to model and analyze financial markets, instruments, and transactions. These techniques help to quantify the risk and return associated with different financial instruments and to design new financial products that meet the needs of investors and issuers.

Numerical methods are a key component of financial engineering, as they provide a powerful tool for solving the complex mathematical equations that underlie financial models. These methods involve the use of computers to perform calculations and simulations, enabling analysts to quickly and accurately evaluate different financial scenarios.

In this chapter, we will provide an overview of the numerical methods commonly used in financial engineering, including:

Finite difference methods
Monte Carlo simulation
Binomial tree methods
Fourier transform methods
PDE methods

We will discuss the basic principles of each method and provide examples of how they are used in financial engineering. We will also examine the strengths and weaknesses of each method, as well as their suitability for different types of financial models.

This chapter is aimed at students with a basic understanding of calculus, probability theory, and financial markets. It is intended to provide an introduction to the numerical methods used in financial engineering, rather than a comprehensive treatment of each method. Students who wish to explore these methods in greater depth should consult the relevant literature and textbooks.

Overall, this chapter aims to provide a solid foundation in numerical methods for financial engineering, enabling students to understand and apply these techniques in their future studies and careers. By the end of this chapter, students should be able to:

Understand the principles behind the different numerical methods used in financial engineering.

M.L.Ruscsak

Evaluate the strengths and weaknesses of each method.
Apply these methods to solve financial engineering problems.
Analyze the results of numerical simulations and apply them to financial decision-making.

We hope that this chapter will provide a useful introduction to the important field of numerical methods in financial engineering. Let us begin our exploration of these methods with finite difference methods.

Overview of numerical methods commonly used in financial engineering, including Monte Carlo simulation and finite difference methods

Financial engineering is a field of study that applies mathematical, statistical, and computational techniques to financial problems. One of the key challenges in financial engineering is pricing complex financial instruments that cannot be valued using closed-form solutions. This requires the development and application of numerical methods to approximate the solution of complex mathematical equations.

Numerical methods are algorithms that use numerical approximations to solve mathematical problems. In financial engineering, numerical methods are used to solve partial differential equations (PDEs) and stochastic differential equations (SDEs) that arise in the pricing of financial derivatives. The two most commonly used numerical methods in financial engineering are Monte Carlo simulation and finite difference methods.

Overview of Numerical Methods in Financial Engineering

Monte Carlo Simulation

Monte Carlo simulation is a numerical method that uses random sampling to solve complex mathematical problems. It was first introduced in the early 20th century by Enrico Fermi and Stanislaw Ulam, and has since become a popular method for pricing financial derivatives.

In the context of financial engineering, Monte Carlo simulation is used to simulate the possible future paths of the underlying asset, using random numbers to generate a set of possible outcomes for the asset price at each time step. The price of the option is then determined by averaging the payoff of the option across the simulated paths. The Monte Carlo simulation method takes into account the risk-free rate of return, the volatility of the underlying asset, the time to expiration of the option, and the strike price of the option.

One of the strengths of the Monte Carlo simulation method is its ability to handle a wide range of complex financial instruments. It can be used to price options with complex payoff structures and exotic features, such as barrier options, Asian options, and basket options. It can also be used to model complex financial instruments that depend on multiple underlying assets, such as options on spreads and options on baskets.

However, one of the limitations of the Monte Carlo simulation method is its computational intensity. It requires a large number of simulations to achieve accurate results, which can be computationally expensive and time-consuming. Additionally, Monte Carlo simulation is subject to variance reduction techniques to increase its efficiency.

Finite Difference Methods

Finite difference methods are numerical methods that approximate the solution of a differential equation at discrete points in space and time. In financial engineering, finite difference methods are used to solve PDEs and SDEs that arise in the pricing of financial derivatives.

In the context of financial engineering, finite difference methods involve discretizing the underlying asset price and time domain, and approximating the partial derivatives in the PDE or SDE using finite differences. The discretized PDE or SDE is then solved using numerical techniques such as the explicit, implicit or Crank-Nicolson schemes.

One of the strengths of finite difference methods is their ability to handle a wide range of financial instruments, including options with complex payoffs and exotic features. They can also be used to model complex financial instruments that depend on multiple underlying assets, such as options on spreads and options on baskets. Finite difference methods can be faster and more computationally efficient than Monte Carlo simulation, making them a popular choice in certain circumstances.

However, one of the limitations of finite difference methods is their accuracy and stability. The numerical approximation of the PDE or SDE can introduce numerical errors and instability, which can lead to inaccurate results. Additionally, finite difference methods can be sensitive to the choice of the discretization scheme, the step sizes in space and time, and the boundary and initial conditions.

Conclusion

In conclusion, numerical methods are a crucial tool in financial engineering for pricing complex financial instruments that cannot be valued using closed-form solutions. Monte Carlo simulation and finite difference methods are two commonly used numerical methods in financial engineering. Monte Carlo simulation is a powerful method for handling a wide range of complex financial instruments that exhibit nonlinear behavior, while finite difference methods are efficient and widely used for pricing options with simple payoff structures. It is important for financial engineers to have a solid understanding of these numerical methods and their underlying principles to ensure accurate and efficient pricing of financial instruments.

M.L.Ruscsak

While both Monte Carlo simulation and finite difference methods have their respective strengths and weaknesses, the choice of which method to use ultimately depends on the specific characteristics of the financial instrument being priced, as well as the computational resources available.

As technology continues to advance, numerical methods in financial engineering are likely to become even more important, enabling the development of increasingly complex financial instruments and strategies. Therefore, it is imperative that financial engineers continue to develop and refine these methods to meet the demands of an ever-evolving financial landscape.

Overall, numerical methods have revolutionized the field of financial engineering, enabling the pricing of complex financial instruments that were previously thought to be impossible to value. As such, they are a critical tool for financial engineers, and will continue to play an essential role in the development and implementation of innovative financial instruments and strategies.

Detailed explanation of Monte Carlo simulation, including the Monte Carlo method and its application in finance

Monte Carlo Simulation Method

The Monte Carlo simulation method is a stochastic simulation method that was introduced in the early 20th century by Enrico Fermi and Stanislaw Ulam. The method involves simulating the possible future paths of the underlying asset, using random numbers to generate a set of possible outcomes for the asset price at each time step. The price of the option is then determined by averaging the payoff of the option across the simulated paths. The Monte Carlo simulation method takes into account the risk-free rate of return, the volatility of the underlying asset, the time to expiration of the option, and the strike price of the option.

The Monte Carlo simulation method is widely used in finance for pricing complex financial instruments such as options, bonds, and derivatives. It allows for the incorporation of various factors that affect the value of these instruments, including market conditions, interest rates, and volatility.

Monte Carlo Method

The Monte Carlo method involves generating random numbers to simulate the possible future paths of the underlying asset. The method uses a computer algorithm to generate a large number of random numbers, which are then used to generate a set of possible outcomes for the asset price at each time step. These outcomes are then used to calculate the expected value of the option, which is the average payoff of the option across all simulated paths.

The Monte Carlo method can handle a wide range of complex financial instruments, including options with multiple factors that affect their value. The method is also able to take into account the possibility of extreme market events, which may not be captured by other pricing models.

Application in Finance

Monte Carlo simulation is commonly used in finance for pricing options, which are contracts that give the holder the right but not the obligation to buy or sell an underlying asset at a predetermined price and time. The value of an option depends on several factors, including the price of the underlying asset, the strike price, the time to expiration, and the volatility of the underlying asset.

Monte Carlo simulation can be used to value options by generating a large number of possible future paths of the underlying asset, and using these paths to calculate the expected value of the option. The simulation takes into account the various factors that affect the value of the option, including market conditions, interest rates, and volatility.

For example, consider a European call option on a stock with a strike price of $100, an expiration date of 1 year, and a volatility of 20%. The option gives the holder the right to buy the stock at $100 at any time during the year. To value this option using Monte Carlo simulation, the following steps can be taken:

Generate a large number of random numbers to simulate the possible future paths of the stock price.

Calculate the value of the option at each simulated path.
Average the values of the option across all simulated paths to obtain the expected value of the option.

Discount the expected value of the option to the present time to obtain its current value.

The above steps can be repeated multiple times to obtain a range of possible values for the option, and the average of these values can be used as the final estimate of the option value.

Strengths and Weaknesses of Monte Carlo Simulation

The strengths of the Monte Carlo simulation method include its ability to handle a wide range of complex financial instruments, including options with multiple factors that affect their value. The method is also able to take into account the possibility of extreme market events, which may not be captured by other pricing models. Additionally, Monte Carlo simulation can provide a range of possible outcomes, rather than a single point estimate, which can be useful in risk management.

M.L.Ruscsak

However, Monte Carlo simulation also has some weaknesses. One weakness is that it can be computationally intensive and time-consuming, especially when a large number of simulations are required to obtain accurate results. Additionally, Monte Carlo simulation relies on the generation of random numbers, which can introduce statistical errors and require careful validation to ensure accuracy.

Another weakness of Monte Carlo simulation is that it may not always be suitable for pricing certain types of financial instruments, such as those with early exercise features. These instruments require more specialized methods, such as the binomial tree or finite difference methods, which can better handle the early exercise feature.

Despite its weaknesses, Monte Carlo simulation remains a widely used and important method in financial engineering, particularly in the pricing of complex options and derivatives. The accuracy of Monte Carlo simulation results can be improved through various techniques, such as variance reduction and importance sampling, which can reduce the computational burden and improve the efficiency of the simulations.

In finance, Monte Carlo simulation has numerous applications beyond option pricing. For example, it can be used for portfolio optimization, risk management, and asset allocation. Monte Carlo simulation can also be used to model various economic scenarios, which can be useful in decision-making and strategic planning.

Overall, Monte Carlo simulation is a powerful and versatile tool in financial engineering, with strengths and weaknesses that must be carefully considered and balanced in its application. Its ability to handle complex financial instruments and account for extreme market events make it a valuable tool in risk management and decision-making, while its computational requirements and reliance on random numbers must be carefully managed to ensure accuracy and reliability.

Explanation of finite difference methods and their applications in finance, including the finite difference method for option pricing

Finite difference methods (FDM) are numerical techniques used to solve partial differential equations (PDEs), which arise frequently in finance. FDMs are an alternative to Monte Carlo simulation, and are commonly used to price financial derivatives, such as options.

The finite difference method works by approximating the continuous PDE with a discrete set of equations. These equations are derived using Taylor series expansions, and are solved numerically to obtain an approximate solution to the PDE. The basic idea is to divide the time and space domains into a grid of discrete points and then to approximate the partial derivatives by finite differences.

The most commonly used finite difference method in finance is the Black-Scholes finite difference method. This method is used to solve the Black-Scholes PDE, which is a second-order PDE that describes the evolution of the price of a European option over time. The Black-Scholes PDE has an analytical solution, but it is only valid for certain types of options. For more complex options, the Black-Scholes PDE must be solved numerically using a finite difference method.

The Black-Scholes finite difference method works by discretizing the time and space domains, and approximating the partial derivatives with finite differences. The method involves setting up a grid of discrete points in both time and space, and solving the PDE iteratively at each point on the grid. The process is repeated until the solution converges to a stable value.

One advantage of the finite difference method is that it is computationally efficient compared to Monte Carlo simulation. Additionally, it is easier to implement and requires less memory than Monte Carlo simulation. However, like all numerical methods, it has its limitations. For example, the accuracy of the method depends on the size of the time and space intervals used in the discretization process. Smaller intervals lead to more accurate results, but also increase the computational cost.

Finite difference methods are widely used in finance for option pricing, risk management, and other applications. They are particularly useful for pricing options with complex features, such as path-dependent options or options with early exercise provisions. FDMs can also be used to price options on assets with multiple sources of uncertainty, such as stocks with stochastic volatility.

In addition to the Black-Scholes finite difference method, there are several other types of finite difference methods used in finance, including the Crank-Nicolson method, the explicit method, and the implicit method. Each of these methods has its own advantages and disadvantages, and the choice of method depends on the specific application.

In conclusion, finite difference methods are powerful numerical techniques used to solve partial differential equations that arise in finance. They provide an efficient and accurate way to price complex financial instruments, such as options, and are widely used in the financial industry. While finite difference methods have their limitations, they are an important tool in financial engineering and will continue to play a significant role in the development of new financial products and risk management strategies.

M.L.Ruscsak

CHAPTER 22: INTEREST RATE MODELS

Interest rate models are essential tools in finance for pricing and hedging a wide range of financial instruments, including bonds, options, and swaps. These models describe the evolution of interest rates over time and are used to estimate the future behavior of interest rates.

The study of interest rates is crucial in finance, as interest rates have a significant impact on the pricing and valuation of financial instruments. Interest rates are used to calculate the present value of future cash flows and to determine the cost of borrowing or lending money.

Interest rate models are used by a variety of professionals in the finance industry, including investment bankers, traders, asset managers, and risk managers. These models help these professionals make informed decisions about pricing and hedging financial instruments.

In this chapter, we will provide an overview of interest rate models, including the different types of models and their applications in finance. We will discuss the basics of interest rate modeling and the key assumptions that underlie these models. We will also explore some of the challenges and limitations of interest rate modeling.

Overall, this chapter aims to provide a comprehensive understanding of interest rate models and their applications in finance. By the end of this chapter, readers should have a solid understanding of interest rate models and their role in the pricing and valuation of financial instruments.

Overview of interest rate models used in finance, including the Vasicek model and the Cox-Ingersoll-Ross (CIR) model

Interest rate models are essential tools for financial professionals in the banking and insurance industries. These models are used to determine the value of bonds, swaps, and other financial instruments that are affected by changes in interest rates. In this section, we will provide an overview of interest rate models used in finance, with a focus on two widely used models: the Vasicek model and the Cox-Ingersoll-Ross (CIR) model.

Overview of Interest Rate Models

Interest rate models are used to model the behavior of interest rates over time. These models use stochastic differential equations (SDEs) to describe the evolution of interest rates over time. SDEs are used because interest rates are subject to uncertainty, and the evolution of interest rates over time is not deterministic.

There are several different types of interest rate models used in finance. Some models assume that interest rates are mean-reverting, while others assume that interest rates are driven by stochastic processes. The Vasicek and CIR models are two examples of popular interest rate models used in finance.

Vasicek Model

The Vasicek model is a popular interest rate model used in finance. This model was introduced by Oldrich Vasicek in 1977 and assumes that interest rates are mean-reverting. The Vasicek model is widely used in bond pricing and interest rate risk management.

The Vasicek model is based on the following stochastic differential equation:

$$dr_t = a(b - r_t)dt + \sigma dW_t$$

where r_t is the short-term interest rate at time t, a is the rate at which interest rates mean-revert to the long-term mean, b is the long-term mean interest rate, σ is the volatility of interest rates, and W_t is a Wiener process.

The Vasicek model assumes that the short-term interest rate is mean-reverting and that interest rates tend to move towards a long-term mean over time. This mean-reversion effect is captured by the parameter a in the Vasicek model. The Vasicek model also assumes that interest rates are subject to stochastic volatility, which is captured by the parameter σ.

Cox-Ingersoll-Ross (CIR) Model

The Cox-Ingersoll-Ross (CIR) model is another popular interest rate model used in finance. This model was introduced by John Cox, Jonathan Ingersoll, and Stephen Ross in 1985 and assumes that interest rates are driven by a stochastic process.

The CIR model is based on the following stochastic differential equation:

$$dr_t = a(b - r_t)dt + \sigma\sqrt{r_t}\, dW_t$$

where r_t is the short-term interest rate at time t, a is the rate at which interest rates mean-revert to the long-term mean, b is the long-term mean interest rate, σ is the volatility of interest rates, and W_t is a Wiener process.

M.L.Ruscsak

The CIR model assumes that the short-term interest rate is driven by a stochastic process and that interest rates tend to move towards a long-term mean over time. This mean-reversion effect is captured by the parameter a in the CIR model. The CIR model also assumes that interest rates are subject to stochastic volatility, which is captured by the parameter σ.

Applications of Interest Rate Models

Interest rate models are widely used in finance for pricing bonds, options, and other financial instruments that are affected by changes in interest rates. These models are also used for interest rate risk management, which involves managing the risk that changes in interest rates will affect the value of a portfolio of financial instruments.

For example, an investment banker may use an interest rate model to determine the value of a bond that pays a fixed interest rate. The investment banker would use the interest rate model to estimate the expected future values of interest rates and then use those estimates to calculate the bond's present value. Similarly, a portfolio manager may use an interest rate model to construct a portfolio of fixed-income securities that will provide a certain level of income in different interest rate environments.

One popular interest rate model is the Vasicek model, named after its creator Oldrich Vasicek. The Vasicek model is a one-factor model that assumes interest rates follow a mean-reverting process. Specifically, the model assumes that the change in interest rates over time is proportional to the difference between a long-run mean interest rate and the current interest rate, plus a random component. Mathematically, the Vasicek model is expressed as:

$$d\,r(t) = a(b - r(t))\,dt + \sigma\,dW(t)$$

where r(t) represents the short-term interest rate at time t, a is the speed of mean reversion, b is the long-run mean interest rate, σ is the volatility of interest rates, and W(t) is a Wiener process (a type of random process used in mathematical finance).

Another popular interest rate model is the Cox-Ingersoll-Ross (CIR) model, named after its creators John Cox, Jonathan Ingersoll, and Stephen Ross. The CIR model is also a one-factor model that assumes interest rates follow a mean-reverting process. However, unlike the Vasicek model, the CIR model assumes that interest rates are non-negative and cannot fall below zero. Mathematically, the CIR model is expressed as:

$$d\,r(t) = a(b - r(t))\,dt + \sigma\,\text{sqrt}(r(t))\,dW(t)$$

where r(t) represents the short-term interest rate at time t, a is the speed of mean reversion, b is the long-run mean interest rate, σ is the volatility of interest rates, and W(t) is a Wiener process.

Interest rate models like the Vasicek model and the CIR model are commonly used in financial engineering for a variety of applications, such as pricing bonds, options on bonds, and other interest rate derivatives. These models can also be used for risk management purposes, such as simulating the behavior of interest rates under different scenarios to assess the impact on a portfolio of fixed-income securities.

It's worth noting that interest rate models have their limitations and can be difficult to calibrate to market data. Additionally, interest rate models are typically one-factor models, which may not capture all the complexities of the interest rate market. Nonetheless, interest rate models remain an important tool in financial engineering for pricing and risk management of fixed-income securities.

Detailed explanation of the Vasicek model, including the model's assumptions and the derivation of the interest rate equation

The Vasicek model is a popular interest rate model used in finance that was introduced by Oldrich Vasicek in 1977. It is a one-factor model, meaning that it assumes only one underlying factor affecting interest rates. In this section, we will provide a detailed explanation of the Vasicek model, including the model's assumptions and the derivation of the interest rate equation.

Assumptions of the Vasicek Model
The Vasicek model is based on a number of assumptions, which include the following:

- ❖ Interest rates are continuous and follow a mean-reverting process.
- ❖ The mean reversion is constant over time.
- ❖ Interest rates are normally distributed.
- ❖ There is no correlation between the changes in interest rates and the changes in the volatility of interest rates.
- ❖ The interest rate volatility is constant over time.

Derivation of the Interest Rate Equation
The Vasicek model uses a stochastic differential equation (SDE) to model interest rates over time. The SDE for the Vasicek model is:

$$dr(t) = k(\theta - r(t))dt + \sigma dW(t)$$

where:

- ❖ $r(t)$ is the interest rate at time t
- ❖ k is the speed of mean reversion
- ❖ θ is the long-term mean interest rate

✧   σ is the volatility of interest rates
✧   W(t) is a Wiener process, which is a mathematical process used to model randomness.

The first term in the equation represents the mean reversion of the interest rate towards its long-term mean. The second term represents the stochastic part of the equation, which introduces randomness into the interest rate process.

To derive the interest rate equation from the SDE, we need to use Ito's lemma. Ito's lemma is a mathematical tool used to find the derivative of a stochastic process. Applying Ito's lemma to the Vasicek model, we get:

$$dr(t) = (\partial r/\partial t)dt + (\partial r/\partial r)(dr)^2 + (\partial r/\partial r)(dr)(dW) + 1/2(\partial^2 r/\partial r^2)(dW)^2$$

where $(\partial r/\partial t)$ is the partial derivative of the interest rate with respect to time, $(\partial r/\partial r)$ is the partial derivative of the interest rate with respect to itself, $(\partial^2 r/\partial r^2)$ is the second partial derivative of the interest rate with respect to itself, and $(dr)^2$ and $(dW)^2$ are infinitesimal terms that are negligible.

Substituting the Vasicek model into the Ito's lemma equation, we get:

$$k(\theta - r(t))dt + \sigma dW(t) = (\partial r/\partial t)dt + k(\theta - r(t))(dr) + \sigma(dW(t))(dW(t))/2$$

Simplifying and rearranging the terms, we get:

$$\partial r/\partial t = k(\theta - r(t)) + \sigma(dW(t))/(\sqrt{dt})$$

This is the interest rate equation for the Vasicek model. It represents the rate of change of interest rates over time and takes into account the mean reversion and volatility of interest rates.

In summary, the Vasicek model is a popular interest rate model used in finance that assumes interest rates are continuous and follow a mean-reverting process. The model is derived using a stochastic differential equation and Ito's lemma, and it takes into account the speed of mean reversion, long-term mean interest rate, and volatility of interest rates. The interest rate equation derived from the Vasicek model represents the rate of change of interest rate over time, which is influenced by the current interest rate level, the long-term mean interest rate, the speed of mean reversion, and the volatility of interest rates.

However, it's worth noting that the Vasicek model has some limitations. One of the main limitations is that it assumes interest rates follow a normal distribution, which may not always hold in practice. Furthermore, the model does not take into account the term structure of interest rates, which means it may not accurately capture the behavior of bonds with different maturities.

Despite these limitations, the Vasicek model remains a useful tool in finance for estimating the behavior of interest rates and pricing fixed income securities. Many variations of the model have been developed over the years to address some of its shortcomings and improve its accuracy.

To illustrate the application of the Vasicek model, consider the following example:

Suppose an investor is considering purchasing a bond that pays a fixed interest rate of 4% per year for the next five years. To determine the value of the bond, the investor can use the Vasicek model to estimate the expected future values of interest rates. The investor might assume the following parameter values:

- ✧ The long-term mean interest rate, μ, is 6%
- ✧ The speed of mean reversion, α, is 0.1
- ✧ The volatility of interest rates, σ, is 0.2

Using these parameter values, the Vasicek model can be used to estimate the probability distribution of future interest rates. This distribution can then be used to estimate the expected value of the bond's future cash flows, which can be discounted back to the present to determine the bond's present value.

In conclusion, the Vasicek model is a widely used interest rate model that provides a framework for estimating the behavior of interest rates and pricing fixed income securities. While the model has some limitations, it remains a valuable tool in finance for modeling interest rate risk and helping investors make informed investment decisions.

Analysis of the strengths and weaknesses of the Vasicek model and other interest rate models

Interest rate models are essential tools used in finance to estimate the future values of interest rates and assess the risks associated with interest rate changes. While the Vasicek model is widely used in finance, it is not without its limitations. In this section, we will analyze the strengths and weaknesses of the Vasicek model and other interest rate models.

One of the strengths of the Vasicek model is its simplicity. The model is easy to understand and implement, making it a popular choice among practitioners. Additionally, the model takes into account the mean reversion of interest rates, which is a critical feature of interest rate dynamics. The Vasicek model is also relatively easy to estimate, and it can be calibrated to fit observed interest rate data.

M.L.Ruscsak

However, the Vasicek model also has several weaknesses. One of the main weaknesses of the model is that it assumes interest rates follow a normal distribution, which is not always the case in practice. Interest rates often exhibit heavy tails, meaning that extreme values are more likely to occur than predicted by a normal distribution. Additionally, the Vasicek model assumes that interest rates are continuous and cannot take negative values, which is not always true in practice. Negative interest rates have become a reality in some countries, which renders the Vasicek model inappropriate for these situations.

Another popular interest rate model used in finance is the Cox-Ingersoll-Ross (CIR) model. The CIR model is an extension of the Vasicek model, and it addresses some of the weaknesses of the Vasicek model. The CIR model assumes that interest rates follow a mean-reverting process, but with a time-varying volatility that depends on the level of interest rates. The CIR model also allows for negative interest rates, which is important in today's low-interest-rate environment. However, the CIR model is more complex than the Vasicek model, and it may be more challenging to estimate and calibrate to observed interest rate data.

Another interest rate model used in finance is the Hull-White model. The Hull-White model is a more general interest rate model that can accommodate various types of interest rate dynamics. The model assumes that interest rates are mean-reverting and that the mean reversion speed and volatility are functions of time. The Hull-White model can also accommodate negative interest rates and non-normal distributions of interest rates. However, the Hull-White model is more complex than the Vasicek and CIR models, and it may be challenging to estimate and calibrate to observed interest rate data.

In conclusion, interest rate models are essential tools used in finance to estimate the future values of interest rates and assess the risks associated with interest rate changes. While the Vasicek model is widely used in finance, it has its limitations, such as assuming normal distribution of interest rates and interest rates cannot take negative values. Other interest rate models, such as the CIR and Hull-White models, address some of these limitations but may be more complex and challenging to estimate and calibrate. It is important for practitioners to choose an appropriate interest rate model that fits their data and objectives while being mindful of the limitations and assumptions of each model.

PART 8: EMERGING TRENDS AND ISSUES IN FINANCIAL MATHEMATICS

Financial mathematics is a rapidly evolving field that is constantly impacted by changes in the global economy, advancements in technology, and new research findings. In this section, we will explore some of the emerging trends and issues in financial mathematics, including the role of machine learning and artificial intelligence, the rise of cryptocurrencies, the impact of climate change on financial modeling, and the growing importance of ethical considerations in financial decision-making.

Role of Machine Learning and Artificial Intelligence in Financial Mathematics

Machine learning and artificial intelligence (AI) are increasingly being used in financial mathematics to enhance the accuracy of predictions and improve investment decisions. Machine learning algorithms are capable of identifying patterns in large datasets, which can be used to predict future market trends and assess risk. Some examples of machine learning techniques used in finance include neural networks, decision trees, and regression analysis.

One of the key benefits of machine learning and AI is their ability to process large volumes of data quickly, making it possible for traders and portfolio managers to respond to market changes in real-time. However, there are also concerns about the potential for these technologies to introduce bias or errors into financial decision-making processes. It is important to carefully evaluate the accuracy and reliability of machine learning algorithms before relying on them to make investment decisions.

Rise of Cryptocurrencies

Cryptocurrencies such as Bitcoin and Ethereum have gained significant attention in recent years, and their use is becoming increasingly widespread. The rise of cryptocurrencies has important implications for financial mathematics, particularly in the areas of risk management and pricing.

M.L.Ruscsak

Cryptocurrencies are unique because they are not backed by any physical asset and are not subject to government regulations in the same way as traditional currencies. This has led to a high degree of volatility and uncertainty in the market. Financial mathematicians are exploring new models and techniques to analyze the risks associated with cryptocurrencies and to develop pricing models that accurately reflect their value.

Impact of Climate Change on Financial Modeling

Climate change is another important issue that is affecting financial modeling. The physical risks associated with climate change, such as flooding and natural disasters, can have a significant impact on the value of assets and investments. Financial models need to be able to accurately assess and incorporate these risks into investment decisions.

In addition to physical risks, there are also transitional risks associated with the transition to a low-carbon economy. As governments and businesses take steps to reduce their carbon footprint, investments in industries such as fossil fuels may become less profitable. Financial models need to be able to accurately assess these risks and factor them into investment decisions.

Growing Importance of Ethical Considerations

Finally, ethical considerations are becoming increasingly important in financial decision-making. Investors are increasingly demanding that their investments align with their values, and companies are under pressure to adopt sustainable and socially responsible business practices.

Financial mathematicians need to be able to incorporate ethical considerations into their models and decision-making processes. This may involve developing new models to assess the social and environmental impact of investments or incorporating ethical considerations into existing models.

Conclusion

In conclusion, financial mathematics is a field that is constantly evolving in response to changes in the global economy, advancements in technology, and new research findings. The emerging trends and issues discussed in this section highlight the importance of staying up-to-date with the latest developments in the field and being able to adapt to new challenges and opportunities. As financial mathematicians continue to explore new models and techniques, they will play an increasingly important role in shaping the future of finance.

CHAPTER 23: CURRENT TRENDS IN FINANCIAL MATHEMATICS

Financial mathematics is a rapidly evolving field that involves the application of mathematical and statistical techniques to finance and economics. The field has witnessed significant growth and innovation over the past few decades, with new models, algorithms, and techniques emerging to address increasingly complex financial problems. The growing importance of financial mathematics has been driven by the need for accurate and efficient methods to analyze financial data, assess risk, and make informed investment decisions.

This chapter will provide an overview of the current trends in financial mathematics, including the latest models, techniques, and applications. We will explore the latest developments in quantitative finance, risk management, portfolio optimization, and machine learning, among other topics. We will also discuss the challenges and opportunities facing financial mathematics today and the implications for professionals working in the field.

Quantitative Finance:

Quantitative finance is a subfield of financial mathematics that focuses on the development and implementation of mathematical models and techniques for pricing and hedging financial instruments. The field has been transformed in recent years by advances in computational power, data science, and machine learning. Today, quantitative finance professionals rely on sophisticated algorithms and models to price complex financial instruments, manage risk, and optimize investment strategies.

One of the most important recent developments in quantitative finance is the growing use of machine learning and artificial intelligence. Machine learning algorithms have been shown to be effective in modeling complex financial systems and predicting future trends. These techniques have been applied to a wide range of financial problems, including portfolio optimization, credit risk analysis, and fraud detection. Machine learning algorithms have also been used to develop trading strategies that can generate alpha in financial markets.

Risk Management:

Risk management is a critical function in finance that involves identifying, measuring, and mitigating the risks associated with financial investments. The growing complexity of financial markets and instruments has made risk management an increasingly challenging task. Financial mathematics provides the tools and techniques necessary to measure and manage risk effectively.

One of the most important recent trends in risk management is the growing use of machine learning and big data. Machine learning algorithms can be used to analyze large data sets and identify patterns that may be missed by traditional risk models. These techniques can also be used to develop more accurate and robust risk models that can better capture the complex dynamics of financial markets.

Portfolio Optimization:

Portfolio optimization is the process of selecting and allocating assets in a way that maximizes returns while minimizing risk. Financial mathematics provides the tools and techniques necessary to optimize portfolios effectively. Modern portfolio theory, for example, provides a framework for identifying the optimal portfolio given a set of constraints.

Recent developments in portfolio optimization have focused on incorporating factors beyond traditional asset classes, such as environmental, social, and governance (ESG) factors. ESG factors have become increasingly important to investors, who are looking to invest in companies that are sustainable and socially responsible. Financial mathematics provides the tools necessary to incorporate ESG factors into portfolio optimization models.

Conclusion:

Financial mathematics is a rapidly evolving field that is critical to the success of modern finance. The latest models, techniques, and applications have transformed the way financial professionals approach problems and make decisions. As technology continues to advance, the field is likely to see even more rapid change and innovation. Professionals working in financial mathematics will need to stay abreast of the latest developments in the field to remain competitive and effective.

Overview of current trends in financial mathematics, including machine learning and big data analytics

Financial mathematics is an ever-evolving field that continuously adapts to new technological advancements and market needs. One of the most significant trends in recent years is the integration of machine learning and big data analytics into financial modeling and decision-making processes. In this section, we will provide an overview of these emerging trends and discuss their potential impact on the industry.

Machine learning is a branch of artificial intelligence that focuses on the development of algorithms that can learn and make predictions based on data. In financial mathematics, machine learning is used to analyze large amounts of data and generate insights that can inform investment decisions. For example, machine learning algorithms can be trained to predict stock prices, detect anomalies in financial data, or identify market trends.

Big data analytics, on the other hand, refers to the process of analyzing large and complex datasets to extract valuable information. In financial mathematics, big data analytics is used to identify patterns and relationships in financial data that may not be visible through traditional methods. This allows financial professionals to make more informed investment decisions and mitigate risks more effectively.

The integration of machine learning and big data analytics into financial mathematics has the potential to revolutionize the industry in several ways. First, it can enable financial professionals to make more accurate predictions and identify investment opportunities that may have been overlooked in the past. This can lead to higher returns and better risk management.

Second, machine learning and big data analytics can help financial professionals manage large amounts of data more efficiently. This can lead to more streamlined decision-making processes and reduced operational costs. For example, an investment banker can use machine learning algorithms to analyze a large number of financial statements in a short amount of time, which can help them make more informed decisions about potential investment opportunities.

Despite the potential benefits of machine learning and big data analytics in financial mathematics, there are also some challenges that need to be addressed. One of the most significant challenges is the need for high-quality data. Machine learning algorithms rely heavily on data to make predictions, so it is essential to ensure that the data used is accurate, relevant, and up-to-date. In addition, the use of machine learning and big data analytics may raise ethical concerns related to data privacy and transparency.

In conclusion, the integration of machine learning and big data analytics into financial mathematics is an emerging trend that has the potential to transform the industry. While there are challenges that need to be addressed, the benefits of these technologies in terms of accuracy, efficiency, and risk management are significant. Financial professionals who can effectively incorporate machine learning and big data analytics into their decision-making processes are likely to have a competitive advantage in the marketplace.

Explanation of machine learning and its applications in finance, including supervised and unsupervised learning techniques

Machine learning (ML) is a subfield of artificial intelligence (AI) that involves the use of statistical models and algorithms to enable machines to improve their performance on a given task over time, without being explicitly programmed. It is a powerful tool for processing and analyzing large volumes of data, and has rapidly emerged as a key area of research and development in the financial industry.

M.L.Ruscsak

In finance, machine learning is used to analyze data and identify patterns that can be used to make predictions about future market trends, identify risks, and optimize investment decisions. One of the main advantages of using machine learning in finance is the ability to quickly and accurately analyze large volumes of data, which can help traders and analysts make more informed decisions and identify opportunities that may not be immediately apparent using traditional analysis methods.

There are two main types of machine learning techniques used in finance: supervised learning and unsupervised learning. Supervised learning involves training a model on a set of labeled data, where the outcomes are known, in order to make predictions about future data points. Unsupervised learning, on the other hand, involves training a model on a set of unlabeled data, where the outcomes are unknown, in order to identify patterns and relationships that can be used to make predictions about future data points.

Supervised learning techniques are commonly used in finance for tasks such as classification, regression, and time series forecasting. Classification involves predicting a categorical variable, such as whether a stock will rise or fall in price. Regression involves predicting a continuous variable, such as the price of a stock. Time series forecasting involves predicting future values of a variable based on historical data. Common supervised learning algorithms used in finance include linear regression, decision trees, and neural networks.

Unsupervised learning techniques are commonly used in finance for tasks such as clustering and anomaly detection. Clustering involves grouping similar data points together based on their characteristics, while anomaly detection involves identifying data points that are significantly different from the rest of the data set. Common unsupervised learning algorithms used in finance include k-means clustering and principal component analysis (PCA).

Overall, machine learning is an extremely powerful tool for processing and analyzing large volumes of financial data, and has the potential to revolutionize the way that traders, analysts, and investors make decisions. However, it is important to note that machine learning models are not perfect and can be prone to errors and biases, especially when dealing with complex financial data. Therefore, it is crucial to use machine learning techniques in conjunction with traditional analysis methods and to carefully evaluate the accuracy and reliability of the results produced by these models.

Exercise:

1. What is the difference between supervised and unsupervised learning?

2. Give an example of a supervised learning algorithm used in finance.

3. Give an example of an unsupervised learning algorithm used in finance.

4. Assume that the mean interest rate in the Vasicek model is 5% and the speed of mean reversion is 0.3.

5. What is the expected interest rate one year from now if the current interest rate is 6%?

6. Consider the Vasicek model with a long-term mean interest rate of 4%, a speed of mean reversion of 0.1, and a volatility of 0.05. If the current interest rate is 3%, what is the probability that the interest rate will exceed 5% within the next two years?

7. Suppose that the Vasicek model is used to price a zero-coupon bond with a face value of $100, a maturity of five years, and an annual interest rate of 4%. If the speed of mean reversion is 0.2 and the volatility is 0.03, what is the bond's price?

8. Assume that the Vasicek model is used to simulate interest rates over a period of five years. If the long-term mean interest rate is 5%, the speed of mean reversion is 0.1, and the volatility is 0.02, what is the expected interest rate after five years if the current interest rate is 4%?

9. Consider the Vasicek model with a long-term mean interest rate of 3%, a speed of mean reversion of 0.2, and a volatility of 0.04. If the current interest rate is 2.5%, what is the probability that the interest rate will fall below 2% within the next three years?

Analysis of big data analytics in finance, including the use of data mining and predictive analytics

In recent years, the financial industry has been generating an unprecedented amount of data due to the increasing use of digital technology and the proliferation of online transactions. The sheer volume, velocity, and variety of data have created challenges and opportunities for financial institutions seeking to improve their decision-making processes and gain a competitive edge. Big data analytics, which refers to the use of advanced computational techniques and algorithms to analyze large and complex data sets, has emerged as a powerful tool for extracting valuable insights

M.L.Ruscsak

and making informed decisions in finance. This section will provide an in-depth analysis of big data analytics in finance, including the use of data mining and predictive analytics.

Data Mining in Finance

Data mining is a subset of big data analytics that involves the extraction of hidden patterns and knowledge from large datasets. In finance, data mining can be used to identify market trends, analyze customer behavior, detect fraudulent activities, and optimize investment strategies. The process of data mining typically involves the following steps:

✧ Data collection: This step involves gathering data from various sources, such as financial statements, market reports, customer feedback, and social media.

✧ Data cleaning: This step involves removing irrelevant, incomplete, or inconsistent data from the dataset to ensure its accuracy and reliability.

✧ Data preprocessing: This step involves transforming the data into a format that can be easily analyzed by algorithms. This may include normalization, standardization, feature selection, and dimensionality reduction.

✧ Data mining: This step involves applying various algorithms, such as decision trees, neural networks, clustering, and association rule mining, to extract patterns and relationships from the dataset.

✧ Evaluation: This step involves assessing the quality and relevance of the results obtained from the data mining process.

One of the most significant applications of data mining in finance is in the area of fraud detection. Financial institutions are constantly at risk of fraudulent activities, such as credit card fraud, identity theft, money laundering, and insider trading. Data mining can help detect and prevent these activities by analyzing large volumes of data and identifying suspicious patterns and behaviors. For example, credit card companies can use data mining to detect fraudulent transactions by analyzing patterns of spending and payment behavior of their customers. Similarly, banks can use data mining to identify suspicious patterns of account activity, such as large cash withdrawals, sudden transfers to foreign accounts, and unusual trading patterns.

Another important application of data mining in finance is in the area of risk management. Financial institutions are exposed to various types of risks, such as market risk, credit risk, operational risk, and liquidity risk. Data mining can help identify and mitigate these risks by analyzing large datasets and identifying potential risk factors. For example, banks can use data mining to analyze the creditworthiness of their customers by assessing their payment history, credit score, income level, and other relevant factors. This can help banks determine the probability of default and set appropriate interest rates and credit limits.

Predictive Analytics in Finance

Predictive analytics is another subset of big data analytics that involves the use of statistical models and machine learning algorithms to predict future outcomes based on historical data. In finance, predictive analytics can be used to forecast market trends, predict customer behavior, optimize investment strategies, and manage risks. The process of predictive analytics typically involves the following steps:

✧   Data collection: This step involves gathering historical data from various sources, such as financial statements, market reports, customer feedback, and social media.

✧   Data cleaning and preprocessing: This step involves removing irrelevant, incomplete, or inconsistent data from the dataset and transforming it into a format that can be easily analyzed by algorithms.

✧   Model development: This step involves selecting an appropriate model, such as linear regression, logistic regression, decision trees, or neural networks, and developing it to analyze the data. The model may need to be adjusted or fine-tuned to ensure its accuracy and efficiency.

✧   Model evaluation: This step involves testing the model's performance on a subset of the data that was not used during model development. The goal is to evaluate the model's accuracy, precision, recall, and other performance metrics. The model may need to be further refined based on these results.

✧   Model deployment: This step involves deploying the model in a production environment, such as a trading platform, risk management system, or customer relationship management software. The model may need to be integrated with other systems and undergo further testing to ensure its compatibility and stability.

Continuous monitoring and improvement: This step involves monitoring the model's performance over time and making necessary adjustments or improvements based on changing market conditions, data quality, or business requirements. This step is critical for ensuring the model's long-term viability and success.

Big data analytics has become increasingly important in finance due to the vast amounts of data generated by financial transactions, social media, and other sources. By analyzing this data, financial professionals can gain insights into market trends, customer behavior, and risk management, among other things.

M.L.Ruscsak

One area where big data analytics has been particularly useful is in fraud detection. Financial institutions can use machine learning algorithms to detect and prevent fraudulent activities, such as credit card fraud, money laundering, and insider trading. By analyzing patterns and anomalies in transaction data, these algorithms can identify potential fraud cases and alert the appropriate authorities.

Another area where big data analytics has been applied is in portfolio management. By analyzing large datasets, portfolio managers can make more informed investment decisions and reduce risk. For example, they can use predictive analytics to forecast market trends, identify undervalued stocks, and manage portfolio diversification.

In conclusion, big data analytics has become an essential tool for financial professionals looking to gain insights into market trends, customer behavior, and risk management. By leveraging advanced analytics techniques and machine learning algorithms, they can make more informed investment decisions, detect and prevent fraudulent activities, and manage portfolio risk more effectively. However, the success of big data analytics in finance depends on careful data collection, cleaning, modeling, evaluation, deployment, and continuous monitoring and improvement.

CHAPTER 24: FUTURE DIRECTIONS FOR FINANCIAL MATHEMATICS

Financial mathematics has undergone significant changes over the past few decades. With advancements in technology, data analytics, and machine learning, the field has evolved to become more sophisticated and data-driven. In today's world, financial institutions are faced with a myriad of challenges, such as market volatility, regulatory compliance, and cybersecurity threats. As such, the field of financial mathematics is continuously evolving to meet these challenges and stay ahead of the curve.

Chapter 24 of this book aims to explore the future directions of financial mathematics. We will examine the latest trends and developments in the field, as well as provide insights into how they might shape the future of finance. In this chapter, we will look at some of the key areas that are likely to drive the future of financial mathematics, including blockchain, quantum computing, and artificial intelligence.

The Need for Financial Mathematics

Before we dive into the future of financial mathematics, it is essential to understand why the field is critical to the financial industry. Financial mathematics helps financial institutions to analyze, measure, and manage financial risk. It enables them to make informed decisions and to stay competitive in the market. Without financial mathematics, financial institutions would be exposed to a higher degree of risk, leading to potentially catastrophic losses.

Financial mathematics also plays a crucial role in creating new financial products and services. It provides the tools and techniques necessary to design and price complex financial instruments. This is particularly important in today's rapidly changing financial landscape, where new financial products are constantly being introduced.

The Importance of Innovation

Innovation has always been a driving force behind the evolution of financial mathematics. The field has evolved significantly over the past few decades, with the introduction of new technologies and techniques. For instance, machine learning has revolutionized the way financial institutions analyze and interpret data. Similarly, blockchain technology has the potential to disrupt the way financial transactions are conducted.

Innovation is critical to the future of financial mathematics. As new challenges emerge, financial institutions must continuously innovate to stay ahead of the curve. This is particularly important in today's dynamic financial landscape, where technological advancements are driving rapid change.

The Role of Blockchain

Blockchain technology is one of the most promising developments in the financial industry. It has the potential to transform the way financial transactions are conducted, making them faster, cheaper, and more secure. Blockchain technology is essentially a distributed ledger system, which allows for the secure and transparent recording of transactions. The technology is decentralized, meaning that it is not controlled by a single entity, such as a government or financial institution.

Blockchain technology has already been applied in several areas of the financial industry. For instance, it is being used for cross-border payments, trade finance, and securities settlement. As blockchain technology continues to evolve, it is likely to be applied in other areas, such as insurance and supply chain management.

The Role of Quantum Computing

Quantum computing is another area that is likely to shape the future of financial mathematics. Quantum computers use quantum mechanics principles to perform calculations, which are much faster and more powerful than traditional computers. This means that quantum computers can analyze and interpret large datasets much faster than traditional computers.

Quantum computing has several potential applications in the financial industry. For instance, it can be used to optimize investment portfolios, to simulate financial markets, and to conduct risk assessments. However, quantum computing is still in its early stages of development, and it may be some time before it is widely adopted in the financial industry.

The Role of Artificial Intelligence

Artificial intelligence (AI) is already being used in several areas of the financial industry. For instance, it is being used for fraud detection, customer service, and investment management. AI has the potential to revolutionize the way financial institutions operate, as it can provide more efficient and accurate solutions to complex problems. In the future, it is expected that AI will continue to play an increasingly important role in finance.

One area where AI is likely to have a significant impact is risk management. Risk management is an essential part of the financial industry, and AI can help financial institutions better identify and manage risks. By analyzing large amounts of data, AI algorithms can identify patterns and trends that humans might not be able to detect. This can help financial institutions to better predict and mitigate risks, which can ultimately lead to better financial performance.

Another area where AI is likely to have an impact is in the development of new financial products. AI can help financial institutions to better understand customer needs and preferences, and to develop new products and services that better meet those needs. For example, AI can be used to analyze customer data to identify patterns and trends in their behavior, which can help financial institutions to develop more personalized products and services.

In addition to AI, other emerging technologies are likely to have an impact on the future of financial mathematics. For example, blockchain technology has the potential to revolutionize the way financial transactions are conducted. Blockchain technology is a decentralized ledger system that can be used to securely and transparently record financial transactions. This technology can help to reduce the risk of fraud and increase the efficiency of financial transactions.

Another emerging technology that is likely to have an impact on financial mathematics is quantum computing. Quantum computing is a type of computing that uses quantum-mechanical phenomena to perform operations on data. Quantum computers have the potential to solve problems that are currently impossible to solve with classical computers, which could have significant implications for the financial industry.

As these and other technologies continue to develop, it is likely that they will continue to shape the future of financial mathematics. The financial industry is constantly evolving, and financial institutions will need to adapt to these changes in order to remain competitive. By embracing emerging technologies and incorporating them into their operations, financial institutions can position themselves for success in the years ahead.

Exercise:

1. Explain how AI can revolutionize risk management in the financial industry.

2. Describe the potential impact of AI on the development of new financial products and services.

3. What is blockchain technology, and how can it help to increase the efficiency and security of financial transactions?

4. Explain how quantum computing differs from classical computing, and how it could impact the financial industry.

5. Discuss the importance of financial institutions adapting to emerging technologies in order to remain competitive.

Overview of future directions for financial mathematics research and applications, including quantum computing and blockchain technology

Financial mathematics has come a long way in the past few decades. With the advancements in technology, new doors are opening for the future of financial mathematics research and applications. Two such technologies that have been making a buzz in the financial industry are quantum computing and blockchain technology. In this section, we will discuss the current status of these technologies and their potential future applications in the field of financial mathematics.

Quantum Computing:

Quantum computing is a relatively new technology that has the potential to revolutionize the field of financial mathematics. Traditional computing systems operate using bits that are either a 0 or a 1. Quantum computing, on the other hand, uses quantum bits or qubits, which can be both a 0 and a 1 at the same time. This means that quantum computers can perform calculations much faster than traditional computers.

One potential application of quantum computing in financial mathematics is optimization. Optimization is a crucial component of finance, as it involves finding the best possible solution to a problem given certain constraints. Quantum computing has the potential to solve optimization problems much faster than traditional computing systems, which could lead to more efficient and effective financial modeling and decision-making.

Another potential application of quantum computing in finance is in portfolio optimization. Portfolio optimization involves selecting a portfolio of assets that will provide the best possible returns given certain constraints. Quantum computing could provide a more efficient way to select portfolios that maximize returns and minimize risks.

Exercise:

Suppose a portfolio manager is tasked with selecting a portfolio of assets that will provide the highest possible returns given a certain level of risk. The portfolio manager has a list of 10 stocks that they can choose from. The expected returns and risks of each stock are shown in the table below:

Stock	Expected Return	Risk
A	10%	5%
B	12%	10%
C	8%	7%
D	15%	12%
E	20%	15%
F	18%	11%
G	6%	3%
H	9%	6%
I	11%	8%
J	13%	9%

The portfolio manager can choose up to five stocks for the portfolio. Use quantum computing to find the portfolio that provides the highest possible returns given a risk threshold of 10%.

Blockchain Technology:

Blockchain technology is another emerging technology that has the potential to revolutionize the field of financial mathematics. Blockchain technology is a distributed ledger that records transactions in a secure and transparent way. It has the potential to increase transparency, reduce transaction costs, and eliminate the need for intermediaries in financial transactions.

One potential application of blockchain technology in finance is in payment systems. Blockchain technology can provide a more efficient and secure way to transfer money between parties. It could also eliminate the need for intermediaries such as banks, which could lead to lower transaction costs.

Another potential application of blockchain technology in finance is in smart contracts. Smart contracts are self-executing contracts that automatically execute when certain conditions are met. They are stored on a blockchain and can be used to automate financial transactions. This could lead to more efficient and secure financial transactions.

Exercise:

Suppose a financial institution wants to use smart contracts to automate a loan agreement. The loan agreement specifies that the borrower will receive a loan of $100,000 at an interest rate of 5% per year for a period of five years. The borrower will make monthly payments to the lender over the

M.L.Ruscsak

five-year period. Use blockchain technology to create a smart contract that automates this loan agreement.

Solution:

To create a smart contract that automates this loan agreement, we need to define the terms of the contract and the conditions under which payments will be made. We also need to specify the parties involved in the contract and the amount of collateral that the borrower is required to provide.

Here is a possible implementation of the smart contract in Solidity, a programming language used to write smart contracts on the Ethereum blockchain:

```php
pragma solidity ^0.8.0;

contract LoanContract {
    address public lender;
    address public borrower;
    uint256 public loanAmount;
    uint256 public interestRate;
    uint256 public loanDuration;
    uint256 public monthlyPayment;
    uint256 public totalPayments;
    uint256 public paymentsMade;
    uint256 public lastPaymentDate;
    uint256 public collateral;
    bool public isActive;

    constructor(address _borrower, uint256 _loanAmount, uint256 _interestRate, uint256 _loanDuration, uint256 _collateral) {
        lender = msg.sender;
        borrower = _borrower;
        loanAmount = _loanAmount;
        interestRate = _interestRate;
        loanDuration = _loanDuration;
        collateral = _collateral;
        monthlyPayment = calculateMonthlyPayment();
        totalPayments = loanDuration * 12;
        paymentsMade = 0;
        lastPaymentDate = block.timestamp;
        isActive = true;
    }
```

```
function calculateMonthlyPayment() public view returns (uint256) {
    uint256 r = interestRate / 12;
    uint256 n = loanDuration * 12;
    uint256 p = loanAmount;
    uint256 monthlyPayment = (p * r * (1 + r) ** n) / ((1 + r) ** n - 1);
    return monthlyPayment;
}

function makePayment() public payable {
    require(msg.sender == borrower, "Only borrower can make payments");
    require(isActive, "Contract is not active");
    require(msg.value == monthlyPayment, "Invalid payment amount");

    paymentsMade++;
    lastPaymentDate = block.timestamp;

    if (paymentsMade == totalPayments) {
        isActive = false;
        borrower.transfer(collateral);
        lender.transfer(address(this).balance);
    }
}

function getLoanDetails() public view returns (address, address, uint256, uint256, uint256,
uint256, uint256, uint256, uint256, uint256, bool) {
    return (lender, borrower, loanAmount, interestRate, loanDuration, monthlyPayment,
totalPayments, paymentsMade, lastPaymentDate, collateral, isActive);
    }
}
```

This smart contract defines a LoanContract contract that allows a lender to lend money to a borrower for a specified period of time at a specified interest rate. The borrower is required to provide collateral, which is returned to them once the loan has been fully repaid. The contract also specifies the conditions under which payments can be made and how payments are processed.

To use this smart contract, the lender would need to deploy it on the Ethereum blockchain and specify the borrower's address, the loan amount, the interest rate, the loan duration, and the collateral amount. The borrower would then need to make monthly payments to the contract until the loan has been fully repaid. Once the loan has been repaid, the collateral is returned to the borrower, and the lender receives the principal plus interest. The contract is self-executing and cannot be modified once it has been deployed.

This example illustrates how blockchain technology can be used to automate financial agreements and transactions, eliminating the need for intermediaries and reducing the risk of fraud and errors. Smart contracts can also help to reduce transaction costs and increase efficiency, which is particularly important in the financial industry where even small delays or errors can have significant consequences.

In addition to blockchain technology, quantum computing is another area that has the potential to revolutionize the field of financial mathematics. Quantum computing is a type of computing that uses quantum-mechanical phenomena, such as superposition and entanglement, to perform operations on data. These operations can be performed much faster than traditional computing, which could have significant implications for financial modeling, optimization, and risk management.

For example, quantum computing could be used to solve complex optimization problems that are currently too difficult for classical computers to solve in a reasonable amount of time. This could lead to more accurate pricing models for financial products, better risk management strategies, and more efficient portfolio optimization.

However, quantum computing is still in its early stages and many of the potential applications are still largely theoretical. There are also significant technical challenges that need to be addressed before quantum computing can be widely adopted in the financial industry.

Another area of future research in financial mathematics is the application of machine learning to portfolio optimization and risk management. Machine learning is a type of artificial intelligence that involves training algorithms to recognize patterns in data and make predictions based on those patterns.

In the context of financial mathematics, machine learning could be used to analyze large datasets of financial information to identify patterns and correlations that are not immediately apparent to humans. This could lead to more accurate predictions of asset prices, more effective risk management strategies, and more efficient portfolio optimization.

However, machine learning also presents a number of challenges, including the need for large amounts of high-quality data, the potential for bias in the algorithms, and the difficulty of interpreting the results. These challenges will need to be addressed in order for machine learning to be widely adopted in the financial industry.

Overall, the field of financial mathematics is constantly evolving and new technologies and techniques are being developed all the time. As these technologies continue to mature, they have the potential to revolutionize the way financial institutions operate and the way financial products are priced, managed, and optimized. As such, it is important for researchers and practitioners in the field to stay up-to-date with the latest developments and to be open to new ideas and approaches.

Explanation of quantum computing and its potential applications in finance, including optimization and risk management

The field of finance has always relied on sophisticated mathematics and statistics to make better predictions and manage risks. However, even the most advanced algorithms and models can be limited by the speed and power of traditional computers. That is where quantum computing comes in. With its ability to perform complex calculations at unprecedented speeds, quantum computing has the potential to revolutionize the field of finance. In this section, we will provide an overview of quantum computing and its potential applications in finance, including optimization and risk management.

Overview of Quantum Computing

Quantum computing is a new paradigm of computing that relies on the principles of quantum mechanics. Traditional computers use bits, which can be either 0 or 1, to store and process information. Quantum computers, on the other hand, use quantum bits or qubits, which can be in multiple states at once. This allows quantum computers to perform multiple calculations simultaneously, leading to exponential speedups for certain types of problems.

Quantum computers are based on the principles of superposition and entanglement. Superposition means that a qubit can be in multiple states at once, whereas entanglement means that two or more qubits can be connected in such a way that the state of one qubit depends on the state of the other qubits.

Quantum computers are still in the early stages of development, and there are many challenges that need to be overcome before they can become practical for commercial use. These challenges include the need for error correction, the need for specialized hardware, and the need for new algorithms and programming languages.

Potential Applications in Finance

Despite these challenges, quantum computing has the potential to revolutionize the field of finance. In particular, quantum computing can be used to solve complex optimization problems that are often encountered in finance. Optimization problems involve finding the best solution to a problem among a large number of possible solutions. For example, a financial institution may want to find the optimal portfolio of investments that maximizes return while minimizing risk. This is a complex optimization problem that can be solved much faster with quantum computing than with traditional computers.

Quantum computing can also be used to improve risk management in finance. Risk management involves identifying and managing potential risks to a financial institution. With its ability to perform complex calculations at unprecedented speeds, quantum computing can help financial institutions to better understand and manage risks.

Another potential application of quantum computing in finance is in the area of fraud detection. Financial institutions are constantly at risk of fraud, and traditional methods of fraud detection can be time-consuming and ineffective. Quantum computing can be used to analyze large amounts of data in real-time, enabling financial institutions to detect and prevent fraud more quickly and efficiently.

Conclusion

Quantum computing has the potential to revolutionize the field of finance by enabling faster and more accurate calculations for complex optimization problems, risk management, and fraud detection. Although quantum computing is still in its early stages of development, it is already being explored by financial institutions and researchers around the world. As quantum computing technology continues to evolve, it is likely that we will see more and more applications of this technology in the field of finance.

Exercise:

Suppose a financial institution wants to optimize its portfolio of investments using quantum computing. The institution has 10 different investments, and it wants to find the optimal combination of investments that maximizes return while minimizing risk. Each investment has a return and a risk factor, as shown in the table below:

Investment	Return	Risk Factor
A	7%	5
B	8%	6
C	9%	8
D	10%	9
E	12%	11

In the previous section, we discussed the potential of quantum computing in finance and how it can be used to optimize portfolios. Let's now dive deeper into this topic and see how quantum computing can be applied to the example problem of optimizing a portfolio of investments.

As mentioned earlier, the financial institution has 10 different investments, each with a return and a risk factor. However, one of the investments, F, is missing its return and risk factor values. To optimize the portfolio using quantum computing, we need to find the optimal combination of investments that maximizes return while minimizing risk.

Quantum computing can be used to solve this problem using an algorithm called quantum annealing. Quantum annealing is a technique that uses quantum mechanics to find the lowest energy state of a system, which in this case corresponds to the optimal combination of investments.

To apply quantum annealing to this problem, we can represent each investment as a qubit, a unit of quantum information that can exist in multiple states at once. The state of each qubit represents whether or not that investment is included in the portfolio. For example, if qubit A is in the "1" state, it means that investment A is included in the portfolio, and if it is in the "0" state, it means that investment A is not included.

To encode the problem of finding the optimal portfolio as a quantum annealing problem, we need to define an objective function that takes into account the return and risk of each investment, as well as the constraints on the total investment amount and the minimum and maximum number of investments in the portfolio. The objective function can be expressed as follows:

$$f(x) = -(r \cdot x - \alpha \cdot \sigma \cdot y)$$

where x is a vector of the qubit states, r is a vector of the investment returns, α is a scalar representing the risk aversion of the investor, σ is a vector of the investment risk factors, and y is a vector of the weights assigned to each investment in the portfolio. The weights represent the percentage of the total investment amount allocated to each investment.

The objective of the optimization problem is to find the values of x and y that minimize the objective function $f(x)$. The constraints on the problem can be expressed as follows:

The total investment amount cannot exceed a certain limit, say $1,000,000.
The portfolio must include at least 3 investments and at most 6 investments.
To solve this problem using quantum annealing, we can use a quantum annealer, a specialized type of quantum computer that is designed to solve optimization problems. Several companies, such as D-Wave and IBM, offer quantum annealers that can be used for financial optimization problems.

In summary, quantum computing has the potential to revolutionize the field of finance by providing faster and more accurate solutions to complex optimization and risk management problems. While the technology is still in its early stages, it is expected to have a significant impact on the financial industry in the coming years.

M.L.Ruscsak

Analysis of blockchain technology and its impact on finance, including its potential to disrupt traditional financial institutions

Analysis of blockchain technology and its impact on finance, including its potential to disrupt traditional financial institutions

Blockchain technology has been one of the most disruptive innovations in recent years, and it has the potential to revolutionize the way financial transactions are conducted. In essence, a blockchain is a decentralized, distributed database that enables secure, transparent, and tamper-proof transactions. It is maintained by a network of nodes that validate and record transactions using complex cryptographic algorithms.

One of the most significant impacts of blockchain technology on finance is its ability to disrupt traditional financial institutions. Historically, banks and other financial institutions have played a critical role in facilitating financial transactions and providing credit to individuals and businesses. However, the rise of blockchain technology has the potential to reduce the role of these intermediaries by enabling peer-to-peer transactions and eliminating the need for trusted third parties.

One of the key advantages of blockchain technology is its ability to provide a high degree of security and transparency. Transactions on a blockchain are recorded in a decentralized and immutable ledger, which means that they cannot be altered or deleted once they have been recorded. This makes blockchain technology ideal for financial applications, as it can help to reduce the risk of fraud and errors.

Another advantage of blockchain technology is its potential to reduce transaction costs. Traditional financial institutions typically charge fees for their services, which can be a significant barrier for individuals and businesses who are seeking to access financial services. However, blockchain technology can enable peer-to-peer transactions without the need for intermediaries, which can help to reduce transaction costs and improve access to financial services.

One of the key applications of blockchain technology in finance is the creation of cryptocurrencies, such as Bitcoin and Ethereum. Cryptocurrencies are digital assets that use blockchain technology to enable secure and transparent transactions. They can be used to store value, make payments, and access financial services without the need for traditional financial institutions.

However, the rise of cryptocurrencies has also raised concerns about their potential to facilitate illicit activities, such as money laundering and terrorist financing. In addition, the volatility of cryptocurrencies can be a significant barrier to their adoption as a mainstream financial instrument.

Despite these challenges, the potential of blockchain technology to disrupt traditional financial institutions is significant. Some of the key applications of blockchain technology in finance include:

Payments: Blockchain technology can enable secure and transparent peer-to-peer payments without the need for traditional financial institutions.

Trade finance: Blockchain technology can help to reduce the time and cost associated with trade finance by enabling secure and transparent transactions between buyers and sellers.

Settlement and clearing: Blockchain technology can enable near-instantaneous settlement and clearing of financial transactions, which can help to reduce counterparty risk and improve efficiency.

Identity management: Blockchain technology can enable secure and transparent identity management, which can help to reduce the risk of fraud and improve access to financial services.

Asset management: Blockchain technology can enable the creation of digital assets, which can be used to represent ownership of physical assets such as real estate or artwork. This can help to improve the liquidity of these assets and enable fractional ownership.

Overall, blockchain technology has the potential to revolutionize the way financial transactions are conducted and disrupt traditional financial institutions. However, its adoption is likely to be gradual and will require collaboration between regulators, financial institutions, and technology companies.

M.L.Ruscsak

CHAPTER 25: CONCLUSION: THE MATHEMATICS OF FINANCE

In this comprehensive guide to the mathematics of finance, we have explored a wide range of mathematical concepts and techniques used in the field of finance. From calculus and statistics to linear algebra and differential equations, we have covered a lot of ground in our quest to understand the complex world of finance.

We began our journey by discussing the fundamental principles of finance, including the time value of money, compound interest, and present and future values. We then moved on to explore the basics of calculus, including limits, derivatives, and integrals, and their applications in finance.

Next, we delved into the world of probability and statistics, including probability distributions, hypothesis testing, and regression analysis. We learned how to use statistical tools to analyze financial data, identify trends and patterns, and make informed decisions.

We then explored linear algebra, including matrices, vectors, and systems of linear equations, and their applications in finance, such as portfolio optimization, risk management, and asset pricing.

Finally, we tackled the complex world of differential equations and their applications in finance, including option pricing and stochastic processes.

Throughout our journey, we have seen how mathematical concepts and techniques are used in a wide range of fields within finance, from investment banking and portfolio management to actuarial science and risk management. We have also seen how advances in technology, such as blockchain and quantum computing, are transforming the way finance is practiced and opening up new opportunities for mathematical research and innovation.

In conclusion, the mathematics of finance is a fascinating and dynamic field that offers a wealth of opportunities for those who are interested in pursuing a career in finance. By mastering the mathematical concepts and techniques covered in this guide, you will be well equipped to tackle the challenges and opportunities of the finance industry and contribute to the ongoing evolution of this exciting field.

Summary of the key concepts and topics covered in the book

Throughout this book, we have covered a wide range of topics related to finance, mathematics, and statistics. The main goal of this book was to provide a comprehensive guide to calculus, statistics, linear algebra, and differential equations, and to explain how these mathematical concepts are used in finance.

In the first part of the book, we introduced the basic concepts of calculus, including limits, derivatives, and integrals. We explained how these concepts are used in finance to analyze rates of change, optimize functions, and calculate probabilities.

The second part of the book focused on statistics, including descriptive and inferential statistics, probability distributions, hypothesis testing, and regression analysis. We demonstrated how these statistical techniques are used in finance to make predictions, estimate risk, and evaluate investment opportunities.

In the third part of the book, we introduced linear algebra, including vectors, matrices, and linear transformations. We explained how these concepts are used in finance to model and analyze complex systems, such as portfolios of investments.

Finally, in the fourth part of the book, we covered differential equations, including first-order and second-order differential equations. We explained how these equations are used in finance to model dynamic systems, such as interest rates and stock prices.

Throughout the book, we provided numerous examples and exercises to help readers understand and apply these mathematical concepts to finance. We also discussed how these concepts are used in various fields, such as investment banking, actuarial science, portfolio management, quantitative analysis, securities trading, financial planning, and financial analysis.

Overall, this book aimed to provide readers with a comprehensive understanding of the mathematics of finance and how these mathematical concepts are used in real-world applications. By mastering these concepts, readers will be better equipped to analyze financial data, make informed investment decisions, and develop strategies to mitigate risk and maximize returns.

Refection on the importance of mathematics in finance and the role of financial mathematics in shaping the future of finance

Mathematics plays a critical role in finance, and it has become increasingly important as the financial industry has become more complex and global. From calculating interest rates to modeling complex financial instruments, mathematics is at the heart of financial analysis and decision-making. In this section, we will reflect on the importance of mathematics in finance and the role of financial mathematics in shaping the future of finance.

One of the key reasons why mathematics is so important in finance is that it provides a rigorous framework for analyzing and understanding financial concepts. For example, the use of mathematical models enables investors to quantify risk and reward and to make informed

M.L.Ruscsak

investment decisions. Mathematics also provides a way to measure financial performance, whether it be in the form of calculating returns, evaluating the effectiveness of different investment strategies, or assessing the financial health of a company.

Moreover, financial mathematics has played a critical role in the development of new financial instruments and markets. For example, the development of options pricing models, such as the Black-Scholes model, enabled the growth of the options market and gave investors new ways to hedge risk and speculate on the direction of asset prices. Similarly, the use of mathematical models in credit risk management has enabled the growth of the credit default swap market, which has become an important tool for managing credit risk in the financial industry.

As the financial industry continues to evolve and become more complex, the importance of mathematics is likely to continue to increase. With the advent of new technologies such as blockchain and artificial intelligence, financial mathematics will play a critical role in enabling these technologies to be applied in the financial industry. For example, the use of mathematical models in machine learning algorithms can enable more accurate predictions of asset prices and improve risk management.

However, it is also important to recognize the limitations of mathematical models in finance. While mathematics provides a rigorous framework for analysis, it cannot capture all of the nuances and complexities of the real world. For example, financial crises, such as the 2008 financial crisis, have highlighted the limitations of mathematical models in predicting market behavior during times of extreme stress.

In conclusion, mathematics plays a crucial role in finance, enabling investors to quantify risk and reward, measure financial performance, and develop new financial instruments and markets. As the financial industry continues to evolve and become more complex, the importance of mathematics in finance is likely to increase, particularly with the advent of new technologies such as blockchain and artificial intelligence. However, it is also important to recognize the limitations of mathematical models in finance and to use them as a tool to inform decision-making, rather than relying on them blindly.

Call to action for readers to continue exploring financial mathematics and its applications in finance.

Financial mathematics is a powerful tool that has been used for decades to understand and analyze financial markets. In this section, we will discuss the importance of financial mathematics and its applications in finance. We will also discuss the benefits of exploring financial mathematics and provide a call to action for readers to continue exploring this field.

Importance of Financial Mathematics

Financial mathematics is important for several reasons. First, it provides a framework for understanding financial markets and the behavior of financial assets. By using mathematical models, we can analyze complex financial data and gain insights into the workings of financial markets.

Second, financial mathematics is essential for risk management. By using mathematical models, we can identify and quantify risks associated with financial assets and portfolios. This helps investors and financial institutions manage their risks and make informed investment decisions.

Finally, financial mathematics is critical for developing new financial products and instruments. Many of the financial products that we use today, such as options, futures, and swaps, are based on mathematical models. Without financial mathematics, we would not have the tools and techniques needed to create these products.

Applications of Financial Mathematics in Finance

Financial mathematics has numerous applications in finance. Some of the key applications include:

Portfolio Management: Financial mathematics is used extensively in portfolio management. By using mathematical models, portfolio managers can optimize their portfolios to achieve their investment objectives while managing risk.

Derivatives Pricing: Financial mathematics is essential for pricing derivatives such as options, futures, and swaps. By using mathematical models, we can determine the fair value of these instruments, which helps investors make informed investment decisions.

Risk Management: Financial mathematics is critical for managing risk in financial markets. By using mathematical models, we can identify and quantify risks associated with financial assets and portfolios, which helps investors and financial institutions manage their risks.

Quantitative Analysis: Financial mathematics is used extensively in quantitative analysis. By using mathematical models, we can analyze financial data and gain insights into the behavior of financial markets.

Algorithmic Trading: Financial mathematics is essential for developing and implementing algorithmic trading strategies. By using mathematical models, traders can create algorithms that can trade financial assets automatically.

Benefits of Exploring Financial Mathematics

M.L.Ruscsak

Exploring financial mathematics has several benefits. First, it can help you develop a deeper understanding of financial markets and the behavior of financial assets. This can be useful for making informed investment decisions and managing risk.

Second, exploring financial mathematics can help you develop valuable skills that are in high demand in the finance industry. Many finance jobs require knowledge of financial mathematics, so developing these skills can help you advance your career.

Finally, exploring financial mathematics can be intellectually rewarding. Financial mathematics is a fascinating and challenging field that can provide a lifetime of intellectual stimulation.

Call to Action

If you are interested in exploring financial mathematics, there are several steps you can take. First, consider taking courses in financial mathematics, calculus, statistics, and linear algebra. These courses will provide you with the foundational knowledge needed to understand and analyze financial markets.

Second, consider reading books and articles on financial mathematics. There are numerous books and articles available on this topic, and reading them can help you develop a deeper understanding of financial mathematics.

Finally, consider seeking out internships or entry-level positions in finance that require knowledge of financial mathematics. These experiences can help you develop practical skills and gain valuable experience in the field.

Conclusion

Financial mathematics is a powerful tool that has numerous applications in finance. By exploring financial mathematics, you can develop a deeper understanding of financial markets, develop valuable skills, and gain intellectual stimulation. We encourage readers to continue exploring financial mathematics and its applications in finance.

APPENDIX: MATHEMATICAL TABLES AND FORMULAS

In finance, mathematics plays a crucial role in modeling, analyzing and predicting financial phenomena, such as asset prices, risk, and returns. Therefore, it is essential for students and practitioners in finance to have access to mathematical tables and formulas that can assist them in performing calculations, solving problems, and interpreting results. In this appendix, we provide a comprehensive set of mathematical tables and formulas that are relevant to finance, including calculus, statistics, linear algebra, and differential equations.

Calculus Formulas:

Calculus is the mathematical study of continuous change. In finance, calculus is used to model and analyze the behavior of financial variables, such as asset prices, interest rates, and portfolio returns. The following are some of the most important calculus formulas in finance:

Derivatives: The derivative of a function $f(x)$ represents the instantaneous rate of change of $f(x)$ with respect to x. The formula for the derivative is:
$$f'(x) = \lim_{h \to 0} [(f(x+h) - f(x))/h]$$

Integration: Integration is the reverse of differentiation. It is used to find the area under a curve. The formula for integration is:
$$\int f(x)\, dx = F(x) + C$$

where $F(x)$ is the antiderivative of $f(x)$, and C is the constant of integration.

Taylor series: A Taylor series is a representation of a function as an infinite sum of terms, where each term is a derivative of the function evaluated at a specific point. The formula for the Taylor series is:
$$f(x) = f(a) + f'(a)(x-a) + f''(a)(x-a)^2/2! + f'''(a)(x-a)^3/3! + \ldots$$

Statistics Formulas:

Statistics is the branch of mathematics that deals with the collection, analysis, interpretation, presentation, and organization of data. In finance, statistics is used to describe and analyze financial data, such as stock prices, interest rates, and portfolio returns. The following are some of the most important statistics formulas in finance:

Mean: The mean is the arithmetic average of a set of numbers. The formula for the mean is:

$$\mu = (x1 + x2 + \ldots + xn)/n$$

where xi is the ith observation, and n is the number of observations.

Variance: The variance is a measure of how spread out a set of numbers is. The formula for the variance is:

$$\sigma^2 = [(x1 - \mu)^2 + (x2 - \mu)^2 + \ldots + (xn - \mu)^2]/n$$

Standard deviation: The standard deviation is the square root of the variance. It measures the dispersion of a set of numbers around the mean. The formula for the standard deviation is:

$$\sigma = \sqrt{[(x1 - \mu)^2 + (x2 - \mu)^2 + \ldots + (xn - \mu)^2]/n}$$

Linear Algebra Formulas:

Linear algebra is the branch of mathematics that deals with linear equations, matrices, vectors, and linear transformations. In finance, linear algebra is used to model and analyze financial systems, such as portfolios, options, and bonds. The following are some of the most important linear algebra formulas in finance:

Matrix multiplication: The product of two matrices A and B is defined as:
$$C = AB$$

where C is a matrix whose (i,j)th element is given by:

$$Cij = \Sigma k{=}1n\ AikBkj$$

Inverse of a matrix: The inverse of a square matrix A is denoted by A^{-1} and is defined as the matrix that satisfies:
$$AA^{-1} = A^{-1}A = I$$

where I is the identity matrix.

3. Determinant of a matrix: The determinant of a square matrix A is denoted by $|A|$ and is defined as:

$$|A| = \Sigma \sigma(\pi)\ a1\pi(1)a2\pi(2)\ldots an\pi(n)$$

where $\sigma(\pi)$ is the sign of the permutation π, and $a1\pi(1)$, $a2\pi(2)$,...,$an\pi(n)$ are the elements of A arranged in the order specified by the permutation π.

Eigenvalues and eigenvectors: If A is a square matrix, a scalar λ is called an eigenvalue of A if there exists a non-zero vector x such that:

$$Ax = \lambda x$$

The vector x is called an eigenvector of A corresponding to the eigenvalue λ.

Diagonalization of a matrix: A square matrix A is said to be diagonalizable if there exists an invertible matrix P and a diagonal matrix D such that:
$$A = PDP^{-1}$$

where D is a diagonal matrix whose diagonal entries are the eigenvalues of A, and P is a matrix whose columns are the eigenvectors of A.

Singular value decomposition (SVD): Every matrix A can be written as:
$$A = U\Sigma V^T$$

where U and V are orthogonal matrices and Σ is a diagonal matrix whose diagonal entries are the singular values of A.

Gaussian elimination: Gaussian elimination is a method for solving systems of linear equations by transforming the augmented matrix of the system into row echelon form and then solving the resulting system of equations.

LU decomposition: LU decomposition is a method for solving systems of linear equations by decomposing the coefficient matrix into a lower triangular matrix L and an upper triangular matrix U, and then solving the resulting system of equations.

Gram-Schmidt orthogonalization: Gram-Schmidt orthogonalization is a method for orthonormalizing a set of linearly independent vectors. This is useful in finance for constructing portfolios of assets with minimal risk.

Linear regression: Linear regression is a statistical method for modeling the relationship between a dependent variable y and one or more independent variables $x_1, x_2,...,x_n$. The relationship is assumed to be linear, and the method finds the best-fit line that minimizes the sum of the squared errors between the observed values of y and the predicted values of y based on the independent variables.

These are some of the most important linear algebra formulas and concepts used in finance. Understanding and applying these concepts can be invaluable for financial analysts, quantitative analysts, and other professionals in the finance industry.

Useful mathematical tables and formulas for financial mathematics

Mathematics is a crucial tool in the field of finance, providing a framework for analyzing and understanding complex financial systems. In this section, we will discuss some of the most useful mathematical tables and formulas in financial mathematics.

Probability Distributions:
Probability distributions are used to model the probability of various outcomes in a financial system. There are several probability distributions used in financial mathematics, including the normal distribution, the student's t-distribution, and the chi-square distribution.

The normal distribution, also known as the Gaussian distribution, is a bell-shaped distribution that is commonly used to model the behavior of financial assets. It is characterized by two parameters, the mean (μ) and the standard deviation (σ).

The student's t-distribution is used to model the behavior of small sample sizes. It is similar to the normal distribution but has fatter tails, which makes it more appropriate for small sample sizes.

The chi-square distribution is used to model the behavior of the sum of squared random variables. It is commonly used in hypothesis testing and confidence interval calculations.

Financial Formulas:
Financial formulas are used to calculate various financial metrics, such as interest rates, present values, and future values. Some of the most important financial formulas include:

Simple Interest: $I = Prt$, where I is the interest, P is the principal, r is the interest rate, and t is the time period.

Compound Interest: $A = P(1 + r/n)^{(nt)}$, where A is the final amount, P is the principal, r is the interest rate, n is the number of compounding periods per year, and t is the time period.

Present Value: $PV = FV/(1 + r)^t$, where PV is the present value, FV is the future value, r is the interest rate, and t is the time period.

Future Value: $FV = PV(1 + r)^t$, where FV is the future value, PV is the present value, r is the interest rate, and t is the time period.

Net Present Value: $NPV = \Sigma(C_t/(1 + r)^t) - C_0$, where NPV is the net present value, C_t is the cash flow at time t, r is the discount rate, and C_0 is the initial investment.

Calculus:

Calculus is used to model and analyze the behavior of financial systems. Some of the most important calculus formulas used in financial mathematics include:

Derivatives: A derivative is a mathematical tool used to measure the rate of change of a function. In finance, derivatives are used to model the behavior of financial assets, such as options and futures contracts.

Integrals: An integral is a mathematical tool used to calculate the area under a curve. In finance, integrals are used to calculate the present value of a stream of cash flows.

Linear Algebra:
Linear algebra is used to model and analyze financial systems, such as portfolios, options, and bonds. Some of the most important linear algebra formulas in finance include:

Matrix multiplication: The product of two matrices A and B is defined as: $C = AB$, where C is a matrix whose (i,j)th element is given by: $C_{ij} = \Sigma_{k=1}^{n} A_{ik}B_{kj}$.

Inverse of a matrix: The inverse of a square matrix A is denoted by A^{-1} and is defined as the matrix that satisfies: $AA^{-1} = A^{-1}A = I$, where I is the identity matrix.

Differential Equations:
Differential equations are used to model and analyze the behavior of financial systems. Some of the most important differential equations used in financial mathematics include:

Black-Scholes Equation: The Black-Scholes equation is a partial differential equation that is widely used in financial mathematics to model the price evolution of European-style options. The equation is named after Fischer Black and Myron Scholes, who developed it in 1973.

The Black-Scholes equation is given by:

$$\partial V/\partial t + 0.5\sigma^2 S^2 \partial^2 V/\partial S^2 + rS\partial V/\partial S - rV = 0$$

where V is the option price, S is the price of the underlying asset, σ is the volatility of the underlying asset, r is the risk-free interest rate, and t is time.

This equation is a parabolic partial differential equation, which means that it is used to model systems where the value of the option depends on both the current value of the underlying asset and the time remaining until the option expires. The Black-Scholes equation is used to calculate the price of European-style options, which are options that can only be exercised on their expiration date.

M.L.Ruscsak

Heat Equation: The heat equation is a partial differential equation that is used to model the diffusion of heat. It is also used in finance to model the diffusion of financial instruments, such as stock prices or interest rates. The heat equation is given by:

$$\partial u/\partial t - \alpha \nabla^2 u = 0$$

where u is the temperature or the value of the financial instrument, t is time, α is a constant that represents the diffusion coefficient, and ∇^2 is the Laplacian operator.

This equation is a parabolic partial differential equation, which means that it is used to model systems where the value of the financial instrument depends on both the current value of the instrument and the time remaining until the option expires.

Wave Equation: The wave equation is a partial differential equation that is used to model wave-like behavior, such as the propagation of sound or light. It is also used in finance to model the propagation of financial shocks, such as sudden changes in interest rates or stock prices. The wave equation is given by:

$$\partial^2 u/\partial t^2 - c^2 \nabla^2 u = 0$$

where u is the wave function or the value of the financial instrument, t is time, c is the wave speed, and ∇^2 is the Laplacian operator.

This equation is a hyperbolic partial differential equation, which means that it is used to model systems where the value of the financial instrument depends on both the current value of the instrument and the rate of change of the instrument.

In conclusion, differential equations are essential tools for financial mathematicians as they provide a way to model and analyze the behavior of financial systems over time. The Black-Scholes equation, the heat equation, and the wave equation are just a few examples of the many differential equations that are used in finance. By understanding these equations and their applications, financial professionals can make more informed decisions and manage risk more effectively.

Bibliography: A list of references cited in the book

Adler, R. J., & Taylor, J. E. (2007). Random Fields and Geometry (Springer Monographs in Mathematics). Springer.

Barber, B. M., & Odean, T. (2000). Trading Is Hazardous to Your Wealth: The Common Stock Investment Performance of Individual Investors. The Journal of Finance, 55(2), 773-806.

Björk, T. (2004). Arbitrage Theory in Continuous Time. Oxford University Press.

Black, F., & Scholes, M. (1973). The Pricing of Options and Corporate Liabilities. Journal of Political Economy, 81(3), 637-654.

Cox, J. C., Ross, S. A., & Rubinstein, M. (1979). Option Pricing: A Simplified Approach. Journal of Financial Economics, 7(3), 229-263.

Derman, E., & Kani, I. (1994). Riding on a Smile. Risk, 7(2), 32-39.

Hull, J. C. (2018). Options, Futures, and Other Derivatives (10th ed.). Pearson.

Merton, R. C. (1973). Theory of Rational Option Pricing. Bell Journal of Economics and Management Science, 4(1), 141-183.

Mishkin, F. S., & Eakins, S. G. (2015). Financial Markets and Institutions (8th ed.). Pearson.

Neftci, S. N. (1996). An Introduction to the Mathematics of Financial Derivatives (2nd ed.). Academic Press.

Shreve, S. E. (2004). Stochastic Calculus for Finance II: Continuous-Time Models (Springer Finance). Springer.

Wilmott, P., Howison, S., & Dewynne, J. (2013). The Mathematics of Financial Derivatives: A Student Introduction (2nd ed.). Cambridge University Press.

Index: An alphabetical list of terms and concepts discussed in the book

A

Actuary, 1, 3, 5, 7, 10, 12, 14, 15, 17, 19, 21, 23, 25, 27, 29, 31, 33, 35, 37, 39, 41, 43, 45, 47, 49, 51, 53, 55, 57, 59, 61, 63, 65, 67, 69, 71, 73, 75, 77, 79, 81, 83, 85, 87, 89, 91, 93, 95, 97, 99, 101, 103, 105, 107, 109, 111, 113, 115, 117, 119, 121, 123, 125, 127, 129, 131, 133, 135, 137, 139, 141, 143, 145, 147, 149, 151, 153, 155, 157, 159, 161, 163, 165, 167, 169, 171, 173, 175, 177, 179, 181, 183, 185, 187, 189, 191, 193, 195, 197, 199, 201, 203, 205, 207, 209, 211, 213, 215, 217, 219, 221, 223, 225, 227, 229, 231, 233, 235, 237, 239, 241, 243, 245, 247, 249, 251, 253, 255, 257, 259, 261, 263, 265, 267, 269, 271, 273, 275, 277, 279, 281, 283, 285, 287, 289, 291, 293, 295, 297, 299, 301, 303, 305, 307, 309, 311, 313, 315, 317, 319, 321, 323, 325, 327, 329, 331, 333, 335, 337, 339, 341, 343, 345, 347, 349, 351, 353, 355, 357, 359, 361, 363, 365, 367, 369, 371, 373, 375, 377, 379, 381, 383, 385, 387, 389, 391, 393, 395, 397, 399, 401, 403, 405, 407, 409, 411, 413, 415, 417, 419, 421, 423, 425, 427, 429, 431, 433, 435, 437, 439, 441, 443, 445, 447, 449, 451, 453, 455, 457, 459, 461, 463, 465, 467, 469, 471, 473, 475, 477, 479, 481, 483, 485, 487, 489, 491, 493, 495, 497, 499, 501, 503, 505,

An actuary is a professional who uses mathematical and statistical methods to analyze and assess financial risk, particularly in the insurance industry.

B

Black-Scholes equation- The Black-Scholes equation is a partial differential equation that models the behavior of financial derivatives, such as options.

C

Capital Asset Pricing Model (CAPM)- The Capital Asset Pricing Model (CAPM) is a financial model that measures the relationship between risk and expected return of an asset, based on the assumption that investors require compensation for the time value of money and risk.

D

Derivatives- Derivatives are financial contracts that derive their value from the underlying assets, such as stocks, bonds, or commodities.

E

Efficient Market Hypothesis (EMH)- The Efficient Market Hypothesis (EMH) is a financial theory that suggests that financial markets are efficient and all available information is already reflected in the prices of financial assets.

F

Financial Engineering- Financial Engineering refers to the use of mathematical modeling and quantitative analysis to design and create financial products, such as derivatives, structured products, and portfolios.

G

Greeks- The Greeks are a set of metrics used in options trading to assess the risk and reward of an options position, including Delta, Gamma, Vega, Theta, and Rho.

H

Hedge Fund - A hedge fund is an investment fund that uses a range of strategies, including leverage, derivatives, and short-selling, to generate returns for investors.

I

Interest Rates - Interest rates are the cost of borrowing or the return on lending, expressed as a percentage of the principal amount.

J

Junk Bonds - Junk bonds are high-yield bonds issued by companies with lower credit ratings and higher default risk.

K

Key Performance Indicators (KPIs) - Key Performance Indicators (KPIs) are financial and non-financial metrics used to evaluate the performance of a business or investment portfolio.

L

Leverage - Leverage is the use of borrowed funds or financial instruments to increase the potential return of an investment or financial transaction.

M

Market Risk- Market risk is the risk of financial loss due to adverse changes in market prices, such as changes in interest rates, exchange rates, or stock prices.

N

Net Present Value (NPV) - Net Present Value (NPV) is a financial metric used to evaluate the profitability of an investment, calculated as the present value of cash inflows minus the present value of cash outflows.

O

Options - Options are financial contracts that give the buyer the right, but not the obligation, to buy or sell an underlying asset at a specified price on or before a specified date.

P

Portfolio Management - Portfolio Management is the process of selecting and managing a group of financial assets, such as stocks, bonds, and derivatives, to achieve specific investment objectives.

Q

Quantitative Analysis - Quantitative Analysis is the use of mathematical and statistical methods to analyze and interpret financial data, such as market trends, asset prices, and risk.

R

Risk Management - Risk Management is the process of identifying, assessing, and mitigating financial risks, such as market risk, credit risk, and operational risk.

S

Securities - Securities are financial instruments that represent ownership or debt in a company, government, or other entity, such as stocks, bonds, and options.

T

Technical Analysis - Technical Analysis is the study of market trends and price patterns in financial assets, using charts, graphs, and other tools to identify potential trading opportunities.

U

Utility Theory- Utility Theory is a financial theory that measures the satisfaction or happiness that an individual or organization derives from different financial outcomes, based on their preferences and expectations.

V

Value at Risk (VaR) - Value at Risk (VaR) is a widely used risk management measure that estimates the maximum loss that a portfolio or investment can suffer over a given time period with a certain degree of confidence. It is a popular tool used by portfolio managers, risk managers, and traders to quantify and manage market risk. VaR is typically expressed as a dollar amount or percentage of the portfolio value.

VaR can be calculated using various methods, including historical simulation, parametric models, and Monte Carlo simulation. Each method has its advantages and disadvantages, and the choice of the method depends on the characteristics of the portfolio and the risk manager's preferences.

The historical simulation method estimates VaR based on historical market data, assuming that future market behavior will be similar to past behavior. This method is easy to implement and does not require any assumptions about the distribution of portfolio returns. However, it is sensitive to the length and quality of historical data and may not capture extreme events that have not occurred in the past.

Parametric models assume that portfolio returns follow a specific probability distribution, such as a normal distribution, and estimate VaR based on the parameters of the distribution. This method is widely used and provides a simple and tractable way to estimate VaR. However, it may not capture the non-normality and skewness of portfolio returns and may be sensitive to the choice of the distribution.

Monte Carlo simulation involves simulating the future values of portfolio positions based on a set of assumed market scenarios and estimating VaR based on the distribution of simulated portfolio returns. This method provides a flexible way to estimate VaR and can capture complex market behaviors and tail risks. However, it requires a significant computational effort and may be sensitive to the assumptions and inputs used in the simulation.

In summary, VaR is a useful tool for measuring and managing market risk, but it is not without limitations and should be used in conjunction with other risk management measures and tools.

W

Wiener Process - The Wiener process, also known as Brownian motion, is a stochastic process that is widely used to model random fluctuations in financial markets and other complex systems. The Wiener process is named after Norbert Wiener, who introduced it in his work on stochastic processes in 1923.

The Wiener process is a continuous-time process that has the following properties:

The process has independent and identically distributed increments.

M.L.Ruscsak

The increments are normally distributed with mean zero and variance proportional to the time interval.

The process has continuous sample paths.

These properties make the Wiener process a simple and powerful tool for modeling random phenomena in finance and other fields. The Wiener process is used to model stock prices, interest rates, exchange rates, and other financial variables. It is also used in physics, biology, and other sciences to model diffusion processes and other stochastic phenomena.

The Wiener process has many interesting properties, such as the scaling property, which states that the process is self-similar and its variance increases linearly with time. The Wiener process is also the basis for the famous Black-Scholes option pricing model, which assumes that stock prices follow a log-normal Wiener process.

X

Exponential Distribution - The exponential distribution is a continuous probability distribution that is widely used in finance and other fields to model the time between independent events that occur at a constant rate. The exponential distribution is a special case of the gamma distribution and has a single parameter, the rate parameter λ.

The probability density function of the exponential distribution is given by:

$f(x) = \lambda e^{\wedge}(-\lambda x)$, for $x \geq 0$

where $\lambda > 0$ is the rate parameter.

The cumulative distribution function of the exponential distribution is given by:

$F(x) = 1 - e^{\wedge}(-\lambda x)$, for $x \geq 0$

The exponential distribution has many interesting properties in finance, particularly in the field of risk management. One important application of the exponential distribution in finance is in modeling the time between defaults of credit portfolios.

For example, suppose a bank has a portfolio of loans, and it wants to calculate the probability that the portfolio will experience a certain number of defaults within a given time frame. If the bank assumes that the time between defaults follows an exponential distribution, it can use the distribution's probability density function to calculate the probability of a default occurring at a specific time. By integrating the density function over the desired time interval, the bank can then determine the probability of a certain number of defaults occurring within that interval.

Another important application of the exponential distribution in finance is in calculating the value at risk (VaR) of a portfolio. VaR is a measure of the maximum loss that a portfolio is expected to experience over a given time horizon, with a specified level of confidence. If the returns of the portfolio are assumed to be normally distributed, the VaR can be calculated using the normal distribution. However, if the returns are not normally distributed, the VaR can be calculated using other distributions, such as the exponential distribution.

In this case, the VaR would be calculated by determining the value of the portfolio that corresponds to the desired level of confidence, based on the cumulative distribution function of the exponential distribution. For example, if the desired level of confidence is 95%, the VaR would be the portfolio value that corresponds to the 95th percentile of the exponential distribution.

Overall, the exponential distribution is a useful tool in finance for modeling the time between independent events, such as defaults or price movements, and for calculating risk measures such as VaR.

www.ingramcontent.com/pod-product-compliance
Lightning Source LLC
Chambersburg PA
CBHW082010190326
41458CB00010B/3138